Joseph Gormley
of Carbon County, Pennsylvania
and His Children

Joseph Gormley
of Carbon County, Pennsylvania
and His Children

Kathryn Chambers Torpey
Alexandria, Virginia

Kathryn Chambers Torpey is a professional genealogist and researcher.
Other Books by Kathryn Chambers Torpey:

John Kennedy of County Donegal, Ulster, Ireland, and His Descendants - A Compiled Genealogy (Including Risk, McCoy, and Pendleton), 2006

William Kennedy of Chester County, Pennsylvania, and His Descendants - A Compiled Genealogy (Including Davis, Smith, Wallace, Russell, and McClure), 2014

Colonial and Revolutionary Kennedy Families from Southeastern Pennsylvania, 2015

The Edwards/Scott Family History - Edinburgh to Philadelphia, 2016

The Chambers Family in Philadelphia Descended from George Chambers Born c 1815 in Ireland, 2016

The Reitze Family in Philadelphia Descended from Christopher Reitze Born 1824 in Hesse-Cassel, Germany, 2017

The Devlin Family in Philadelphia Descended from Peter Devlin Born c 1810 in Ireland (the female perspective), 2018

The McCauley Family in Philadelphia including the Wallace & Patton Families from Mullaghinch, County Londonderry, Ireland, 2019

Imprint: Kindle Direct Publishing Platform

ISBN-13: 9781703333299

Torpey Books
5035 Domain Place
Alexandria, VA
22311-5066

IN MEMORY OF

Thelma Steigerwalt Gormley

Contents

FOREWORD

This family history documents what is known about the origins and life of Joseph and Margaret (Montgomery) Gormley and each of their twelve children. The purpose of the narration is to document for posterity the origins of the Gormley family in the Bann Valley of County Londonderry, Ireland, and to trace their lives in America during the mid-to-late 19th Century and early 20th Century.

The research for this family history was conducted in two general time frames. The first family tree was compiled by my father, William Scott Chambers, in the 1950s. The balance of the research contained in this family history was conducted between 1995 and 2003 at the National Archives, the Library of Congress, and the Daughters of the American Revolution Library in Washington, D.C.; the National Genealogical Society Library then located in Arlington, Virginia; and at National Archives II in College Park, Maryland. Substantial research was also conducted at the Latter-Day Saints Family History Center located in McLean, Virginia. Other repositories visited included the Free Library of Philadelphia, the Philadelphia City Archives, the Genealogical Society of Pennsylvania, and the Historical Society of Pennsylvania all in Philadelphia; the Camden County Historical Society in Camden, New Jersey; the Gloucester County Historical Society in Woodbury, New Jersey; and the New Jersey State Archives in Trenton, New Jersey. Also visited was the Adriance Public Library in Poughkeepsie, New York.

A tour was made of Summit Hill, Lansford, Jim Thorpe, and Mahoning Township in Carbon County with Robert C. Gormley, great-grandson of James M. Gormley. Locations visited in Summit Hill included the Old Presbyterian Cemetery, the GAR Cemetery, and the home of Thelma Steigerwalt Gormley who was then living in the house originally occupied by Samuel and Margaret (Glenn) Gormley Allen. The visit to Lansford included a stop at the Lehigh Navigation Coal Company shops and the No. 9 coal tunnel. The visit to Mahoning Township included an inspection of the property once owned by Margaret (Montgomery) Gormley where the barn was still found to be standing. Additional site visits were made to the U.S. Soldiers' and Airmen's Home National Cemetery in Washington, D.C.; the National Military Cemetery in Gettysburg, Pennsylvania; the Poughkeepsie Rural Cemetery in Poughkeepsie, New York; Mount Moriah Cemetery in Philadelphia; and Ardsley Memorial Park operated by the Hillside Cemetery Company in Roslyn, Pennsylvania.

Professional researchers employed in this endeavor included Joan Meyer and Charles Seng for research in Carbon County, Pennsylvania; Karen Gensey for research in Bethlehem, Pennsylvania; Lynn Jefferies and June Zublic for research in Camden County, New Jersey; Susan Koelble for research in Philadelphia; Mary Lou Davison for research in Poughkeepsie, New York; Frederick Smith for research in Albany, New York; Barbara Hodges for research in Lyon County, Nevada; and Edwina Case Skyles for research in Chicago, Illinois. Scholars and historians consulted for their expertise in Carbon County research included Dan Wilson, Jack Sterling, and John Koehler, the Weatherly Historian who is also President of the Union Cemetery in Weatherly. Also contacted was Tom Dombroski of Hazleton, Pennsylvania, a member of Co.

K, 81st Pennsylvania Volunteer Infantry, an organization dedicated to preserving the memory of those men who served in this regiment during the Civil War.

With respect to Irish records, Lavonne Bradfield of San Antonio, Texas, provided copies from her personal files of original marriage, baptismal, and church membership records from the First Garvagh Presbyterian Church. She also provided a copy of a transcription she made of the headstone of Mary Ann Wallace in the Aghadowey Presbyterian Cemetery in County Londonderry, Ireland, that pertains to the subjects of this family history.

The following institutions and facilities were contacted by mail for information. In Pennsylvania: the Division of Vital Statistics in New Castle, the Lehigh County Clerk's Office in Allentown, the Bethlehem Area Public Library and the Nisky Hill Cemetery in Bethlehem, the First Presbyterian Church of Panther Valley in Summit Hill, and the Presbyterian Historical Society, the Temple University Urban Archives, and Girard College in Philadelphia. In Alabama: the Montgomery County Genealogical Society, Oakwood Cemetery, and the State of Alabama Department of Archives and History in Montgomery and the Autauga County Genealogical Society in Prattville. In South Carolina: the Charleston Public Library and the City of Charleston Archives in Charleston. In New York: the New York State Archives in Albany and the Dutchess County Genealogical Society, the Dutchess County Historical Society, the Miller Funeral Home, the Vassar College Alumnae and Alumni Association, and the Poughkeepsie City Clerk's Office in Poughkeepsie. In New Jersey: the New Jersey Vital Statistics Office in Trenton and Clover Leaf Park Cemetery in Woodbridge. In California: the Placer County Clerk - Recorder's Office in Auburn and the Native Daughters of the Golden West in San Francisco. In Illinois: the Railroad Retirement Board in Chicago.

Brief contact and a limited exchange of information was made with the descendants of four of the children of Joseph and Margaret (Montgomery) Gormley. The descendants of their daughter, Letitia (Gormley) Wallace, contacted were Linda Butler of Poughkeepsie, New York, Kandee (Butler) Shafer of Pleasant Valley, New York, and Wayne Butler of Orlando, Florida. These three contacts were made possible via preliminary correspondence with Harry Brown of Newburgh, New York, Blanche Ceneskie of Westerville, Ohio, and Elizabeth Johnson of Concord, North Carolina, who are related to the Wallace/Butler family through their uncle, William Witzenbocker, who married Mary Wallace. The descendants of their daughter, Matilda (Gormley) Boyd, contacted were Ellen (Boyd) Gehring and her daughter, Janice (Gehring) Eidem, both of Summit Hill, and their cousin, James S. Boyd, retired Pennsylvania State Trooper. The descendant of their daughter, Jane (Gormley) Erwin, contacted was Henry Kindt Erwin of Allentown, Pennsylvania. The descendants of their son, William B. Gormley, contacted were Jean (Buss) Troxell of Lancaster, Pennsylvania, and Nancy (Riley) Gerechoff of Deal, New Jersey. These two contacts were made possible via preliminary contact with Jessica Fahey-Petrack of Lehighton, Pennsylvania, who is related to the Gormley/Hartman family through her aunt, Mary Catherine (Hartman) Gormley, the wife of William B. Gormley.

By far, the greatest contribution to this work came from contact made with Robert C. Gormley, a great-great-grandson of Joseph and Margaret (Montgomery) Gormley who descends collaterally from their son, James M. Gormley, his son, Robert M. Gormley, and his son, Palmer

R. Gormley. Mr. Gormley is a family historian and Civil War military memorabilia aficionado who has studied the Gormley family history for more than thirty years. His records, family papers, personal recollections, and friendship with some of the descendants of the families of Smith Gormley, James Gormley, and Robert Gormley served as the foundation for much of the research contained in this family history.

Kathryn Chambers Torpey
October 28, 2019

DESCENDANT CHART

Children of Joseph and Margaret (Montgomery) Gormley

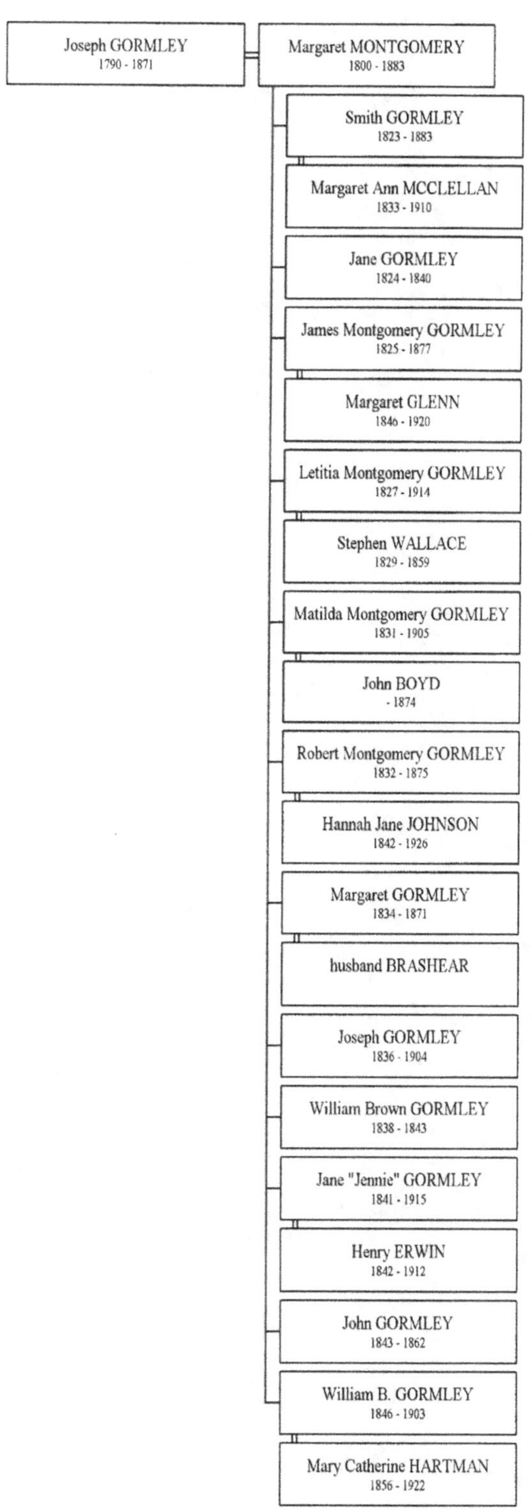

The Gormley Family History

Gormley is an anglicized version of an ancient Irish surname whose original spelling variations included O'Gairmleadhaigh, O'Gormshuil, and O'Gormshuiligh. Their original territory, known as Cinel Moen (their tribe name), was located in the modern Barony of Raphoe in County Donegal. In the 14th Century, the Gormleys were driven out of that area by the O'Donnells. Their new homeland was on the other side of the River Foyle in County Tyrone between the townlands of Derry and Strabane. Like many of the small independent septs in northwest Ireland, the Gormleys eventually sank into obscurity after the plantation of Ulster. By the 17th Century, the descendants of the Gormleys were located chiefly in the counties of Armagh and Londonderry.[1,2] True to form, the subjects of this family history first make their appearance in that part of County Londonderry known as the Bann Valley.

THE GORMLEY FAMILY IN IRELAND

The Bann Valley

The Bann Valley is in the most eastwardly part of County Londonderry. It was once primarily an agricultural area with farmlands extending southward throughout the valley in the direction of Kilrea and Garvagh. The valley was fed by the Bann River which flowed through Ulster separating County Londonderry from County Antrim. The Bann River drained Lough Neagh to the north where it met the sea at Coleraine, then the second largest city in the county.

First Garvagh Presbyterian Church

The First Garvagh Presbyterian Church has a long history in the Bann Valley. Documentary evidence exists of a minister at the church as early as 1660. He was succeeded by many other Presbyterian ministers including the Reverend Mr. James Brown who was ordained at First Garvagh on December 1, 1795.[3] He served as minister of the First Garvagh Presbyterian

---

[1]Edward MacLysaght, *Irish Families - Their Names Arms and Origins*, (Dublin, Ireland: Hodges Figgis & Co., LTD, 1957), 163.

[2]For a scholarly account of the history of the O'Gormley family branch of the Ceneal Moain lineage within the northern Ui Neill dynasty see Dr. Brian Deeny's "Ceneal Moain and the O'Gormleys in East Donegal and West Tyrone," *Familia*, Volume 2, No. 6, 1990, Ulster Historical Foundation, p. 39 - 56.

[3]James McConnell, *Fasti of the Irish Presbyterian Church, 1613 - 1840*, (Belfast, Ireland: The Presbyterian Historical Society, 1951), Part IX, p. 191, # 766, FHL Microfilm Roll 0994080,

Church until his assistant, James Miller, was ordained on February 18, 1840. The Reverend Brown died on May 20, 1850 at the age of 88 and in the 55th year of his ministry.[4] It is largely through his records which begin in 1795 that the history of the Gormley and the Montgomery families in the Bann Valley have been preserved.

The baptism of Joseph Gormley does not appear in the records of the First Garvagh Presbyterian Church because the records begin in 1795 and he was born before that year. Nevertheless, based on a review of the existing baptismal records there appears to have been only one Gormley family in the area so it is possible that Joseph Gormley may have been the son of James Gormley of Ballyagan, Desertoghill Parish, County Londonderry.[5]

The baptism of Margaret Megomery (sic) appears in the records of the First Garvagh Presbyterian Church on March 24, 1801.[6] She was from Magheramore, Desertoghill Parish, County Londonderry. Based on an analysis of two church censuses, her parents were probably Robert and Agnes Montgomery and her grandparents may have been Robert and Jennet Montgomery also of Magheramore.[7,8]

---

says:

> BROWN, James; 4th s. of John Brown, farmer, Co. Antrim: b. 1762: educ. Glas.: M.A.(Glas.), 1789: lic. Route Pres., 1792: ord. Garvagh (1st), 1 Dec., 1795: Clerk of Route Pres., 18 -34: ret. 1839: d. 20 May 1850. Rev. Clarke Huston, Macosquin, was a son-in-law.

[4]William Dool Killen, *History of Congregations of the Presbyterian Church in Ireland and Biographical Notices of Eminent Presbyterian Ministers and Laymen with Signification of Names of Places*, (Belfast, Ireland: J. Cleeland, 1886), 147, FHL Microfilm Roll 0908207.

[5]Baptisms of the Children of James Gormley, First Garvagh Presbyterian Church, Garvagh, Errigal Parish, County Londonderry, Ireland, Public Records Office of Northern Ireland, Belfast, Northern Ireland, Microfilm MIC/1P/257 include the following:

> 20 July 1797 Elizabeth Gormley of Ballyagan Deseroghill Parish
> 20 January 1800 John son of James Gormley of Ballyagan, Dertoghill Parish
> 22 July 1801 Samuel Gormley of Ballyagan, Dertoghill Parish
> 11 March 1808 James son of James Gormley of Ballyagan, Dertoghill Parish
> 22 March 1810 John son of James Gormley of Ballyagan, Dertoghill Parish

[6]Baptism of Margaret Megomery (sic), March 24, 1801, First Garvagh Presbyterian Church, Garvagh, Errigal Parish, County Londonderry, Ireland, Public Records Office of Northern Ireland, Belfast, Northern Ireland, Microfilm MIC/1P/257.

[7]Visitation of the Reverend James Brown to Maghrimore (sic), July 1818. A copy of the original record of the First Garvagh Presbyterian Church, Errigal Parish, County Londonderry, Ireland, was provided to Kathryn C. Torpey on September 9, 2003 by Lavonne Bradfield,

The Reverend James Brown recorded the marriage of Joseph Gormley to Peggy Megomery (sic) on May 23, 1822.[9] Beginning in the Summer of 1825, he also made a record of the names of their three oldest children when he visited the members of the Congregation living in Maghrimore.[10,11] That is, he entered the following information in his book about the subjects of this family history:

> Robert McGumery
> Joseph Gormley
> Margaret Gormley
> Smyth Gormley
> Jane Gormley
> Jas Gormley

The Reverend James Brown also dutifully recorded the baptisms of all of the remaining

---

<<LBradfield@satx.rr.com>>. The record was provided to Lavonne Bradfield by a member of the First Garvagh Presbyterian Church. The record states:

> Robt McGumery
> Agnes, his wife
> Mary
> Jennet
> Robt
> Margt

[8]Visitation of the Reverend James Brown to Mach More (sic), 1796, First Garvagh Presbyterian Church, Garvagh, Errigal Parish, County Londonderry, Ireland, Public Records Office of Northern Ireland, Belfast, Northern Ireland, Microfilm MIC/1P/257, states:

> Robert McGummery
> Jennet McGummery
> Mary McGummery
> Robt McGummery

[9]Marriage of Joseph Gormley and Pegey Megomery, May 23, 1822, First Garvagh Presbyterian Church, Garvagh, Errigal Parish, County Londonderry, Ireland, Public Records Office of Northern Ireland, Belfast, Northern Ireland, Microfilm MIC/1P/257.

[10]Visitation of the Reverend James Brown Beginning in the Summer of 1825 - Maghrimore (sic). A copy of the original record of the First Garvagh Presbyterian Church, Errigal Parish, County Londonderry, Ireland, was provided to Kathryn C. Torpey by Lavonne Bradfield, <<LBradfield@satx.rr.com>>, on September 9, 2003. The record was provided to Lavonne Bradfield by a member of the First Garvagh Presbyterian Church.

[11]i.e., Magheramore, Desertoghill Parish, County Londonderry.

children of Joseph and Margaret (Montgomery) Gormley who were born in Ireland except for the baptism of Matilda Gormley.[12] The baptisms appear as follows in the records of the First Garvagh Presbyterian Church:

> 22 June 1827 Letitia daughter to Joseph Gormley of Magheramore Parish of Desertoghill
> 2 January 1832 Robert son to Joseph Gormley of Mullinabrone Parish of Aghadowey
> 27 March 1834 Mar't daughter of Joseph Gormley of Mullinabrone Parish of Aghadowey
> 18 July 1836 Joseph son to Jos Gormley of Mullinabrone Parish of Aghadowey
> 5 December 1838 William Brown son to Joseph Gormley of Mullinabrone Parish of Aghadowey

The baptism of Matilda Gormley may have escaped being recorded by the Reverend James Brown because it occurred around the time the Gormley family is thought to have moved from Magheramore in Desertoghill Parish to Mullinabrone in Aghadowey Parish.

Irish Census Enumerations

The 1831 census of County Londonderry is one of the few Irish census schedules to have survived the fire at the Public Records Office in Dublin in 1922. In that census schedule, Joseph Gormley and his household, which included his wife, six children, and a servant, were enumerated in the Bann Valley as follows:

CO. LONDONDERRY, PARISH OF AGHADOWEY, TOWNLAND OF MULLANABRONE

Jos[h] Gormley

Number of House:	24	
Number of Families:	1	
Number of Persons in Family:		
Males:	4 (i.e., Joseph, Smith, James, Robert)	
Females:	4 (i.e., Margaret, Jane, Letitia, Matilda)	
Servants:	1	
Religion:		
Established Church:	0	
Catholic:	1	
Presbyterian:	8[13]	

The Tithe Applotment

The Tithe Applotment was a tax based on how much land a person occupied. It was paid

----

[12]Baptisms of the Children of Joseph Gormley, First Garvagh Presbyterian Church, Garvagh, Errigal Parish, County Londonderry, Ireland, Public Records Office of Northern Ireland, Belfast, Northern Ireland, Microfilm MIC/1P/257.

[13]1831 Irish Census (population), County Londonderry, Parish of Aghadowey, Townland of Mullanabrown (sic), page 16, FHL Microfilm Roll 0597160.

by rural inhabitants to support the clergy of the Church of Ireland. Persons of all denominations were required to pay the tithe because the Church of Ireland was the Established Church until 1871.

Joseph Gormley was duly recorded in the Tithe Applotment for the Church of Ireland, Diocese of Derry, Parish of Aghadowey, Mullanabrone (sic) that was certified on July 3, 1832. The register indicated that he was possessed of (owned or rented) 7 acres, 1 rod, and 0 perches valued at 4 pounds, 7 pence, and 9 shillings. His tithe on the property was 7 pence, 3 shillings.[14,15] This appears to be the last record created by Joseph Gormley in the Bann Valley before his departure for America.

JOURNEY TO A NEW LIFE

Joseph Gormley's Arrival in America

Joseph Gormley is reported to have been one of the early settlers in Summit Hill.[16] According to family legend, he came to America alone and, after he was established in Summit Hill, he sent to Ireland for the rest of his family.[17]

Joseph Gormley reported in his Declaration of Intention that he arrived at the Port of New York on Sunday, May 20, 1838, from Londonderry with the intent to settle in Summit Hill, then in Northampton County, Pennsylvania.[18] Nevertheless, his name does not appear on the Port of

---

[14]Tithe Applotment, County Londonderry, Diocese of Derry, Parish of Aghadowey, Townland of Mullanabrone, Certified 3 July 1832, Dated 12 August 1833, Rec'd 11 September 1833, FHL Microfilm Roll 0258443.

[15]Reverend Thomas H. Mullin, B.A., B.D., *Aghadowey - A Parish and its Linen Industry*, (Belfast, Ireland: Century Services, Ltd., 1972), p. unknown, also contains the reference to the assessment of Joseph Gormley in 1833 for 7 acres in Mullinabrone (sic).

[16]Fred Brenckman, *History of Carbon County, Pennsylvania*, (Harrisburg, Pennsylvania: James J. Nungesser, Publisher, 1913), 324.

[17]Letter dated November 7, 2003 from Robert C. Gormley, 334 Brownsburg Road, Newtown, Pennsylvania 18940 to Kathryn C. Torpey, 5035 Domain Place, Alexandria, Virginia 22311-5066 contains a copy of an article by Ed Gildea entitled "Summit Hill Woman Murdered in China" that appeared in a June 1973 issue of *The Valley Gazette*. In the article John M. Gormley, great-grandson of Joseph and Margaret (Montgomery) Gormley, related the family legend concerning the arrival of Joseph Gormley in Summit Hill.

[18]Declaration of Intention of Joseph Gormley, Court of Common Pleas, Northampton County, Pennsylvania, December 20, 1842, Carbon County Courthouse, Jim Thorpe,

New York passenger manifests and no vessels arrived at the Port of New York directly from Londonderry between May 13, 1838 and May 26, 1838.[19,20]

Since no vessels appeared to have arrived at the Port of New York directly from Londonderry during the time period in question, the search for Joseph Gormley was widened to include the Port of Philadelphia. An examination of the passenger lists of vessels arriving at the Port of Philadelphia revealed that the Ship Erin arrived from Londonderry on Monday, May 21, 1838, after a voyage that lasted 36 days.[21] Aboard that ship was a passenger by the name of Joseph Grimsley who was stated to be 33 years old.[22] Despite the obvious errors in spelling and age, the entry on the passenger manifest for the Ship Erin is believed to refer to the arrival in America of the subject of this family history.

The accuracy of information contained on ship passenger manifests was not a high priority prior to 1882.[23] Errors in spelling, age, occupation, and nationality were common and came about because, during the time Joseph Gormley arrived in America, most Irish people traveling in steerage usually did so without any formal papers such as passports and visas to document their identity. In addition, many of the passengers from Ulster, including Joseph Gormley, were illiterate and spoke English with a distinctly rural Irish accent that was quite

---

Pennsylvania.

[19]Notice, "Shipping List for the Week Ending May 19, 1838," *New York Herald*, Monday, May 21, 1838, p. 1, Library of Congress, Washington, D.C.

[20]Notice, "Shipping List for the Week Ending May 26, 1838," *New York Herald*, Monday, May 28, 1838, p. 1, Library of Congress, Washington, D.C.

[21]Notice, "Ship Arrivals," *Philadelphia Public Ledger*, Tuesday, May 22, 1838, p. 2, Library of Congress, Washington, D.C., says:

> ARRIVED
> Br ship Erie (sic), Wilkinson, Londonderry, 36 days.

[22]Entry for Joseph Grimsley, Ship Erin Passenger Manifest, May 21, 1838, p. 8, line 181, Passenger Lists of Vessels Arriving at Philadelphia, PA, 1800-1882, Records of the U.S. Customs Service, Records Group 36, National Archives Microfilm Publication M425, Roll 53.

[23]Passenger manifests created prior to 1882 are known as Customs Passenger Lists. They were provided to the Collector of Customs when the vessels arrived in port. Beginning in 1882, the U.S. Congress enacted legislation designed to regulate and restrict immigration. Passenger manifests created as a result of this legislation are known as Immigration Passenger Lists. They were provided to immigration officials when the vessels arrived in port. These later lists usually contain more accurate information than the earlier lists.

difficult to understand. It is likely that the ticket agent and the shipping clerk who heard Joseph Gormley state his name and age may have heard him say something other than what he actually said. This incorrect information would have been entered on the passenger manifest. When the Ship Erin arrived at the Port of Philadelphia, Captain Wilkinson would have submitted the passenger manifest to the Collector of Customs (rather than to an immigration official) and the passengers, including Joseph Gormley, would have been allowed to disembark the vessel and make their way in America without any official processing other than a brief stop at a quarantine station to identify any passengers who were sick, injured, or carrying a communicable disease.

The Family's Arrival in America

Margaret (Montgomery) Gormley and the nine children officially arrived at the South Street Seaport on the East River in the Port of New York on December 12, 1839, abroad the Ship Sheridan.[24] According to the notice of arrival that appeared in the New York Herald, the Ship Sheridan departed Liverpool on November 14, 1839.[25]

The Gormley family was listed on the Ship Sheridan passenger manifest as follows:

Gormley, Margaret	34
, Smith	15
, Jane	13
, James	11
, Litcher (sic)	10
, Matilda	8
, Robert	7
, Margaret	5
, Joseph	3
, William	1

It is unknown whether Margaret (Montgomery) Gormley and the children were traveling alone or in the company of other wives and children making the same journey or whether they were met by someone they knew when the ship docked in New York. In any case, they made their way out of New York and are said to have arrived by train in Mauch Chunk sometime after

---

[24]Entry for Margaret Gormley and Children, Ship Sheridan Passenger Manifest, December 12, 1839, page 3, line 19, Passenger List of Vessels Arriving at New York, NY, 1820-1897, Records of the U.S. Customs Service, Record Group 36, National Archives Microfilm Publication M237, Roll 40.

[25]Notice, "Ship Arrivals," *New York Herald*, Wednesday, December 11, 1839, p. 5, Library of Congress, Washington, D.C., says:

ARRIVED
Packet ship Sheridan, Lepeyster, fm Liverpool, Nov 14, mdz to E.K. Collins.

7

the last stagecoach had departed for Summit Hill so they had to walk the whole nine miles up the hill in the dark to their new home. As they walked along the old wagon road, they were reported to have been terrified by the sounds of the night including the noisy call of the Katydids, a large grasshopper which was then plentiful in America, but unknown in Ireland.[26]

THE GORMLEY FAMILY IN AMERICA

Joseph and Margaret (Montgomery) Gormley

Joseph Gormley was born November 21, 1790 or November 21, 1792 in County Londonderry, Ireland.[27,28] He died October 8, 1871 or October 9, 1871 in Mahoning Township, Carbon County, Pennsylvania.[29,30] Joseph Gormley married Margaret Montgomery, daughter of Robert and Agnes Montgomery, on May 23, 1822 at Garvagh, Errigal Parish, County Londonderry, Ireland.[31,32,33] She was born April 5, 1800 in Magheramore, Desertoghill Parish,

---

[26]Letter dated November 7, 2003 from Robert C. Gormley, 334 Brownsburg Road, Newtown, Pennsylvania 18940 to Kathryn C. Torpey, 5035 Domain Place, Alexandria, Virginia 22311-5066 contains a copy of an article by Ed Gildea entitled "Summit Hill Woman Murdered in China" that appeared in a June 1973 issue of *The Valley Gazette* in which John M. Gormley, great-grandson of Joseph and Margaret (Montgomery) Gormley, related the family legend concerning the arrival of Margaret (Montgomery) Gormley and the children in Summit Hill.

[27]Will of Margaret Gormley, May 29, 1878, November 8, 1883, Will Book 1, page 431, Carbon County, Pennsylvania, FHL Microfilm Roll 1290573 says: "Joseph Gormley born Nov. 21st 1790 (sic)."

[28]Margaret Gormley, Civil War Dependent Relative Pension Application File, MO 246,903, Records of the Veterans Administration, Record Group 15, National Archives, Washington, D.C., contains an affidavit from Joseph Gormley's doctor, P.D. Keiser, saying that Joseph Gormley was 79 (sic) when he died on October 9 (sic), 1871 (i.e., born c. 1792).

[29]Will of Margaret Gormley, May 29, 1878, November 8, 1883, Will Book 1, page 431, Carbon County, Pennsylvania, FHL Microfilm Roll 1290573 says: "Joseph Gormley died Oct 8th (sic)1871."

[30]Margaret Gormley, Civil War Dependent Relative Pension Application File, MO 246,903, Records of the Veterans Administration, Record Group 15, National Archives, Washington, D.C., says Joseph Gormley, husband of the applicant, died October 9 (sic), 1871 in Summit Hill, Pennsylvania.

[31]Visitation of the Reverend James Brown to Maghrimore (sic), July 1818. A copy of the original record of the First Garvagh Presbyterian Church, Errigal Parish, County Londonderry, Ireland, was provided to Kathryn C. Torpey by Lavonne Bradfield,<<LBradfield@satx.rr.com>>,

County Londonderry, Ireland.[34,35,36] She probably died November 3, 1883 in Summit Hill, Carbon County, Pennsylvania.[37,38] Nevertheless, two other sources state her death date was

on September 9, 2003. The record was provided to Lavonne Bradfield by a member of the First Garvagh Presbyterian Church. The record states:

> Robt McGumery
> Agnes, his wife
> Mary
> Jennet
> Robt
> Margt

[32]Marriage of Joseph Gormley and Pegey Megomery, May 23, 1822, First Garvagh Presbyterian Church, Garvagh, Errigal Parish, County Londonderry, Ireland, Public Records Office of Northern Ireland, Belfast, Northern Ireland, Microfilm MIC/1P/257.

[33]Margaret Gormley, Civil War Dependent Relative Pension Application File, MO 246,903, Records of the Veterans Administration, Record Group 15, National Archives, Washington, D.C., says "...the declarant (i.e., Margaret Gormley) was married to the father of said son at Garvah (sic) Ireland on the ___ day of July (sic) 1822, A.D. by Rev. James Brown;..."

[34]Will of Margaret Gormley, May 29, 1878, November 8, 1883, Will Book 1, page 431, Carbon County, Pennsylvania, FHL Microfilm Roll 1290573 says: "Margaret Gormley born April 5th, 1800."

[35]Baptism of Margaret Megomery, March 24, 1801, First Garvagh Presbyterian Church, Garvagh, Errigal Parish, County Londonderry, Ireland, Public Records Office of Northern Ireland, Belfast, Northern Ireland, Microfilm MIC/1P/257.

[36]Entry for Margaret Gormley and Children, Ship Sheridan Passenger Manifest, December 12, 1839, page 3, line 19, Passenger List of Vessels Arriving at New York, NY, 1820-1897, Records of the U.S. Customs Service, Record Group 36, National Archives Microfilm Publication M237, Roll 40 says 34, i.e. born 1805 in Ireland.

[37]Margaret Gormley, Civil War Dependent Relative Pension Application File, MO 246,903, Records of the Veterans Administration, Record Group 15, National Archives, Washington, D.C., says Margaret Gormley, the applicant, died November 3, 1883 at Summit Hill, Pennsylvania.

[38]Will of Margaret Gormley, May 29, 1878, November 8, 1883, Will Book 1, page 431, Carbon County, Pennsylvania, FHL Microfilm Roll 1290573 says: "Margaret Gormley died Nov. 3rd 1883."

November 4, 1883 or November 7, 1883.[39,40] Joseph Gormley and his wife, Margaret (Montgomery) Gormley, were both buried in the Old Presbyterian Cemetery in Summit Hill, Carbon County, Pennsylvania.[41,42,43]

LIFE IN SUMMIT HILL. In the late 1830s, Joseph Gormley and his family would have found that Summit Hill was no more than a small village situated at an elevation of more than 1,600 feet above sea level in Mauch Chunk Township, Northampton County, Pennsylvania.

Summit Hill was about nine miles from the town of Mauch Chunk (now known as Jim Thorpe). Its major claim to fame was that it was the site of the discovery of anthracite coal by Philip Ginder in 1791. In addition to back-breaking jobs, the village of Summit Hill probably furnished its early residents with little more than a commanding view of the surrounding area from a local high point on Sharp Mountain known as Mt. Jefferson.

Although the view from the mountain may have been different from the scene back home

---

[39]Letter dated June 12, 1997 from Robert C. Gormley, 334 Brownsburg Road, Newtown, Pennsylvania 18940 to Kathryn C. Torpey, 5035 Domain Place, Alexandria, Virginia 22311-5066 contains extracts from the Records of the First Presbyterian Church of Summit Hill and Tamaqua as prepared by an elderly member of the church which state:

> VOLUME II (1873-1903)
> REGISTER OF MEMBERS:
> Mrs. Joseph Gormley   DIED 11/4 (sic)/1883
> Hanna (sic) Gormley   ADMISSION 1/13/1877

[40]Estate of Margaret Gormley, Summit Hill, # 1309, Carbon County Courthouse, Jim Thorpe, Pennsylvania, contains a deposition from Margaret Allen and a deposition from William Gormley dated c. February 14, 1888 that both state she died November 7 (sic), 1883.

[41]Will of Margaret Gormley, May 29, 1878, November 8, 1883, Will Book 1, page 431, Carbon County, Pennsylvania, FHL Microfilm Roll 1290573 implies that both she and Joseph Gormley were buried in Summit Hill.

[42]Letter dated October 8, 1996 from Robert C. Gormley, 334 Brownsburg Road, Newtown, Pennsylvania 18940 to Kathryn C. Torpey, 5035 Domain Place, Alexandria, Virginia 22311-5066 states that Joseph and Margaret (Montgomery) Gormley were both buried in the Old Presbyterian Cemetery in Summit Hill.

[43]Margaret Gormley, Civil War Dependent Relative Pension Application File, MO 246,903, Records of the Veterans Administration, Record Group 15, National Archives, Washington, D.C., contains an affidavit from Joseph Gormley's doctor, P.D. Keiser, stating that Joseph Gormley was buried in Summit Hill.

in Ireland, many of the neighbors may have been the same. Immigrants from Ireland such as
Joseph Gormley may have been attracted to Summit Hill through the work of men like Alexander
McLean who came from Farrenlester, Dunboe Parish, County Londonderry, Ireland. After he
arrived in Summit Hill about 1820, Alexander McLean quickly became involved in the fledgling
anthracite coal mining operation by hauling coal via mule team from the coal quarries in Summit
Hill to Mauch Chunk. Later, he is said to have signed a contract with the Lehigh Navigation
Coal Company to become a mine operator and manager.[44] At that point, he would have been in a
position to offer jobs to the men back home and, perhaps, that is exactly what he did which
would account for the high number of immigrants to Summit Hill from the Bann Valley between
1830 and 1850.[45]

      FIRST PRESBYTERIAN CHURCH OF SUMMIT HILL AND TAMAQUA. After their arrival in
Summit Hill, Joseph and Margaret (Montgomery) Gormley joined the First Presbyterian Church
of Summit Hill and Tamaqua. This church was established on April 19, 1839. In May 1844, the
congregation became independent of Tamaqua and was renamed the First Presbyterian Church of
Summit Hill. The congregation worshiped in the local schoolhouse until a church was erected in
1847.[46]

The date Joseph Gormley joined the church is unknown because the Membership
Register bearing his name is undated. The date his wife, Margaret (Montgomery) Gormley,
joined the church has been reported differently by various sources. That is, the minutes of the
church are said to state that Margaret (Montgomery) Gormley was admitted on examination on
December 10, 1841, while the Membership Register is reported to say she joined the church on

---

[44]Joan Campion, *Smokestacks and Black Diamonds - A History of Carbon County,
Pennsylvania*, (Easton, Pennsylvania: Canal History and Technology Press, 1997), 35, states that
the Lehigh Coal & Navigation Company (LC&N) was founded in 1821 by Josiah White and
Erskine Hazard as a merger of two companies - the Lehigh Coal Company established to mine
coal and establish a road from the mines in Summit Hill to the Lehigh River, and the Lehigh
Navigation Company established to provide transportation for the coal to market by way of the
Lehigh River. By 1839, LC&N owned about 8,000 acres of coal land in the eastern end of
Pennsylvania's southern anthracite field. Its coal operations were run by a subsidiary known as
the Lehigh Navigation Coal Company (LNC). The LNC was headquartered in Lansford. The
LNC's company towns were Summit Hill, Nesquehoning, Coaldale, Lansford, and Tamaqua.

[45]E-mail dated February 1, 2001 from Dan Wilson, dan.wilson@asu.edu to
BannValley@4qd.co.uk describing the early settlement of Summit Hill and the surrounding area.

[46]Fred Brenckman, *History of Carbon County, Pennsylvania*, (Harrisburg, Pennsylvania:
James J. Nungesser, Publisher, 1913), 331.

December 16, 1841 or December 16, 1842[47,48] or on September 12, 1842.[49]

    The baptisms of Joseph and Margaret (Montgomery) Gormley's three youngest children appear as follows in the records of the church:

REGISTER OF BAPTISMS:

NO.	CHILD	PARENTS	BORN	BAPTIZED
40	Peggy (sic) Jane	Joseph & Jane (sic) Gormley	1841	May 16, 1841
89	John	Joseph & Jane (sic) Gormley	August 5, 1843	-
133	William	Joseph & Jane (sic) Gormley	-	April 7, 1847[50]

---

[47]Letter dated June 12, 1997 from Robert C. Gormley, 334 Brownsburg Road, Newtown, Pennsylvania 18940 to Kathryn C. Torpey, 5035 Domain Place, Alexandria, Virginia 22311-5066 contains extracts from the Records of the First Presbyterian Church of Summit Hill and Tamaqua as prepared by an elderly member of the church which state:

VOLUME I (1839 - 1873)
REGISTER OF MEMBERS:
Joseph Gormley   DIED
Margaret, wife of Joseph   Received in Membership 12/16/1841(sic)

[48]E-mail dated October 10, 1999 from Dan Wilson, dan.wilson@asu.edu to Kathryn C. Torpey, 5035 Domain Place, Alexandria, Virginia 22311-5066 contains extracts from the Records of the First Presbyterian Church of Summit Hill as prepared by Jack Sterling which state:

Minutes:
Gormley, Margaret, wife of Joseph - admitted by exam 10 Dec 1841
Membership Register
51 Gormley, Margaret, wife - 16 Dec 1842 (sic)

[49]E-mail dated February, 5, 2000 from Dan Wilson, dan.wilson@asu.edu to Kathryn C. Torpey, 5035 Domain Place, Alexandria, Virginia 22311-5066 contains extracts from the Records of the First Presbyterian Church of Summit Hill as prepared by Jack Sterling which state:

51 Margaret, wife of Joseph Gormley, admitted by exam - 12 Sept 1842 (sic)

[50]Letter dated November 13, 2003 from Edith Ann Szczecina, Secretary, First Presbyterian Church of Panther Valley, 44 West White Street, P.O. Box 36, Summit Hill, Pennsylvania 18250 to Kathryn C. Torpey, 5035 Domain Place, Alexandria, Virginia 22311-5066 provided copies of three pages of the baptismal register containing entries # 34 to # 140, inclusive.

COAL MINING IN SUMMIT HILL. According to the 1840 census, Joseph Gormley was employed in mining in Mauch Chunk Township, presumably in Summit Hill.[51] In that capacity, he would have engaged in quarrying coal in the "Old Mines." The coal, which was originally hoisted to the surface in buckets, was loaded into cars that were hauled out of the "Old Mines" by mule teams through passages cut in the rocks and transported, via a wagon road that ran through the forest, to Mauch Chunk where it was loaded on barges and carried to Philadelphia via the Lehigh River. In 1844, a tunnel was driven through the rocks southwest of the "Old Mines."[52] This event formally introduced the era of underground mining operations to the area. Joseph Gormley is thought to have worked in these underground mining operations until 1847 when he bought property in Mahoning Township.[53]

NATURALIZATION. Joseph Gormley signed his Declaration of Intention with his mark on December 20, 1842, when he swore before the Court of Common Pleas of Northampton County, Pennsylvania, that it was his bona fide intention to become a Citizen of the United States and to renounce forever all allegiance and fidelity to the Queen of Great Britain and Ireland of whom he was at that time a subject.[54] On March 25, 1845, Joseph Gormley signed his Petition for

---

[51]1840 U.S. Census (population), Pennsylvania, Northampton County, Mauch Chunk Township, page 212, line 21, National Archives Microfilm Publication M704, Roll 479, Household of Jos. Gramley (sic) states:

MAUCH CHUNK TOWNSHIP, NORTHAMPTON COUNTY, PENNSYLVANIA

Jos. Gramley (sic)
Free white persons:

Males:	2	(Under 5) - i.e., Joseph & William Brown
	1	(5-10) - i.e., Robert
	1	(10-15) - i.e., James
	1	(15-20) - i.e., Smith
	1	(30-40) - i.e., Joseph
Females:	1	(Under 5) - i.e., Margaret
	1	(5-10) - i.e., Matilda
	2	(10-15) - i.e., Jane & Letitia
	1	(30-40) - i.e., Margaret

NOTE: 1 Person Employed in Mining

[52]*Summit Hill Borough Centennial 1889-1989, The Town that Began the Industrial Revolution in America*, http://legionpost316.virtualave.net/summit_hill.htm, downloaded September 25, 2003.

[53]Deed from James O'Brian to Joseph Gormley, October 8, 1847 (recorded October 28, 1847), Volume 2, p. 177, Deeds, Volumes 1-3, 1843-1851, Carbon County, Pennsylvania, FHL Microfilm Roll 2208973.

[54]Declaration of Intention of Joseph Gormley, Court of Common Pleas, Northampton County, Pennsylvania, December 20, 1842, Carbon County Courthouse, Jim Thorpe,

Citizenship with his mark when he took the Oath of Allegiance before the Court of Common Pleas of Northampton County, Pennsylvania.[55]

FARMING IN MAHONING TOWNSHIP. Over time, Joseph and Margaret (Montgomery) Gormley owned two properties in Mahoning Township, described as the richest agricultural district in Carbon County.[56]

The first property, consisting of 46 acres, was purchased by Joseph Gormley on October 8, 1847, from James O'Brian.[57] The property was bounded by the land of Casper Frederick, Jonas Horn, John Seager, Esquire, Thomas Trumbo[ur], and Wilson Hough. A small portion of the property, consisting of about 60 yards (i.e., 11-1/4 perches), was bounded by the Mahoning Creek.

Undoubtedly, the purchase of this 46 acre property represented the culmination of years of hard work on the part of Joseph Gormley. At the age of 57, he could now count himself among the landowners of Mahoning Township.

Gone were the days of being a sub-tenant on someone else's property in Ireland where he was obliged to pay rent forever to an absentee landlord's overseer. Being industrious and strongly ambitious of upward mobility, Joseph Gormley willingly spent nine years of his life working in the coal mines of Summit Hill for the sake of his children. He wanted to be sure that they would be independent after he was gone. Rather than leaving his children the legacy of debt and obligation, Joseph Gormley wanted to die knowing that they would be free and independent. As far as Joseph Gormley was concerned, owning a farm and engaging in agriculture was definitely a step in the right direction.

Pennsylvania.

[55]Petition for Citizenship and Oath of Allegiance of Joseph Gormley, Court of Common Pleas, Northampton County, Pennsylvania, March 25, 1845, Carbon County Courthouse, Jim Thorpe, Pennsylvania. It is unclear why Joseph Gormley was naturalized in the Court of Common Pleas of Northampton County. He lived in that part of Northampton County that became Carbon County in 1842. His naturalization documents were found in the Carbon County Courthouse located in Jim Thorpe, so it is possible that Joseph Gormley may have been naturalized in Carbon County by the Court of Common Pleas of Northampton County acting on behalf of Carbon County.

[56]Fred Brenckman, *History of Carbon County, Pennsylvania*, (Harrisburg, Pennsylvania: James J. Nungesser, Publisher, 1913), 255.

[57]Deed from James O'Brian to Joseph Gormley, October 8, 1847 (recorded October 28, 1847), Volume 2, p. 177, Deeds, Volumes 1-3, 1843-1851, Carbon County, Pennsylvania, FHL Microfilm Roll 2208973.

In the 1850 census and in the 1860 census, Joseph Gormley was enumerated as a farmer living on his property in Mahoning Township.[58,59] In the 1860 agricultural census the property was described as a farm consisting of 44 acres (improved), valued at $1,950.00.[60] Also enumerated on the farm were farming implements and machinery valued at $75.00. Livestock on the farm included 2 horses, 5 cows, 2 sheep, and 4 swine valued at $300.00. The farm produced 100 bushels of rye, 150 bushels of Indian Corn, 100 bushels of oats, 10 lbs. of wool, 100 bushels of Irish potatoes, 80 bushels of buckwheat, 150 lbs. of butter, and 10 tons of hay. The value of animals slaughtered was estimated at $75.00.

It appears from the land records that on February 13, 1852, Joseph and Margaret (Montgomery) Gormley sold their 46 acres adjacent to the Mahoning Creek to their oldest son,

---

[58]1850 U.S. Census (population), Pennsylvania, Carbon County, Mahoning Township, page 388, lines 11-18, National Archives Microfilm Publication M432, Roll 762, Household of Joseph Gormley enumerated directly beside Wilson Huff (sic) as follows:

MAHONING TOWNSHIP, CARBON COUNTY, PENNSYLVANIA, OCTOBER 23, 1850

Joseph Gormley	55 M	Farmer $1800	Ireland
Margaret	48 F		Do
Margaret	15 F		Do
Joseph	14 M		Do
Jane	9 F		Penna
John	7 M		Do
William	3 M		Do
Margaret Gaston	7 F		Do

[59]1860 U.S. Census (population), Pennsylvania, Carbon County, Mahoning Township, page 972, lines 11-20, National Archives Microfilm Publication M653, Roll 1089, Household of Joseph Gomly (sic) enumerated directly beside Wilson Hough (sic) as follows:

MAHONING TOWNSHIP, CARBON COUNTY, PENNSYLVANIA, JUNE 27, 1860

Joseph Gomly (sic)	67 M	Farmer $2000 $500	Ireland
Margaret	59 F		
Robt	25 M	Lab	
John	16 M		Pa
Wm	13 M		
Jas. Boyd	8 M		
Margaret	5 F		
Smith Gomly (sic)	36 M	Farmer	
Marg	23 F		Ireland
Marg	1 F		

[60]1860 U.S. Census (agricultural), Pennsylvania, Carbon County, Mahoning Township, page 5 & 6, National Archives Microfilm Publication T1138, Roll 12.

Smith Gormley, for the sum of $1,200.00 and subject to the following condition:

> ...subject always nevertheless to the support and maintenance well and truly furnished and made of the same Joseph Gormley and Margaret his wife upon and out of the said premises during and for their natural lifetime respectively and also to the support and maintenance of Jane, John, and William children of the said Joseph and Margaret until severally fourteen years of age and no longer.[61]

Eight years later, on November 14, 1860, Joseph and Margaret (Montgomery) Gormley signed a Quit Claim releasing their son, Smith Gormley, from the requirement of maintenance and support because their youngest child had attained the age of fourteen.[62] Smith Gormley paid his parents $300.00 at the time they signed the release. Two years later, on April 1, 1862, Smith Gormley sold the 46 acre property adjacent to the Mahoning Creek to William Mullen.[63]

Reminiscences about the farm in Mahoning Township were contained in a letter written by Margaret (Gormley) Brashear, the daughter of Joseph and Margaret (Montgomery) Gormley, who was living in Shanghai.   In her letter dated July 11, 1870 which is addressed to her brother, Robert Gormley, she wrote:

> ...when I receive your letter it takes me far back I can remember things I had forgotten I look back and cannot realize I ever worked in the fields in Mahoning...[64]

About a year prior to Smith Gormley being released from his obligation to support his parents and three youngest siblings in conjunction with the 46 acre property adjacent to the Mahoning Creek, Margaret (Montgomery) Gormley bought a second piece of property consisting of 50 acres for $200.00 from John McLaughlin.[65] This second property was situated adjacent to

---

[61]Deed from Joseph Gormley & Wife to Smith Gormley, February 13, 1852 (recorded April 10, 1852), Volume 5, p. 86, Deeds, Volumes 4-7, 1851-1855, Carbon County, Pennsylvania, FHL Microfilm Roll 2208974.

[62]Deed of Release from Joseph Gormley & Wife to Smith Gormley, November 14, 1860 (recorded November 16, 1860), Volume 10, p. 554, Deeds, Volumes 10-12, 1859-1864, Carbon County, Pennsylvania, FHL Microfilm Roll 2208976.

[63]Deed from Smith Gormley & Wife to William Mullen, April 1, 1862 (recorded April 16, 1862), Volume 11, p. 426, Deeds, Volumes 10-12, 1859-1864, Carbon County, Pennsylvania, FHL Microfilm Roll 2208976.

[64]Letter dated May 17, 1997 from Robert C. Gormley, 334 Brownsburg Road, Newtown, Pennsylvania 18940 to Kathryn C. Torpey, 5035 Domain Place, Alexandria, Virginia 22311-5066 provided copies of these letters for transcription.

[65]Deed from John McLaughlin to Margaret Gormley, May 28, 1859 (recorded June 27,

the land of James Sinyard, Robert Neal, George Kimmerer, James Murphy, and Caleb Lownes. Joseph and Margaret (Montgomery) Gormley and their three youngest children are thought to have moved to this property in 1862 after Smith Gormley sold the 46 acre property adjacent to the Mahoning Creek.

In the 1870 census, Joseph Gormley, his wife, and their youngest son, William Gormley, were enumerated living on the 50 acre property in Mahoning Township.[66] Given their advanced age, it is likely that Joseph and Margaret (Montgomery) Gormley were being supported by their children including their youngest son, William Gormley. On May 22, 1876, five years after the death of Joseph Gormley, Margaret (Montgomery) Gormley sold the 50 acre property in Mahoning Township to Robert Black of the City of Philadelphia for $1,200.00.[67] Today, the only remaining original structure on the property is the barn.[68]

DECLINE AND DEATH OF JOSEPH GORMLEY. Given that the 46 acre property in Mahoning Township was purchased by Joseph Gormley on October 8, 1847 and sold to his son, Smith Gormley, on February 13, 1852, it is likely that Joseph Gormley was unable to perform much work on the farm. In fact, the maintenance and support clause in the deed of sale for Smith Gormley suggests that Joseph Gormley was in declining health as early as 1852.[69]

1859), Volume 10, p. 6, Deeds, Volumes 10-12, June 1859-March 1864, Carbon County, Pennsylvania, FHL Microfilm Roll 2208976.

[66]1870 U.S. Census (population), Pennsylvania, Carbon County, Mahoning Township, page 172, lines 38-40, National Archives Microfilm Publication M593, Roll 1320, Household of Joseph Gormley enumerated directly beside James Murphy as follows:

MAHONING TOWNSHIP, CARBON COUNTY, PENNSYLVANIA, JULY 27, 1870

Gormley, Joseph	81 M	Laborer	Ireland
, Margaret	71 F	Keeping House	Ireland
, William	21 M	Laborer	Pa

[67]Deed from Margaret Gormley to Robert Black, May 22, 1876 (recorded May 22, 1876), Volume 23, p. 212, Deeds, Volumes 22-23, 1875-1877, Carbon County, Pennsylvania, FHL Microfilm Roll 2209192.

[68]The site visit on June 24, 1997 to Margaret (Montgomery) Gormley's property in Mahoning Township, Carbon County, Pennsylvania, was made by Kathryn C. Torpey in the company of Robert C. Gormley, great-grandson of James and Margaret (Glenn) Gormley.

[69]There is a mysterious probate document filed in the Carbon County Courthouse in Jim Thorpe which is said to be part of the Estate of Joseph Gormley, Mahoning Township, # 0144, in which a minor by the name of Robert Gormley petitioned the court to appoint him a guardian due to the death of his father, Joseph Gormley, late of the Township of Mahoning, deceased. James

His daughter, Margaret (Gormley) Brashear, also mentioned her father and his deteriorating health in each of her three letters from Shanghai dated December 23, 1869, July 11, 1870, and March 12, 1871, respectively.[70]

Given the clause in the deed of sale to Smith Gormley and the grave concern of Margaret (Gormley) Brashear about ever again seeing her father alive, it is apparent that Joseph Gormley was not well so he and his wife, Margaret (Montgomery) Gormley, probably relied heavily on their children for most of their income in their later years. This conclusion is further supported by Margaret (Montgomery) Gormley's descriptions of the poor state of Joseph Gormley's health in her application for a Civil War dependent relative pension (i.e., mother's pension) based on the tragic death of their son, John Gormley, during the Civil War.[71]

In fact, the records contained in Margaret (Montgomery) Gormley's application for a dependent relative pension reveal that Joseph Gormley was an invalid by 1862. This is the same year that Smith Gormley sold the 46 acre farm adjacent to the Mahoning Creek and his parents,

---

Broderick was appointed as Robert Gormley's guardian. It is unclear what, if anything, the petition has to do with the Joseph Gormley who is the subject of this family history. Since no other Joseph Gormley is known to have been living in Mahoning Township in 1852, the petition, which was approved by the court on March 4, 1852, is included for its reference value. It read as follows:

> To the honorable the Judges of the Court of the County of Carbon of March Term 1852.
>
> The Petition of Robert Gormley son of Joseph Gormley, late of the Township of Mahoning in said county, deceased - Humbly showeth
>
> That the said petitioner is a minor above the age of fourteen years and hath no guardian appointed to take care of his person and estate. Your petitioner therefore prays your honors to appoint some fit person as guardian.
>
> And he will pray   Robert Gormley

[70]Letter dated May 17, 1997 from Robert C. Gormley, 334 Brownsburg Road, Newtown, Pennsylvania 18940 to Kathryn C. Torpey, 5035 Domain Place, Alexandria, Virginia 22311-5066 provided copies of these letters for transcription.

[71]Margaret Gormley, Civil War Dependent Relative Pension Application File, MO 246,903, Records of the Veterans Administration, Record Group 15, National Archives, Washington, D.C., contain affidavits by Margaret Gormley dated August 3, 1881, the Summit Hill Postmaster dated July 2, 1881, and Joseph Gormley's doctor, P.D. Keiser, dated August 1, 1881, concerning his physical condition and by George Murphy and Monroe Smith, dated June 12, 1883, and by Samuel Allen and Matthew E. Sinyard, dated July 22, 1883, concerning John Gormley's financial support of his parents.

Joseph and Margaret (Montgomery) Gormley, and their three youngest children all moved to the 50 acre property in Mahoning Township purchased solely by Margaret (Montgomery) Gormley in 1859.

The affidavits in Margaret (Montgomery) Gormley's application for a dependent relative pension clearly attest to the fact that Joseph and Margaret (Montgomery) Gormley were heavily dependent on their deceased son, John Gormley, who gave them all the money he earned working for the farmers in Mahoning Township prior to his enlistment in the Union Army during the Civil War. John Gormley's support of his parents was confirmed by the postmaster and the neighbors of the Gormley family who said that Joseph Gormley's son, John Gormley, did all he could to support his parents before his enlistment in the Union Army by working for local farmers and giving his earnings to his parents. After John Gormley's enlisted in the Union Army and up until the time of his death in 1862, he was reported to have sent all his money home to his parents.

Samuel Allen and Matthew Sinyard, who were personally acquainted with Joseph Gormley, said that he was not able to earn a living due to debility (although they acknowledged that he did the chores around the house), and his son, John Gormley, always, as far as they knew, gave his parents all the money or goods he received in payment for his work with the farmers in Mahoning Township. After John Gormley enlisted in the Union Army, Samuel Allen and Matthew Sinyard both agreed that John Gormley sent all his money home to his parents.[72,73]

Joseph Gormley's poor health was confirmed by his doctor, P.D. Keiser, a physician who lived in Mahoning Township. Doctor Keiser reported that he became the family physician in 1864 and that Joseph Gormley was, by that time, a worn out old man. Doctor Keiser further reported that Joseph Gormley had not been able to do a day's work for many years prior to the time of his death.

According to Doctor Keiser, Joseph Gormley died in 1871 shortly after having had an inflammation of the lungs.

MARGARET (MONTGOMERY) GORMLEY, WIDOW OF JOSEPH. After the death of Joseph Gormley, it is unclear how long Margaret (Montgomery) Gormley remained on her 50 acre property in Mahoning Township. She was assessed for real and personal property in Mahoning Township from 1861 to 1872, but not thereafter even though she did not sell the 50 acre property

---

[72]Samuel Allen was the second husband of Margaret (Glenn) Gormley, the widow of James Gormley, son of Joseph and Margaret (Montgomery) Gormley.

[73]The relationship of Matthew Sinyard to Ellen Sinyard, the wife of James Boyd, son of Matilda (Gormley) Boyd, is unknown.

until May 22, 1876.[74,75] It was not until a year later, on May 22, 1877, that Margaret (Montgomery) Gormley bought property in Summit Hill from James Ford.[76] And, at the time she bought the property in Summit Hill, she was stated to be living in Ashton.

On May 29, 1878, Margaret (Montgomery) Gormley executed her will in which she stated that she was living in a house that she owned in Summit Hill that she was bequeathing to her youngest son, William Gormley.[77] The house was located at 75 East White Street.

On June 9, 1879, at the age of 79, Margaret (Montgomery) Gormley appeared before the Court of Common Pleas in Carbon County and swore that she was entitled to a dependent relative pension as the mother of John Gormley who served in the Union Army and died of wounds and typhoid fever during the Civil War.[78] It is unclear why Margaret (Montgomery) Gormley waited so long to exercise her right to a dependent relative pension. She never received the pension because she died before the application process was finalized.

In the 1880 census, Margaret (Montgomery) Gormley was enumerated in Summit Hill with her daughter-in-law, Hannah Jane (Johnson) Gormley, the widow of Robert Gormley.[79]

---

[74]Margaret Gormley, Civil War Dependent Relative Pension Application File, MO 246,903, Records of the Veterans Administration, Record Group 15, National Archives, Washington, D.C., contains a statement by the Commissioner's Clerk of Carbon County and Custodian of the Records of Assessment Books of the County dated February 7, 1882 to the effect that Margaret (Montgomery) Gormley was assessed for real and personal property in Mahoning Township from 1861 to 1872 and not thereafter.

[75]Deed from Margaret Gormley to Robert Black, May 22, 1876 (recorded May 22, 1876), Volume 23, p. 212, Deeds, Volumes 22-23, 1875-1877, Carbon County, Pennsylvania, FHL Microfilm Roll 2209192.

[76]Deed from James Ford to Margaret Gormley, May 22, 1877 (recorded July 10, 1877), Volume 24, p. 112, Deeds, Volumes 24-26, 1877-1881, Carbon County, Pennsylvania, FHL Microfilm Roll 2209193.

[77]Will of Margaret Gormley, May 29, 1878, November 8, 1883, Will Book 1, page 431, Carbon County, Pennsylvania, FHL Microfilm Roll 1290573.

[78]Margaret Gormley, Civil War Dependent Relative Pension Application File, MO 246,903, Records of the Veterans Administration, Record Group 15, National Archives, Washington, D.C.

[79]1880 U.S. Census (population), Pennsylvania, Carbon County, Summit Hill, page 349D, lines 22-28, National Archives Microfilm Publication T9, Roll 1107, Household of Margaret Gormley:

THE DEATH OF MARGARET (MONTGOMERY) GORMLEY. According to two depositions contained in Margaret (Montgomery) Gormley's estate file, she moved to the home of Margaret (Glenn) Gormley Allen, the widow of James Gormley where she lived for about three years before she died. She was in bad health for a considerable period of time before her death. During the last seven weeks before her death she was confined to bed continuously and required constant care and nursing. Her son, William Gormley, who was then living in Summit Hill with his wife and family, and Margaret (Glenn) Gormley Allen, nursed her during her final illness. Margaret (Glenn) Gormley Allen cared for her during the day and William Gormley attended her during the night. She is believed to have died at the home of her daughter-in-law, Margaret (Glenn) Gormley Allen, on November 3, 1883.[80]

THE WILL OF MARGARET (MONTGOMERY) GORMLEY. Margaret (Montgomery) Gormley executed her will on May 29, 1878, at which time she stated in the document that she was in good health and of sound mind.[81] In her will, she bequeathed the house she then occupied in Summit Hill to her son, William Gormley, for his use as long as he lived. At his death, the house was to become the property of his children.

In a petition filed by the Lehigh Valley Trust and Safe Deposit Company on March 12, 1904, on behalf of two of the children of William Gormley, the house in question was described as follows:

> All that certain lot or piece of ground situate on the North side of East White Street, in the borough of Summit Hill, Carbon County, Pennsylvania, being designated as lot # 75 East White Street, BOUNDED and described as follows: to wit - BEGINNING at a point being corner of said lot, and lot # 73 and East White Street, and extending eastwardly a front of thirty (30) feet, and thence extending of that same width northwardly one hundred and twenty-five (125) feet to a twenty-foot wide alley. BOUNDED North by the said

---

SUMMIT HILL, MAUCH CHUNK TOWNSHIP, CARBON COUNTY, PENNSYLVANIA, JUNE 9, 1880:

Gormley, Margaret	F 80	Keeps house	Ireland
Gormley, Hannah	F 35	At home	Pa
, Joseph	M 13	Picks Slate	Pa
, Mary	F 11	At school	Pa
, Robert	M 9	At school	Pa
, Margaret	F 6		Pa
, William	M 4		Pa

[80]Estate of Margaret Gormley, Summit Hill, # 1309, Carbon County Courthouse, Jim Thorpe, Pennsylvania, contains the deposition of Margaret (Glenn) Gormley Allen and the deposition of William Gormley.

[81]Will of Margaret Gormley, May 29, 1878, November 8, 1883, Will Book 1, page 431, Carbon County, Pennsylvania, FHL Microfilm Roll 1290573.

alley, South by East White Street, East by lot # 77 and West by lot # 73.[82]

Margaret (Montgomery) Gormley also made the following specific monetary bequests in her will to be paid to her heirs after payment of all necessary expenses of her funeral and putting a headstone on her grave and that of her husband:

Mary Ann Wallis (sic), daughter of Letitia	$100.00
Margaret Gormley, daughter of Robert	$200.00
Joseph Gormley, son of Robert	$100.00
John Gormley, son of James	$100.00
Matilda Gormley, daughter of William	$100.00
Remaining four sons of James (unnamed)	$50.00 each
Letitia, my daughter	$100.00

She appointed M.E. Sinyard as her executor.[83] The will was witnessed by Joseph Nevins and Palmer O'Donnell.

In a codicil to her will executed on October 31, 1883, just days before she died, Margaret (Montgomery) Gormley made void the bequest to Mary Ann Wallis (sic), daughter of Letitia (Gormley) Wallace, because she had paid Mary Ann Wallis (sic) $100.00 on or about March 25, 1883, and she reduced the bequest to Margaret Gormley, daughter of Robert Gormley, to $100.00. The codicil was witnessed by her son, William Gormley, and her daughter-in-law, Margaret (Glenn) Gormley Allen.

The will and the codicil were both signed with Margaret (Montgomery) Gormley's mark.

THE BURIAL OF JOSEPH AND MARGARET (MONTGOMERY) GORMLEY. The Old Presbyterian Cemetery in Summit Hill was the final resting place of Joseph and Margaret (Montgomery) Gormley, their son, James Gormley, and their grandson, Joseph Gormley, the son of James and Margaret (Glenn) Gormley.[84] Their daughter, Jane Gormley, who may have died between 1840-1841 at about the age of 15 and their grandson, Samuel Gormley, the son of James

---

[82]Estate of William Gormley, Lehigh County, # 3065, Carbon County Courthouse, Jim Thorpe, Pennsylvania.

[83]M. E. Sinyard is probably a reference to Matthew Sinyard. Matthew Sinyard's farm was immediately across from Margaret (Montgomery) Gormley's 50 acre property in Mahoning Township. The Sinyard farmhouse was still standing on the property in 2004.

[84]Letter dated October 8, 1996 from Robert C. Gormley, 334 Brownsburg Road, Newtown, Pennsylvania 18940 to Kathryn C. Torpey, 5035 Domain Place, Alexandria, Virginia 22311-5066 describes from his memory the type of monument and stones installed in the Gormley plot at the Old Presbyterian Cemetery and reports on who was buried in the plot.

and Margaret (Glenn) Gormley, also appear to be buried in the same plot.[85] The cemetery may also have been the burial location of their son, William Brown Gormley, who died in early childhood probably between 1843-1846.

The Gormley monument in the Old Presbyterian Cemetery is reported to have been impressive. It may have been commissioned by Margaret (Gormley) Brashear who mentioned her intention to erect a suitable memorial to her parents in her letter from Shanghai dated March 12, 1871:

> ...I am sorry my letter did not reach in time for my dear old father to hear from me how much I would give only to see him now but I hope I shall see him yet before he dies at any rate if I do not have that pleasure on earth all I can do is to erect a handsome monument to their memory...[86]

According to Robert C. Gormley, the great-grandson of James Gormley, the Gormley monument was in the shape of an obelisk with inscriptions and scripture on all its sides. There were perhaps three small stones around the base each containing the initials of the deceased. Undoubtedly these small stones included the headstones of Joseph Gormley and Margaret (Montgomery) Gormley because Margaret (Montgomery) Gormley specifically authorized in her will the expense of "putting a headstone on my grave and that of my husband, Joseph

---

[85]Letter dated May 12, 2004 from Robert C. Gormley, 334 Brownsburg Road, Newtown, Pennsylvania 18940 to Kathryn C. Torpey, 5035 Domain Place, Alexandria, Virginia 22311-5066 contains a copy of a page from a small notebook that may show the names of people buried in the Old Presbyterian Cemetery whose surname began with the letter G. The whereabouts of the original notebook are unknown, but may be in the possession of the GAR Cemetery in Summit Hill. The photocopy of the page from the notebook is in the possession of Robert C. Gormley and states the following with respect to the Gormley burials:

> Buried on Lot
> James Gormley, soldier
> Joe Gormley
> Margaret M. Gormley
> Samel (sic) Gormley
> Joe Gormley
> [Jane] Gormley
>
> Robert Gormley gave
> for general use 1934 $10.00

[86]Letter dated May 17, 1997 from Robert C. Gormley, 334 Brownsburg Road, Newtown, Pennsylvania 18940 to Kathryn C. Torpey, 5035 Domain Place, Alexandria, Virginia 22311-5066 provided copies of these letters for transcription.

Gormley."[87] In addition to the small stones, the Gormley plot also contained a large slab covering the grave of their son, James Gormley, but no name was inscribed upon its surface.

Sadly, the Old Presbyterian Cemetery fell into deep neglect. In June 1972, the cemetery was cleared of all but one tombstone and converted into a public memorial park.[88] The official records of the Old Presbyterian Cemetery do not contain any mention of the Gormley burials.[89,90]

PORTRAIT OF JOSEPH GORMLEY. A portrait of Joseph Gormley, the family patriarch, was reportedly in the possession of Mary Alice (Gormley) Lindsay, one of the descendants of James Gormley. This portrait was formerly in the possession of her father, John M. Gormley, who was the executor of the estate of Robert M. Gormley, the son of Robert and Hannah Jane (Johnson) Gormley. The portrait is thought to have been part of the estate of Robert M. Gormley.[91,92]

------

[87]Will of Margaret Gormley, May 29, 1878, November 8, 1883, Will Book 1, page 431, Carbon County, Pennsylvania, FHL Microfilm Roll 1290573.

[88]Letter dated October 8, 1996 from Robert C. Gormley, 334 Brownsburg Road, Newtown, Pennsylvania 18940 to Kathryn C. Torpey, 5035 Domain Place, Alexandria, Virginia 22311-5066 states that he was familiar with the Gormley plot having visited it when growing up in Summit Hill and that the cemetery was cleared in June 1972.

[89]Letter dated June 12, 1997 from Robert C. Gormley, 334 Brownsburg Road, Newtown, Pennsylvania 18940 to Kathryn C. Torpey, 5035 Domain Place, Alexandria, Virginia 22311-5066 containing extracts of Volumes I, II, and III of the Records of the First Presbyterian Church of Summit Hill and Tamaqua and the Presbyterian Cemetery in Summit Hill as prepared by an elderly member of the church states that no records were found concerning the stones for any Gormley burials.

[90]Summit Hill Presbyterian Cemetery Web Page, <<freepages,genealogy.rootsweb.com/~mccem/sh-presbcem.htm>>, downloaded September 10, 2003 contains a list of 156 names of those buried in the Old Presbyterian Cemetery. It was prepared from the cemetery plot map. The name Gormley does not appear on the plot map, however, the 156 names on the plot map only represent a partial listing of those buried in the cemetery

[91]Letters dated March 12, 2002 and January 21, 2003 from Robert C. Gormley, 334 Brownsburg Road, Newtown, Pennsylvania 18940 to Kathryn C. Torpey, 5035 Domain Place, Alexandria, Virginia 22311-5066 state that the watercolor of Joseph Gormley may be in the possession of his second cousin, Mary Alice (Gormley) Lindsay.

[92]Letter dated November 7, 2003 from Robert C. Gormley, 334 Brownsburg Road, Newtown, Pennsylvania 18940 to Kathryn C. Torpey, 5035 Domain Place, Alexandria, Virginia 22311-5066 contains a copy of an article by Ed Gildea entitled "Summit Hill Woman Murdered

Smith Gormley was born March 16, 1823 in Magheramore, Desertoghill Parish, County Londonderry, Ireland.[93,94,95] He died March 18, 1883 in Buck Mountain, Lausanne Township, Carbon County, Pennsylvania.[96,97] He married Margaret Ann McClellan, the daughter of James

---

in China" that appeared in a June 1973 issue of *The Valley Gazette* which included a photograph of John M. Gormley, holding a painting of his great-grandfather, Joseph Gormley.

[93]Visitation of the Reverend James Brown Beginning in the Summer of 1825 lists Smyth, Jane and James Gormley, children of Joseph and Margaret Gormley, living in Maghrimore (sic). A copy of the original record of the First Garvagh Presbyterian Church, Errigal Parish, County Londonderry, Ireland, was provided to Kathryn C. Torpey by Lavonne Bradfield, <<LBradfield@satx.rr.com>>, on September 9, 2003. The record was provided to Lavonne Bradfield by a member of the First Garvagh Presbyterian Church.

[94]Entry for Margaret Gormley and Children, Ship Sheridan Passenger Manifest, December 12, 1839, page 3, line 19, Passenger List of Vessels Arriving at New York, NY, 1820-1897, Records of the U.S. Customs Service, Record Group 36, National Archives Microfilm Publication M237, Roll 40 says Smith 15, i.e. born 1824 in Ireland.

[95]Letter dated February 15, 1999 from Robert C. Gormley, 334 Brownsburg Road, Newtown, Pennsylvania 18940 to Kathryn C. Torpey, 5035 Domain Place, Alexandria, Virginia 22311-5066 reports the results of his site visit to Union Cemetery in Weatherly where he found the Gormley burial site. The headstone (and photo) reads as follows:

> Smith Gormley
> Born March 16 1823
> Died March 18 1882 (sic)
> 57 Yrs. (sic) & 2 D.

[96]Margaret A. Gormley, Navy Widows and Other Dependents File (Approved), 1861-1910, WO 9008, WC 7535, U.S. Marine Corps, Records of the Veterans Administration, Record Group 15, National Archives Microfilm Publication M1279, Fiche 6745 states Smith Gormley died March 18, 1883. Note: Pension indexed under Smith Gromley (sic).

[97]Letter dated February 15, 1999 from Robert C. Gormley, 334 Brownsburg Road, Newtown, Pennsylvania 18940 to Kathryn C. Torpey, 5035 Domain Place, Alexandria, Virginia 22311-5066 reports the results of his site visit to the Union Cemetery in Weatherly where he found the Gormley burial site. The headstone (and photo) reads as follows:

> Smith Gormley
> Born March 16 1823
> Died March 18 1882 (sic)

and Margaret McClellan, on November 1, 1857 in Buck Mountain aka Clifton, Lausanne Township, Carbon County, Pennsylvania.[98,99] She was born February 12, 1833 in Ireland.[100,101] She died July 26, 1910 in Mahanoy City, Schuylkill County, Pennsylvania.[102,103,104] They are both

---

57 Yrs. (sic) & 2 D.

[98]Margaret A. Gormley, Navy Widows and Other Dependents File (Approved), 1861-1910, WO 9008, WC 7535, U.S. Marine Corps, Records of the Veterans Administration, Record Group 15, National Archives Microfilm Publication M1279, Fiche 6745 states, (1) per the widow on 4 September 1890, that she and Smith Gormley were married on November 1, 1857 (sic) in Clifton (sic), Pennsylvania by the Rev. J. Ormond; (2) per the Rev. J.W. Bischoff on August 31, 1891 who was then in custody of the records of the Presbyterian Church of Eckley, Pennsylvania that the entry in the church marriage register says November 1, 1858 (sic), in Clifton (sic), Pennsylvania, by the Reverend J. Ormond; and (3) per Andrew Boyd on August 31, 1891 that he was a witness to the marriage that took place at Buck Mountain (sic). Note: Pension indexed under Smith Gromley (sic).

[99]*Gazetteer or Geographical Dictionary of the World*, (Philadelphia, Pennsylvania: J.B. Lippincot, 1880) 316 says:

> **Buck Mountain, or Clifton,** a mining post-village of Carbon co., Pa., on the line of Luzerne co., in Lausanne township, on the Drifton Branch Railroad, 2 miles S.E. of Eckley. Here is a colliery.

[100]Letter dated February 15, 1999 from Robert C. Gormley, 334 Brownsburg Road, Newtown, Pennsylvania 18940 to Kathryn C. Torpey, 5035 Domain Place, Alexandria, Virginia 22311-5066 reports the results of his site visit to Union Cemetery in Weatherly where he found the Gormley burial site containing the birth and death date inscription for Margaret (McClellan), Gormley.

[101]1910 U.S. Census (population), Pennsylvania, Schuylkill County, Mahanoy City, E.D. 43, page 9A, line 1, National Archives Microfilm Publication T624, Roll 1417, Household of John Lowe says:

> MAHANOY CITY, WARD 5, SCHUYLKILL COUNTY, PENNSYLVANIA
> Margarett (sic) Gormley   MIL F W 77 Wd born: Ireland immigration: 1849

[102]Letter dated February 15, 1999 from Robert C. Gormley, 334 Brownsburg Road, Newtown, Pennsylvania 18940 to Kathryn C. Torpey, 5035 Domain Place, Alexandria, Virginia 22311-5066 reports the results of his site visit to Union Cemetery in Weatherly where he found the Gormley burial site containing the birth and death date inscription for Margaret (McClellan) Gormley.

[103]Margaret A. Gormley, Navy Widow, # 7535, Pension Payment Cards, Veterans

buried in Union Cemetery, Weatherly, Carbon County, Pennsylvania.[105,106]

U.S. CENSUS ENUMERATIONS. In the 1840 census, Smith Gormley appears to be enumerated with his parents in Mauch Chunk Township.[107]

In the 1850 census, Smith Gormley was enumerated in Lausanne Township where he is thought to have been living in Buck Mountain then one of the most prosperous villages in the coal fields of Carbon County.[108] Its wealth was due largely to the fact that the coal produced at Buck Mountain was of the very finest grade in terms of its steaming quality and its almost total lack of smoke when burned. In fact, during the Civil War, coal from Buck Mountain was used extensively by the United States Navy because this fuel made vessels less conspicuous to the enemy as targets and it also facilitated secrecy in the movement of ships.[109]

Administration, 1907-1933, M850, Roll 865 records the date of death of Margaret A. Gormley as July 26, 1910. The final pension payment for Margaret A. Gormley was made to Alice Lowe on November 30, 1910.

[104]Death Certificate for Margaret A. Gormley, July 26, 1910, # 68876 & # 253, Pennsylvania Division of Vital Statistics, New Castle, Pennsylvania 16103 does not contain the names of her parents.

[105]E-mail dated October 22, 1998 from Robert C. Gormley, 334 Browning Road, Newtown, Pennsylvania 18940 to Kathryn C. Torpey, 5035 Domain Place, Alexandria, Virginia 22311-5066 states that he went to Weatherly and found Smith Gormley, his wife, Margaret (McClellan) Gormley, and three of their children buried in Union Cemetery in Weatherly.

[106]Letter dated October 12, 1999 from Jack Koehler, 108 Hudsondale Street, Weatherly, Pennsylvania 18255 to Kathryn C. Torpey, 5035 Domain Place, Alexandria, Virginia 22311-5066 reports that there is no Presbyterian cemetery in Weatherly. He is the President of Union Cemetery. He confirmed that Smith Gormley is buried in Union Cemetery. His wife and three of his children - Maggie, James, and Martha - are buried with him.

[107]1840 U.S. Census (population), Pennsylvania, Northampton County, Mauch Chunk Township, page 212, line 21, National Archives Microfilm Publication M704, Roll 479, Household of Jos. Gramley (sic).

[108]1850 U.S. Census (population), Pennsylvania, Carbon County, Lausanne Township, page 233, lines 24-35. National Archives Microfilm Publication M432, Roll 762, Household of William Cambell (sic).

[109]Fred Brenckman, *History of Carbon County, Pennsylvania*, (Harrisburg, Pennsylvania: James J. Nungesser, Publisher, 1913), 224.

The entry in the 1850 census is difficult to discern. That is, Smith Gormley appears to be enumerated in this census schedule along with two other people of the same surname one of whom has an unrecognizable first name and the other who possibly may be his younger brother, Robert Gormley. The threesome was living with the family of William Cambell (sic) and beside the family of James Boyd. The entry is as follows:

LAUSANNE TOWNSHIP, CARBON COUNTY, PENNSYLVANIA, AUGUST 24, 1850

Smith Gaennely (sic)	28 M	Hosler	Ireland	
Maldusia "	28 M or F	Miner	Ireland	
Robert Garmeny (sic)	20 M	Laborer	Ireland[110]	

Between 1850 and 1860, Smith Gormley was a busy man. On February 13, 1852, he bought his father's farm in Mahoning Township for $1,200.00. In the deed, Smith Gormley is described as "son of the parties of the first part." The sale was contingent on Smith Gormley agreeing to support and maintain his parents during and for their natural lifetime and to support and maintain his three youngest siblings - Jane, John and William - until each child turned fourteen.[111]

In the 1860 census, Smith Gormley was enumerated living on the Gormley family farm in Mahoning Township with his wife and baby daughter.[112] Also living on the property were both his parents, three of his brothers - Robert, John, and William - and two of the children of his sister, Matilda (Gormley) Boyd. As the oldest son, Smith Gormley had, apparently, assumed responsibility for maintenance and support of the extended family. That arrangement ended on November 16, 1860 when Smith Gormley was legally relieved of any further obligation to support his parents and his three youngest siblings after his parents executed a Deed of Release to that effect and he paid them an additional $300.00.[113]

---

[110]1850 U.S. Census (population), Pennsylvania, Carbon County, Lausanne Township, page 233, lines 24-35. National Archives Microfilm Publication M432, Roll 762. Household of William Cambell (sic).

[111]Deed from Joseph Gormley & Wife to Smith Gormley, February 13, 1852 (recorded April 10, 1852), Volume 5, p. 86, Deeds, Volumes 4-7, 1851-1855, Carbon County, Pennsylvania, FHL Microfilm Roll 2208974, image 138, <<www.familysearch.org>>, appears to indicate that at the time Smith Gormley purchased the farm he was living somewhere other than in Carbon County because he is referred to in the deed as "late of said County", i.e., Carbon County.

[112]1860 U.S. Census (population), Pennsylvania, Carbon County, Mahoning Township, page 972, lines 11-20, National Archives Microfilm Publication M653, Roll 1089, Household of Joseph Gomly (sic).

[113]Deed of Release from Joseph Gormley & Wife to Smith Gormley, November 14, 1860

MARRIAGE TO MARGARET ANN McCLELLAN. Smith Gormley and Margaret McClellan were married by the Rev. J. Ormond, pastor of the Presbyterian Church of Eckley, on November 1, 1857 at Buck Mountain, also known as Clifton, Lausanne Township. Carbon County, Pennsylvania.[114,115]

SERVICE IN THE CIVIL WAR. In 1862, after Smith Gormley and his wife sold the Gormley family farm in Mahoning Township they removed to Lausanne Township where they lived in Buck Mountain.[116] On June 3, 1863, Smith Gormley enlisted as a private in Company G of the 34th Regiment of the Pennsylvania Volunteer Militia.[117,118] He is said to have enlisted in Weatherly which is about five miles southwest of Buck Mountain.[119] After his brief tour of duty in the militia, Smith Gormley enlisted in the U.S. Marine Corps on September 21, 1864. He was

---

(recorded November 16, 1860), Volume 10, p. 554, Deeds, Volumes 10-12, 1859-1864, Carbon County, Pennsylvania, FHL Microfilm Roll 2208976, image 300, <<www.familysearch.org>>.

[114]Margaret A. Gormley, Navy Widows and Other Dependents File (Approved), 1861-1910, WO 9008, WC 7535, U.S. Marine Corps, Records of the Veterans Administration, Record Group 15, National Archives Microfilm Publication M1279, Fiche 6745. Note: Pension indexed under Smith Gromley (sic).

[115]Ninth Presbyterian Church, Marriages, 1850-1908, Philadelphia, Pennsylvania, FHL Microfilm Roll 0505481 (item 1) reveals on page 174, No. 1116, 1865, that there was a second Smith Gormley living in Philadelphia who married a Mary Jane Patterson on August 21, 1865. Their witnesses were Jane Gormley and Martha Smith. The relationship, if any, between the two Smith Gormleys is unknown.

[116]Deed from Smith Gormley & Wife to William Mullen, April 1, 1862 (recorded April 16, 1862), Volume 11, p. 426, Deeds, Volumes 10-12, 1859-1864, Carbon County, Pennsylvania, FHL Microfilm Roll 2208976.

[117]Samuel P. Bates, *History of the Pennsylvania Volunteers - 1861 - 1865*, (Harrisburg, Pennsylvania: B. Singlerly, State Printer, 1871). Volume X:1252, says:

> Smith Gormerly (sic), 34th Regiment, Co. G. mustered in June 3, 1863, mustered out August 24, 1863

[118]J.D. Laciar, *Patriotism of Carbon County, Pennsylvania*, (Mauch Chunk, Pennsylvania, n.s., 1867), 98, says:

> Gormly (sic), Smith

[119]E-mail dated November 3, 1997 from Robert C. Gormley, 334 Brownsburg Road, Newtown, Pennsylvania 18940 to Kathryn C. Torpey, 5035 Domain Place, Alexandria, Virginia 22311-5066 says Smith Gormley enlisted in Weatherly in 1863.

assigned to duty at the Navy Yard in Washington, D.C., where he remained until February 5, 1866. The war being over, Smith Gormley simply left his duty station without being officially discharged. Twenty-four years later, on September 4, 1890, when his widow, Margaret (McClellan) Gormley, applied for a Navy widow's pension, she learned that Smith Gormley was listed as a deserter. After a great deal of effort, she had his name cleared.[120]

THE LATER YEARS. After leaving the U.S. Marine Corps, Smith Gormley returned to Buck Mountain where he lived out the rest of his days. This is consistent with the content of several affidavits contained in Margaret (McClellan) Gormley's application for a Navy widow's pension in which the various testators speak of being well acquainted with the family of Smith Gormley while they lived in Buck Mountain going back over forty years.[121]

Smith Gormley's relationship with his family of origin is less clear. In a letter from Shanghai dated December 23, 1869, his sister, Margaret (Gormley) Brashear, made a cryptic remark about her brother.[122] In the letter, which was directed to her brother, Robert Gormley, she asked him if he knew where Smith Gormley was and what Smith Gormley was doing while at the same time stating that she didn't think anyone in the family should associate with Smith Gormley.

The reason for Margaret (Gormley) Brashear's comment about Smith Gormley is unclear. Her most frequent complaints in her three surviving letters from Shanghai concern the lengthy wait for letters from home and the deteriorating state of her parents' health. So, Smith Gormley may not have been keeping in touch with his sister on a regular basis or she may have decided that he was not helping out enough with their parents after they released him from his legal obligation to support and maintain them for the rest of their lives.[123]

---

[120]Margaret A. Gormley, Navy Widows and Other Dependents File (Approved), 1861-1910, WO 9008, WC 7535, U.S. Marine Corps, Records of the Veterans Administration, Record Group 15, National Archives Microfilm Publication M1279, Fiche 6745 contains a letter dated July 23, 1891, stating the charge of desertion against Smith Gormley was removed and a certificate of discharge would be issued stating February 5, 1866, as the date he left the service. Note: Pension indexed under Smith Gromley (sic).

[121]Margaret A. Gormley, Navy Widows and Other Dependents File (Approved), 1861-1910, WO 9008, WC 7535, U.S. Marine Corps, Records of the Veterans Administration, Record Group 15, National Archives Microfilm Publication M1279, Fiche 6745. Note: Pension indexed under Smith Gromley (sic).

[122]Letter dated May 17, 1997 from Robert C. Gormley, 334 Brownsburg Road, Newtown, Pennsylvania 18940 to Kathryn C. Torpey, 5035 Domain Place, Alexandria, Virginia 22311-5066 provided copies of these letters for transcription.

[123]Deed of Release from Joseph Gormley & Wife to Smith Gormley, November 14, 1860

In the 1870 census, Smith Gormley and his family were enumerated in Lausanne Township.[124] Since the Borough of Weatherly was separate from Lausanne Township in 1870, it is most probable that Smith Gormley and his family were still living in Buck Mountain at the time. The Gormleys were enumerated as follows:

LAUSANNE TOWNSHIP, CARBON COUNTY, PENNSYLVANIA, OCTOBER 7, 1870

Gormly (sic), Smith	46 M	Laborer	Ireland	Citizen of U.S.A.
, Margaret	36 F	Keeping house	Ireland	
, Margaret	12 F		Pa.	
, Mary	9 F		Pa.	
, Allice (sic)	6 F		Pa.	
, Matilda	3 F		Pa.	
, Martha	2/12 (Nov)		Pa.	
McClenna, (sic) Margaret 75			Ireland	

In the 1880 census, Smith Gormley and his household were definitely enumerated a Buck Mountain.[125] The enumeration as follows:

BUCK MOUNTAIN, LAUSANNE TOWNSHIP, CARBON COUNTY, PENNSYLVANIA, JUNE 15, 1880

Smith Gormley	M 57	Ireland	Laborer
Margaret Gormley	F 46	Ireland	Keeps House
Alice C. Gormley	F 17	Pa	At Home
Matilda Gormley	F 12	Pa	At School
Martha Gormley	F 11	Pa	
James A. Gormley	M 6	Pa	
Robt. L. Gormley	M 2	Pa	
Margaret McClelland (sic)	F 87	Pa (sic)	Mother-in-law

THE DEATH OF SMITH GORMLEY. According to documents contained in Margaret (McClellan) Gormley's application for a Navy widow's pension, Smith Gormley died on March 18, 1883, probably in Buck Mountain since the mines in Buck Mountain were in operation until November 18, 1883, eight months after Smith Gormley's death.[126] Margaret (McClellan)

(recorded November 16, 1860), Volume 10, p. 554, Deeds, Volumes 10-12, 1859-1864, Carbon County, Pennsylvania, FHL Microfilm Roll 2208976.

[124]1870 U.S. Census (population), Pennsylvania, Carbon County, Lausanne Township, page 127, lines 26-33, National Archives Microfilm Publication M593, Roll 1320, Household of Smith Gormly (sic).

[125]1880 U.S. Census (population), Pennsylvania, Carbon County, Buck Mountain, page 298D, lines 7-14, National Archives Microfilm Publication T9, Roll 1107, Household of Smith Gormley.

[126]Fred Brenckman, *History of Carbon County, Pennsylvania*, (Harrisburg, Pennsylvania:

Gormley's application for a Navy widow's pension also contains affidavits that state the Reverend J.P. Moffat, minister of the Presbyterian Church in Weatherly, officiated at his funeral and the undertaker was Mr. E.T. Wurner (sic) also of Weatherly.[127,128] Smith Gormley was buried in Union Cemetery in Weatherly where he still rests today.[129]

MARGARET ANN (McCLELLAN) GORMLEY, WIDOW OF SMITH. Margaret (McClellan) Gormley appears to have spent her final years living with her daughter, Alice (Gormley) Lowe. In the 1900 census, she can be found living in Mahanoy City on East Center Street with her son-in-law and daughter, John W. and Alice (Gormley) Lowe.[130] She was enumerated as follows:

MAHANOY CITY, SCHUYLKILL COUNTY, PENNSYLVANIA, JUNE 8, 1900
Gormley, Margrat (sic)   MIL   W F   b Feb 1835   Widow
8 (sic) children, 4 living   b Ireland
1850 (year of immigration)

In the 1910 census, Smith Gormley's widow, Margaret (McClellan) Gormley, was still living in Mahanoy City at 1332 East Center Street with her son-in-law and daughter, John W.

James J. Nungesser, Publisher, 1913), 224, says the mines at Buck Mountain were in operation until November 18, 1883, when they were closed in the belief that the available supply of coal had been exhausted.

[127]Margaret A. Gormley, Navy Widows and Other Dependents File (Approved), 1861-1910, WO 9008, WC 7535, U.S. Marine Corps, Records of the Veterans Administration, Record Group 15, National Archives Microfilm Publication M1279, Fiche 6745. Note: Pension indexed under Smith Gromley (sic).

[128]Letter dated December 23, 2003 from Jack Koehler, 108 Hudsondale Street, Weatherly, Pennsylvania 18255 to Kathryn C. Torpey, 5035 Domain Place, Alexandria, Virginia 22311-5066 reports that he is in possession of all the records of the Presbyterian Church in Weatherly including the records of the Reverend James Moffat, but a review of these records did not reveal a death date for Smith Gormley. He also checked with the local undertaker, but his records are almost non-existent until the 1890s.

[129]Letter dated October 23, 1999 from Jack Koehler, 108 Hudsondale Street, Weatherly, Pennsylvania 18255 to Kathryn C. Torpey, 5035 Domain Place, Alexandria, Virginia 22311-5066 reports that he is the President of the Union Cemetery and that Smith Gormley is buried in Union Cemetery. His wife and three of his children - Maggie, James, and Martha - are buried with him.

[130]1900 U.S. Census (population), Pennsylvania, Schuylkill County, Borough of Mahanoy City, E.D. 161, page 16, lines 82-88, National Archives Microfilm Publication T623, Roll 1484, Household of John W. Lowe.

and Alice (Gormley) Lowe.[131] She was enumerated as follows just a few months before she died:

MAHANOY CITY, SCHUYLKILL COUNTY, PENNSYLVANIA, APRIL 19, 1910
Gormley, Margarett (sic)   MIL   W F   77   Widow
8 (sic) children, 4 living   b Ireland
1849 (year of immigration)

THE CHILDREN OF SMITH AND MARGARET ANN (McCLELLAN) GORMLEY. Smith and Margaret (McClellan) Gormley are known to have had seven children - Margaret, Mary, Alice, Matilda, Martha, James, and Robert. Three of their children - Margaret, Martha, and James - died young. They are buried in the same plot with their parents in Union Cemetery in Weatherly.[132]

Their oldest surviving daughter **Mary Anna Gormley** removed to Philadelphia where she married Harry Leopold Burkart.[133] According to family legend, Mary (Gormley) Burkart's husband played with John Philip Sousa's band. He is said to have been stricken ill with ptomaine poisoning while on tour and died en route home to Philadelphia.[134] In 1900, Henry and Mary (Gormley) Burkart can be found living at 2556 N. 16th Street where Harry Burkart was working as a tailor. Enumerated with them was their only son, Robert Burkart, and Mary (Gormley) Burkart's brother, Robert L. Gormley.[135] In the 1910 census, Henry and Mary

---

[131]1910 U.S. Census (population), Pennsylvania, Schuylkill County, Borough of Mahanoy City, E.D. 43, page 8B, lines 93-100 and page 9A, line 1, National Archives Microfilm Publication T624, Roll 1417, Household of John W. Lowe.

[132]Letter dated October 23, 1999 from Jack Koehler, 108 Hudsondale Street, Weatherly, Pennsylvania 18255 to Kathryn C. Torpey, 5035 Domain Place, Alexandria, Virginia 22311-5066 reports that he is the President of Union Cemetery and that Smith Gormley is buried in Union Cemetery. His wife and three of his children - Maggie, James, and Martha - are buried with him.

[133]Marriage of Harry Lenpold (sic) Burkart and Mary Anna Gormley, February 26, 1885, Central Presbyterian Church, Philadelphia, Pennsylvania, Pennsylvania Marriages, 1709-1940, FHL Microfilm Roll 505525.

[134]Notes and documents provided on October 27, 1999 by Robert C. Gormley, 334 Brownsburg Road, Newtown, Pennsylvania 18940 to Kathryn C. Torpey, 5035 Domain Place, Alexandria, Virginia 22311-5066 contains a picture postcard with a photograph of Harry and Mary (Gormley) Burkett (sic) and their only son, Robert. The postcard contains the notation on the back about Harry Burkett (sic) playing with Sousa's band and his death from ptomaine poisoning while on tour with the band.

[135]1900 U.S. Census (population), Pennsylvania, Philadelphia County, Philadelphia, E.D.

33

(Gormley) Burkart were still living at the same address with their son, Robert Burkart, but in that enumeration, Harry Burkart was listed as a musician with an orchestra.[136] In the 1920 census, Harry and Mary (Gormley) Burkart were enumerated at 5847 Washington Avenue living with their son, Robert Burkart. Harry Burkart was working as a musician at a theater and his son was working as a clerk at a bank.[137] Harry and Mary (Gormley) Burkart died in 1920 and 1922, respectively.[138,139] They are both buried in Hillside Cemetery, Roslyn, Montgomery County, Pennsylvania.[140,141] In the 1930 census, their son, Robert Burkart, was enumerated with his wife, Lydia May (Stief) Wagstaff Burkart, living at 5650 Pine Street in Philadelphia where he was employed as a salesman for an oil and gas company.[142]

Their second oldest surviving daughter **Alice Gormley** married John W. Lowe on March 10, 1888 in Mahanoy City, Schuylkill County, Pennsylvania.[143] John Lowe was born in Nova

---

691, page 6B, line 100 and page 7A, lines 1-4, National Archives Microfilm Publication T623, Roll 1470, Household of Harry L. Burkart.

[136]1910 U.S. Census (population), Pennsylvania, Philadelphia County, Philadelphia, E.D. 645, page 5B, lines 76-78, National Archives Microfilm Publication T624, Roll 1402, Household of Harry L. Burkart.

[137]1920 U.S. Census (population), Pennsylvania, Philadelphia County, Philadelphia, E.D. 1774, page 6B, lines 51-53, National Archives Microfilm Publication T625, Roll 1647, Household of Harry L. Burkhart (sic).

[138]Death Certificate of Harry L. Burkart, February 20, 1920, Philadelphia, Pennsylvania, Pennsylvania Death Certificates, 1906-1966, <<www.ancestry.com>>, downloaded May 9, 2019.

[139]Death Certificate of Mary A. Burkart, September 1, 1922, Philadelphia, Pennsylvania, Pennsylvania Death Certificates, 1906-1966, <<www.ancestry.com>>, downloaded May 9, 2019.

[140]Find-A-Grave Memorial # 198596714, Harry L. Burkart (no headstone photograph), added April 24, 2019, Hillside Cemetery, Roslyn, Montgomery County, Pennsylvania, <<www.findagrave.com>>.

[141]Find-A-Grave Memorial # 198596433, Mary A. Gormley Burkart (no headstone photograph), added April 24, 2019, Hillside Cemetery, Roslyn, Montgomery County, Pennsylvania, <<www.findagrave.com>>.

[142]1930 U.S. Census (population), Pennsylvania, Philadelphia County, Philadelphia, E.D. 51-524, page 1A, lines 4-5, National Archives Microfilm Publication T626, Roll 2141, Household of Robert T. Burkart.

[143]Marriage of John Lowe and Alice M. Gormley, February 26, 1885, First Presbyterian

Scotia, Canada, immigrated to the United States between 1871 and 1874, and worked as a coal miner. They had six children: James, Hilda, Harry, Margaret, John, and Kathryn all of whom were privileged to know their grandmother, Margaret Ann (McClellan) Gormley, the widow of Smith Gormley, who lived with them from at least 1900 until she died on July 26, 1910.[144,145,146,147] John W. and Alice (Gormley) Lowe resided in Mahanoy City until their death in 1939 and 1931, respectively.[148,149] They are both buried at the German Protestant Cemetery in Mahanoy City.[150,151] Also buried in the German Protestant Cemetery is their grandson, Captain Robert T. Lowe, a Flying Fortress pilot stationed in Italy during World War II. After the war, he

----

Church, Mahanoy City, Schuylkill County, Pennsylvania, U.S. Presbyterian Church Records, 1701-1970, <<www.ancestry.com>>, downloaded May 9, 2019.

[144]1900 U.S. Census (population), Pennsylvania, Schuylkill County, Borough of Mahanoy City, E.D. 161, page 16, lines 82- 88, National Archives Microfilm Publication T623, Roll 1484, Household of John W. Lowe.

[145]1910 U.S. Census (population), Pennsylvania, Schuylkill County, Borough of Mahanoy City, E.D. 43, page 8B, lines 93-100 and page 9A, line 1, National Archives Microfilm Publication T624, Roll 1417, Household of John W. Lowe.

[146]1920 U.S. Census (population), Pennsylvania, Schuylkill County, Mahanoy City, Ward 5, E.D. 63, page 5B, lines 78-84, National Archives Microfilm Publication T625, Roll 1650, Household of John W. Lowe.

[147]1930 U.S. Census (population), Pennsylvania, Schuylkill County, Mahanoy City, E.D. 54-58, page 7A, line 50 and page 7B, lines 51-54, National Archives Microfilm Publication T626, Roll 2145, Household of John W. Lowe.

[148]Death Certificate of John W. Lowe, March 25, 1939, Mahanoy City, Schuylkill County, Pennsylvania, Pennsylvania Death Certificates, 1906-1966, <<www.ancestry.com>>, downloaded May 9, 2019.

[149]Death Certificate of Alice Lowe, March 18, 1931, Mahanoy City, Schuylkill County, Pennsylvania, Pennsylvania Death Certificates, 1906-1966, <<www.ancestry.com>>, downloaded May 9, 2019.

[150]Find-A-Grave Memorial # 198641815, John W. Lowe (headstone photograph), added April 26, 2019, German Protestant Cemetery, Mahanoy City, Schuylkill County, Pennsylvania, <<www.findagrave.com>>.

[151]Find-A-Grave Memorial # 198595870, Alice Gormley Lowe (headstone photograph), added April 24, 2019, German Protestant Cemetery, Mahanoy City, Schuylkill County, Pennsylvania, <<www.findagrave.com>>.

was part of the Homebound Task Force whose job it was to fly the infantry troops of the Fifth Army from Naples to Casablanca which was the first leg of their journey back to the States. Tragically, he was killed in a plane crash in the performance of his duties in this capacity on May 26, 1945, in Italy.[152]

Their youngest surviving daughter, **Matilda Gormley** married Alfred/Alford McCollough/McCullough. They had three daughters, Edith, Hazel and Emily.[153,154,155] He died April 30, 1913 at the age of 51 in Winton, Lackawanna County, Pennsylvania.[156] She died on June 12, 1946 at the age of 78 in Kingston, Luzerne County, Pennsylvania.[157] They are both buried at Oak Lawn Cemetery and Mausoleum in Hanover, Luzerne County, Pennsylvania.[158,159]

------

[152]News Story, *The Evening Times,* "Capt. R.T. Lowe Killed in Plane Crash in Italy," Monday, June 11, 1945, Sayre, Pennsylvania, <<www.newspapers.com>>, downloaded October 3, 2019.

[153]Death Certificate of Edith M. Vincent, August 1, 1957, Kingston, Luzerne County, Pennsylvania, Pennsylvania Death Certificates, 1906-1966, <<www.ancestry.com>>, downloaded May 10, 2019, says parents were Alfred McCollough (sic) and Matilda Gormley

[154]Death Certificate of Hazel Rubury, March 9, 1959, Kingston, Luzerne County, Pennsylvania, Pennsylvania Death Certificates, 1906-1966, <<www.ancestry.com>>, downloaded May 10, 2019, says parents were Alfred McCollough (sic) and Matilda Gormley

[155]Death Certificate of Emily M. Lampman, August 15, 1962, Wilkes-Barre, Luzerne County, Pennsylvania, Pennsylvania Death Certificates, 1906-1966, <<www.ancestry.com>>, downloaded May 10, 2019, says parents were Alford McCollough (sic) and Matilda Gormley

[156]Death Certificate of Alfred McCollough (sic), April 30, 1913, Winton, Lackawanna County, Pennsylvania, Pennsylvania Death Certificates, 1906-1966, <<www.ancestry.com>>, downloaded May 10, 2019.

[157]Death Certificate of Matilda J. McCullough (sic), June 12, 1946, Kingston, Luzerne, Pennsylvania, Pennsylvania Death Certificates, 1906-1966, <<www.ancestry.com>>, downloaded May 10, 2019.

[158]Find-A-Grave Memorial # 99529381, Alfred (sic) McCollough (headstone photograph), added October 24, 2012, Oak Lawn Cemetery & Mausoleum, Hanover, Luzerne County, Pennsylvania, <<www.findagrave.com>>. Note: Duplicate Find-A-Grave Memorial # 143451434 for Alford (sic) McCollough, added March 7, 2015, was deleted May 24, 2019.

[159]Find-A-Grave Memorial # 147056856, Mathilda (sic) J. McCollough (headstone photograph), added May 27, 2015, Oak Lawn Cemetery & Mausoleum, Hanover, Luzerne County, Pennsylvania. Also see duplicate Find-A-Grave Memorial # 143451507 for Matilda

Their only surviving son, **Robert Leonard Gormley**, never married. He enlisted in the U.S. Army on June 21, 1898, at Philadelphia, Pennsylvania. He served in Troop I of the 6th Cavalry during the Spanish-American War. He was discharged on January 22, 1899, at Fort Sill, Oklahoma.[160] He lived in several states after the war including at the U.S. Home for Disabled Veterans in Danville, Vermilion County, Illinois from where he applied for a Spanish-American War pension on September 12, 1927.[161] Later, he moved to Peoria, Peoria County, Illinois, where on February 23, 1934, he applied for Veterans Compensation based on his Spanish-American War service.[162] He died on January 16, 1947 in St. Louis City, Missouri.[163] He was buried at Jefferson Barracks National Cemetery in Lemay, St. Louis County, Missouri.[164]

(sic) McCollough, added March 7, 2015, <<www.findagrave.com>>.

[160]U.S. Army Register of Enlistments, 1798-1914, National Archives Microfilm Publication M233, Roll 39, <<www.ancestry.com>> says:

> Gormley, Robert L. born: Buck Mountain; age: 21y5m; occupation: clerk

[161]General Index to Pension Files, 1861-1934, National Archives Microfilm Publication T288, Roll 181 says:

> Gormley, Robert L. I Co 6 U.S. Cav
> 1927 Sept 12   SO 1,591,568   SC A-3-23-26   ILL
> C-2,295,856

[162]Veterans Compensation Application of Robert Leonard Gormley, February 23, 1934, Pennsylvania, Spanish War Compensation, 1898-1934, <<www.ancestry.com>>, downloaded May 10, 2019.

[163]Death Certificate of Robert L. Gormley, January 16, 1947, St. Louis City, Missouri, Missouri Death Certificates, 1910-1968, Missouri Digital Heritage, <<www.sos.mo.gov/mdh>>, downloaded May 10, 2019.

[164]Find-A-Grave Memorial # 81311491, Robert Leonard Gormley (headstone photograph), added December 1, 2011, Jefferson Barracks National Cemetery, Lemay, St. Louis County, Missouri, <<www.findagrave.com>>, downloaded April 29, 2019.

Jane Gormley was probably born c. 1824 in Magheramore, Desertoghill Parish, County Londonderry, Ireland.[165,166] She probably died c. 1840-1841 in Ashton, Mauch Chunk Township, Northampton County, Pennsylvania.[167]

THE LIFE OF JANE GORMLEY. The following records of this child have survived:

The first is the 1825 visitation of the Reverend James Brown, minister of the First Garvagh Presbyterian Church.[168]

The second is the 1839 ship passenger list documenting the family's arrival in New York.[169]

---

[165]Visitation of the Reverend James Brown Beginning in the Summer of 1825 lists Jane Gormley, a child of Joseph and Margaret Gormley, living in Maghrimore (sic). A copy of the original record of the First Garvagh Presbyterian Church, Errigal Parish, County Londonderry, Ireland, was provided to Kathryn C. Torpey by Lavonne Bradfield, <<LBradfield@satx.rr.com>>, on September 9, 2003. The record was provided to Lavonne Bradfield by a member of the First Garvagh Presbyterian Church.

[166]Entry for Margaret Gormley and Children, Ship Sheridan Passenger Manifest, December 12, 1839, page 3, line 19, Passenger List of Vessels Arriving at New York, NY, 1820-1897, Records of the U.S. Customs Service, Record Group 36, National Archives Microfilm Publication M237, Roll 40 says 13 (sic), i.e. born 1826 in Ireland.

[167]Letter dated June 12, 1997 from Robert C. Gormley, 334 Brownsburg Road, Newtown, Pennsylvania 18940 to Kathryn C. Torpey, 5035 Domain Place, Alexandria, Virginia 22311-5066 containing extracts of Volumes I, II, and III of the Records of the First Presbyterian Church of Summit Hill and Tamaqua and the Presbyterian Cemetery in Summit Hill as prepared by an elderly member of the church document the birth of a second daughter named Jane Gormley in 1841.

[168]Bann Valley Families Genealogical Data, <<http://www.4qd.co.uk/bann/>>, Extracts of the Visitations of the Reverend James Brown Beginning in the Summer of 1825, downloaded December 2, 2000, lists Jane Gormley, a child of Joseph and Margaret Gormley, living in Magheramore.

[169]Entry for Margaret Gormley and Children, Ship Sheridan Passenger Manifest, December 12, 1839, page 3, line 19, Passenger List of Vessels Arriving at New York, NY, 1820-1897, Records of the U.S. Customs Service, Record Group 36, National Archives Microfilm Publication M237, Roll 40.

The third is the 1840 census where Jane Gormley appears to have been enumerated, by inference, with her parents in Mauch Chunk Township.[170]

Thereafter, there is no further record of this Jane Gormley.

THE DEATH OF JANE GORMLEY. Jane Gormley is thought to have been hit and killed by a coal car in Ashton when she was about 15 years old. This tragic accident was originally thought to refer to the family matriarch, Margaret (Montgomery) Gormley, but two depositions contained in Margaret (Montgomery) Gormley's estate file make it very clear that she died at the age of 82 after an illness that lasted seven weeks.[171,172]

It is far more likely that the subject of this accident was Jane Gormley. According to family legend, the accident occurred on the No. 1 plane, one of the two planes used by the Lehigh Navigation Coal Company to haul coal to Summit Hill from the Panther Valley mines which included Ashton.[173] Local residents often picked coal in that area for use in their homes. Coal fell from the coal cars as they were being moved up the planes making it available, albeit illegally, to those willing to risk picking between the rails. In this case, the risk proved to be too great.

----

[170]1840 U.S. Census (population), Pennsylvania, Northampton County, Mauch Chunk Township, page 212, line 21, National Archives Microfilm Publication M704, Roll 479, Household of Jos. Bramley (sic).

[171]Letter dated November 7, 2003 from Robert C. Gormley, 334 Brownsburg Road, Newtown, Pennsylvania 18940 to Kathryn C. Torpey, 5035 Domain Place, Alexandria, Virginia 22311-5066 contains a copy of an article by Ed Gildea entitled "Summit Hill Woman Murdered in China" that appeared in a June 1973 issue of *The Valley Gazette* in which John M. Gormley, great-grandson of Joseph and Margaret (Montgomery) Gormley, relates the inaccurate family legend concerning the death of Margaret (Montgomery) Gormley. In the article John M. Gormley is quoted as saying the following:

> An accident in Lansford, which was then known as Ashton, took the life of Mrs. Gormley. She was killed when struck by a coal car.

[172]Estate of Margaret Gormley, Summit Hill, # 1309, Carbon County Courthouse, Jim Thorpe, Pennsylvania, contains the two depositions. One was made by her son, William Gormley, and the other was made by her former daughter-in-law, Margaret (Glenn) Gormley Allen.

[173]Letter dated January 2, 2004, from Robert C. Gormley, 334 Brownsburg Road, Newtown, Pennsylvania 18940 to Kathryn C. Torpey, 5035 Domain Place, Alexandria, Virginia 22311-5066.

THE BURIAL OF JANE GORMLEY. The Gormley family maintained a plot at the Old Presbyterian Cemetery in Summit Hill. Jane Gormley may have been buried in this family plot even though the name Gormley does not appear in any of the cemetery records.[174,175,176,177]

---

[174]Letter dated May 12, 2004 from Robert C. Gormley, 334 Brownsburg Road, Newtown, Pennsylvania 18940 to Kathryn C. Torpey, 5035 Domain Place, Alexandria, Virginia 22311-5066 contains a copy of a page from a small notebook that may show the names of people buried in the Old Presbyterian Cemetery whose surname began with the letter G. The whereabouts of the original notebook are unknown, but may be in the possession of the GAR Cemetery in Summit Hill. The photocopy of the page from the notebook is in the possession of Robert C. Gormley and states the following with respect to the Gormley burials:

> Buried on Lot
> James Gormley, soldier
> Joe Gormley
> Margaret M. Gormley
> Same (sic) Gormley
> Joe Gormley
> [Jane] Gormley

[175]Letter dated October 8, 1996 from Robert C. Gormley, 334 Brownsburg Road, Newtown, Pennsylvania 18940 to Kathryn C. Torpey, 5035 Domain Place, Alexandria, Virginia 22311-5066 states that he was familiar with the Gormley plot having visited it when growing up in Summit Hill and that the cemetery was cleared in June 1972.

[176]Letter dated June 12, 1997 from Robert C. Gormley, 334 Brownsburg Road, Newtown, Pennsylvania 18940 to Kathryn C. Torpey, 5035 Domain Place, Alexandria, Virginia 22311-5066 containing extracts of Volumes I, II, and III of the Records of the First Presbyterian Church of Summit Hill and Tamaqua and the Presbyterian Cemetery in Summit Hill as prepared by an elderly member of the church states that the name Gormley does not appear in the cemetery records.

[177]Summit Hill Presbyterian Cemetery Web Page, <<freepages,genealogy.rootsweb.com/~mccem/sh-presbcem.htm>>, downloaded September 10, 2003 contains a list of 156 names of those buried in the Old Presbyterian Cemetery. It was prepared from the cemetery plot map. The name Gormley does not appear on the plot map, however, the 156 names on the plot map only represent a partial listing of those buried in the cemetery

James Montgomery Gormley was probably born c. 1825 in Magheramore, Desertoghill Parish, County Londonderry, Ireland.[178,179] He died July 15, 1877 at Lansford, Carbon County, Pennsylvania.[180] He married Margaret Glenn, the daughter of James and Elizabeth (Bacon) Glenn, on April 11, 1866 in Summit Hill, Carbon County, Pennsylvania.[181] She was born August 20, 1846 in Ashton, Mauch Chunk Township, Carbon County, Pennsylvania.[182,183] She died May

---

[178]Visitation of the Reverend James Brown Beginning in the Summer of 1825 lists Jas. Gormley, a child of Joseph and Margaret Gormley, living in Maghrimore (sic). A copy of the original record of the First Garvagh Presbyterian Church, Errigal Parish, County Londonderry, Ireland, was provided to Kathryn C. Torpey by Lavonne Bradfield, <<LBradfield@satx.rr.com>>, on September 9, 2003. The record was provided to Lavonne Bradfield by a member of the First Garvagh Presbyterian Church.

[179]Entry for Margaret Gormley and Children, Ship Sheridan Passenger Manifest, December 12, 1839, page 3, line 19, Passenger List of Vessels Arriving at New York, NY, 1820-1897, Records of the U.S. Customs Service, Record Group 36, National Archives Microfilm Publication M237, Roll 40 says 11 (sic), i.e. born 1828 in Ireland.

[180]Letter dated July 1, 1997 from Robert C. Gormley, 334 Brownsburg Road, Newtown, Pennsylvania 18940 to Kathryn C. Torpey, 5035 Domain Place, Alexandria, Virginia 22311-5066 contains an unsourced copy of the *Gormley Family Bible* containing the following entry:

James Gormley Sr Died July 15 1877 aged 45 (sic) years

[181]Letter dated July 1, 1997 from Robert C. Gormley, 334 Brownsburg Road, Newtown, Pennsylvania 18940 to Kathryn C. Torpey, 5035 Domain Place, Alexandria, Virginia 22311-5066 contains an unsourced copy of the *Gormley Family Bible* containing the following entry:

James Gormley married to Margaret Glenn April 11th A.D.1866

[182]Death Certificate for Margaret Allen, May 21, 1920, # 61600 & # 37, Pennsylvania Division of Vital Statistics, New Castle, Pennsylvania 16103 states she was born August 20, 1846.

[183]Conversation on June 24, 1997 with Robert C. Gormley, 334 Brownsburg Road, Newtown, Pennsylvania 18940 in which he stated that Margaret Glenn was born in Ashton.

21, 1920 in Summit Hill, Carbon County, Pennsylvania.[184,185] James Montgomery Gormley was buried in the Old Presbyterian Cemetery in Summit Hill, Carbon County, Pennsylvania.[186,187] His widow, Margaret (Glenn) Gormley, and her second husband, Samuel Allen, are buried together in the GAR Cemetery, Summit Hill, Carbon County, Pennsylvania.[188,189]

U.S. CENSUS ENUMERATIONS. In 1840, James Gormley appears to have been present with his family in Mauch Chunk Township.[190] In 1850, he may be enumerated in Schuylkill, Schuylkill County, Pennsylvania as a laborer named James Ginday (sic) (25y) born in Ireland.[191]

---

[184]Death Certificate for Margaret Allen, May 21, 1920, # 61600 & # 37, Pennsylvania Division of Vital Statistics, New Castle, Pennsylvania 16103.

[185]Letter dated July 1, 1997 from Robert C. Gormley, 334 Brownsburg Road, Newtown, Pennsylvania 18940 to Kathryn C. Torpey, 5035 Domain Place, Alexandria, Virginia 22311-5066 contains an unsourced copy of the *Gormley Family Bible* containing the following entry:

Margaret Allen died May 21 - 1920 aged 73 yrs 9 months

[186]Letter dated June 24, 1997 from Robert C. Gormley, 334 Brownsburg Road, Newtown, Pennsylvania 18940 to Kathryn C. Torpey, 5035 Domain Place, Alexandria, Virginia 22311-5066 states that James Gormley's grave was marked with a slab that had no visible engraving.

[187]Summit Hill Presbyterian Cemetery Web Page, <<freepages.genealogy.rootsweb.com/~mccem/sh-presbcem.htm>>, downloaded September 10, 2003, contains a list of 156 names provided by Margaret Sides from the old cemetery plot map. The name Gormley does not appear on the list, however, the list is only a partial listing of those buried there.

[188]Site visit on June 24, 1997 to the GAR Cemetery, Summit Hill, Carbon County, Pennsylvania, in the company of Robert C. Gormley, great-grandson of James and Margaret (Glenn) Gormley.

[189]Letter dated October 8, 1996 from Robert C. Gormley, 334 Brownsburg Road, Newtown, Pennsylvania 18940 to Kathryn C. Torpey, 5035 Domain Place, Alexandria, Virginia 22311-5066 says the GAR Cemetery in Summit Hill once contained a Civil War cannon which fell pray to a World War II scrap drive, but, otherwise, the cemetery remains much as it was forty-five years earlier when Robert C. Gormley moved away except that it's a bit larger now.

[190]1840 U.S. Census (population), Pennsylvania, Northampton County, Mauch Chunk Township, page 212, line 21, National Archives Microfilm Publication M704, Roll 479, Household of Jos. Gramley (sic).

[191]1850 U.S. Census (population), Pennsylvania, Schuylkill County, Schuylkill, page 299B, line 17, National Archives Microfilm Publication M432, Roll 827, Household of Conrad

SERVICE IN THE CIVIL WAR. The whereabouts of James Gormley at the time of the 1860 census is unknown. Family legend has it that he ran off to Philadelphia, in opposition to his parents' wishes, to enlist in the Union forces during the Civil War. He is said to have stayed, briefly, with one of his sisters (either Matilda or Letitia) in Philadelphia, and then enlisted under the name James Montgomery to confuse any who would try to find and retrieve him.[192,193]

This family legend is consistent with the compiled military service record of a James Montgomery who enlisted on June 18, 1863, in Company B of the 33rd Regiment of the Pennsylvania Volunteer Militia for the duration of the emergency.[194] The James Montgomery in question enrolled in Philadelphia and was mustered out in Philadelphia on August 1, 1863.[195] In between those dates, he appears on the rolls of his company in Harrisburg, Pennsylvania. The Record of Events for Company B, 33rd Pennsylvania Militia Infantry described the activities of the company including that they saw action on July 1, 1863, at Carlisle and again on July 13, 1863, between 6 and 8:30 PM at Hagerstown. Company B also had 10 men under the command of Captain Stephen Souder in the skirmish at Oyster Point in connection with the 71st New York Militia.[196]

Graber.

[192]Letter dated September 2, 1996 from Robert C. Gormley, 334 Brownsburg Road, Newtown, Pennsylvania 18940 to Kathryn C. Torpey, 5035 Domain Place, Alexandria, Virginia 22311-5066.

[193]Letter dated April 6, 1997 from Robert C. Gormley, 334 Brownsburg Road, Newtown, Pennsylvania 18940 to Kathryn C. Torpey, 5035 Domain Place, Alexandria, Virginia 22311-5066 states that family legend has it that James Gormley's widow may have applied for a Civil War widow's pension, but was unsuccessful because her late husband's discharge papers bearing the name James Montgomery had been lost. On April 23, 1997, the Civil War pension name index and the organizational index were consulted, but nothing was found for a James Gormley who served under the name James Montgomery.

[194]Letter dated October 8, 1996 from Robert C. Gormley, 334 Brownsburg Road, Newtown, Pennsylvania 18940 to Kathryn C. Torpey, 5035 Domain Place, Alexandria, Virginia 22311-5066 says that given that James Gormley's brothers, Smith and Robert, both enlisted in the 1863 Emergency Militia Regiments, it is likely that James Gormley would have followed suit.

[195]Union Compiled Military Service Record of James Montgomery, Co. B, 33rd Pennsylvania Militia (Emergency 1863), Records of the Adjutant General's Office, Record Group 94, National Archives, Washington, D.C.

[196]Record of Events, Co. B, 33rd Pennsylvania Militia Infantry (1863 Emergency), Compiled Records Showing Service of Military Units in Volunteer Union Organizations,

Robert C. Gormley reports that while attending Dickinson College in Carlisle he often noted the damage to the columns in the old courthouse portico caused by the Confederate artillery. Little did he know at that time that his great-grandfather, James Gormley, was part of the action.[197]

SOJOURN IN CALIFORNIA. After James Gormley's discharge from the militia in August 1863, he appears to have removed to California. He may have been accompanied on this trip by his brother-in-law, John Boyd.[198] They may have been searching for gold. During James Gormley's stay in California, he joined a secret society in Visalia, California, known as the Independent Order of Good Templars, Lodge # 48.[199] He was admitted to membership on February 19, 1864 in the name James Montgomery presumably because that was the name listed on his Civil War discharge papers.[200] Having paid all demands against him and being under no charge whatsoever, the organization issued him a membership certificate in the Independent Order of Good Templars that was dated August 26, 1864.[201] Although his membership certificate in the Independent Order of Good Templars survived, his Civil War military discharge papers disappeared on his way back home from California when he lost his trunk during the journey.[202]

National Archives Microfilm Publication M595, Roll 172.

[197]Letter dated May 17, 1997 from Robert C. Gormley, 334 Brownsburg Road, Newtown, Pennsylvania 18940 to Kathryn C. Torpey, 5035 Domain Place, Alexandria, Virginia 22311-5066.

[198]Letter dated May 17, 1997 from Robert C. Gormley, 334 Brownsburg Road, Newtown, Pennsylvania 18940 to Kathryn C. Torpey, 5035 Domain Place, Alexandria, Virginia 22311-5066 states that John Boyd and James Gormley may have traveled together to California.

[199]The Independent Order of Good Templars was a secret society founded in 1851 in Utica, New York. It stood for total abstinence and no license and was probably, at one time, the strongest foe to the legalized liquor traffic in the United States and Canada.

[200]Letters dated October 8, 1996 and November 17, 1996 from Robert C. Gormley, 334 Brownsburg Road, Newtown, Pennsylvania 18940 to Kathryn C. Torpey, 5035 Domain Place, Alexandria, Virginia 22311-5066 state that he is in possession of the original membership certificate belonging to his great-grandfather.

[201]Letter dated August 5, 1997 from Robert C. Gormley, 334 Brownsburg Road, Newtown, Pennsylvania 18940 to Kathryn C. Torpey, 5035 Domain Place, Alexandria, Virginia 22311-5066 provided a copy of the Certificate of Membership.

[202]Conversation on June 24, 1997 with Robert C. Gormley, 334 Brownsburg Road, Newtown, Pennsylvania 18940 in which he related the family tradition concerning the loss of James Gormley's Civil War military discharge papers.

MARRIAGE TO MARGARET GLENN. Eventually, James Gormley arrived home where, according to an entry in the *Gormley Family Bible*, he married Margaret Glenn on April 11, 1866.[203] They were married by Pastor John White. Margaret Glenn was from Ashton. Her parents were James and Elizabeth (Bacon) Glenn and she had at least seven siblings - Letitia, Anna, Elizabeth, Samuel, James, Ellen, and Mary.[204,205]

NATURALIZATION. James Gormley was naturalized on September 25, 1868, in the Carbon County Court of Common Pleas. Because he arrived in the United States as a minor, his naturalization was a one-step process in that it omitted the waiting period between the Declaration of Intention and the Petition for Citizenship. He executed both documents on the same date.[206,207] In his paperwork, he declared that he arrived in the Port of New York in 1840 (sic) from Liverpool with the intention of settling in Coaldale. He signed his papers with his name. His witnesses were Samuel Allen and Henry Williamson.[208]

---

[203]Letter dated July 1, 1997 from Robert C. Gormley, 334 Brownsburg Road, Newtown, Pennsylvania 18940 to Kathryn C. Torpey, 5035 Domain Place, Alexandria, Virginia 22311-5066 contains an unsourced copy of the *Gormley Family Bible* containing the following entry:

James Gormley married to Margaret Glenn April 11th A.D.1866

[204]1850 U.S. Census (population), Pennsylvania, Carbon County, Mauch Chunk Township, page 304B, lines 29-39, National Archives Microfilm Publication M432, Roll 762, Household of James Glenn, enumerated Margaret Glenn with her parents and siblings as follows:

Margaret Glenn   5   b. Pennsylvania.

[205]1860 U.S. Census (population), Pennsylvania, Carbon County, Mauch Chunk Township, page 218, lines 38-40 and page 219, lines 1-4, National Archives Microfilm Publication M563, Roll 1089, Household of James Glenn enumerated Margaret Glenn with her parents and siblings as follows:

Margaret Glenn   15   b Pennsylvania.

[206]Declaration of Intention of James Gormley, Court of Common Pleas, Carbon County, Pennsylvania, September 25, 1868, Carbon County Courthouse, Jim Thorpe, Pennsylvania.

[207]Petition for Citizenship and Oath of Allegiance of James Gormley, Court of Common Pleas, Carbon County, Pennsylvania, September 25, 1868, Carbon County Courthouse, Jim Thorpe, Pennsylvania.

[208]Samuel Allen was the second husband of James Gormley's widow, Margaret (Glenn) Gormley and Henry Williamson sold 50 acres of land in Mahoning Township to John Boyd on June 22, 1852 and again on April 1, 1865.

In accordance with U.S. naturalization law, James Gormley should have become a citizen of the United States at the time his father, Joseph Gormley, naturalized on March 25, 1845, provided James Gormley arrived in the United States as a minor and had not yet reached his majority (i.e., the age of 21) at the time of his father's naturalization. Since James Gormley chose to naturalize on his own in 1868, he may not have been a minor at the time of his father's naturalization in 1845.

The original naturalization certificate of James Gormley was in the possession of James Gormley's grandson, John M. Gormley, the son of James and Martha Haines (Lewis) Gormley. Unfortunately, its present whereabouts is unknown.[209]

MARRIED LIFE TOGETHER. James and Margaret (Glenn) Gormley were married eleven years, 1866-1877. According to family tradition, their six sons - John, Samuel, Joseph, James, William, and Robert - were all born in Carbon County.[210]

In the 1870 census, however, James Gormley (30y) (sic), his wife, Margaret (24y) and his two oldest sons, John (4y) and Samuel (2y) were living in Rahn, Schuylkill County, Pennsylvania where he worked as a miner.[211] This is consistent with the obituary of his oldest son, John, which says he was born in 1867 in Coaldale.[212] The family may have moved to Carbon County after 1870 because the coal company operated mines, shops, and administrative offices in the immediate area of Lansford beginning in 1870.[213]

His sister, Margaret (Gormley) Brashear, seemed somewhat mystified about where James Gormley actually lived when she wrote the following to their brother, Robert Gormley, in her letter of July 11, 1870, from Shanghai:

---

[209]Letter dated April 6, 1997 from Robert C. Gormley, 334 Brownsburg Road, Newtown, Pennsylvania 18940 to Kathryn C. Torpey, 5035 Domain Place, Alexandria, Virginia 22311-5066.

[210]Conversation of June 24, 1997 with Robert C. Gormley, 334 Brownburg Road, Newtown, Pennsylvania 18940.

[211]1870 U.S. Census (population), Pennsylvania, Schuylkill County, Rahn, page 371B, lines 13-16, National Archives Microfilm Publication M593, Roll 1448, Household of James Gormelly (sic).

[212]Coaldale is in Schuylkill County.

[213]Fred Brenckman, *History of Carbon County, Pennsylvania*, (Harrisburg, Pennsylvania: James J. Nungesser, Publisher, 1913), 212, says that the Lehigh Coal & Navigation Company removed its construction and repair shops and the offices from Summit Hill to Lansford during 1870-1871.

... I received a very kind letter from James a few months ago and have not answered it yet
but think I shall this steamer but do not know where to address it I see it was mailed in
Tamaqua but he gives me no address to send to I have come to the conclusion I will not
write this steamer to him...[214,215]

Yet, James Gormley did keep in touch with the family as is clearly attested to by a letter directed to him by his niece, Mary Ann Wallace, in which she said:

Phila. Dec 15 1871
Dear Uncle, I am almost ashamed to write to you now after waiting so long but
had nothing to say and I was waiting for mother to come from the country. I
received your letter and I was very glad to hear that the baby was better but sorry
to hear that Johney was sick but hope he is better by this time...[216]

DEATH OF JAMES GORMLEY. James Gormley died on July 15, 1877.[217] According to family tradition, he died of cholera morbus.[218] He was buried beneath a large slab in the Old Presbyterian Cemetery in Summit Hill. The slab had no name inscribed upon its surface.[219]

---

[214]Tamaqua is in Schuylkill County.

[215]Letter dated May 17, 1997 from Robert C. Gormley, 334 Brownsburg Road, Newtown, Pennsylvania 18940 to Kathryn C. Torpey, 5035 Domain Place, Alexandria, Virginia 22311-5066 provided copies of these letters for transcription.

[216]The original letter was in the possession of Robert C. Gormley, 334 Brownsburg Road, Newtown, Pennsylvania 18940, until March 1, 1997, when he gave it to Kathryn C. Torpey, 5035 Domain Place, Alexandria, Virginia 22311-5066. Robert C. Gormley is the great-grandson of James Gormley, the recipient of the letter, and Kathryn C. Torpey is the great-granddaughter of Mary Ann (Wallace) McCauley, the author of the letter.

[217]Letter dated July 1, 1997 from Robert C. Gormley, 334 Brownsburg Road, Newtown, Pennsylvania 18940 to Kathryn C. Torpey, 5035 Domain Place, Alexandria, Virginia 22311-5066 contains an unsourced copy of the *Gormley Family Bible* containing the following entry:

James Gormley Sr Died July 15 1877 aged 45 (sic) years

[218]Jeanette L. Jerger, M.D.. *A Medical Miscellany for Genealogists*, (Bowie, Maryland: Heritage Books, Inc.), 27 states that cholera morbus, also known as cholera infantum and summer complaint, was a disease of infants and young children characterized by vomiting, severe diarrhea, and fever. If was of short duration and death frequently occurred within three to five days. It is unclear whether James Gormley died of cholera morbus or cholera, an acute infectious disease characterized by severe diarrhea, vomiting, and inflammation of the colon. The end result was the same.

[219]Letter dated June 24, 1997 from Robert C. Gormley, 334 Brownsburg Road, Newtown,

RE-MARRIAGE OF WIDOW. In the 1880 census, Margaret (Glenn) Gormley, the widow of James Gormley, and her children were enumerated in Lansford Borough living directly beside her brother-in-law, William Gormley, and his family.[220] The enumeration was as follows:

LANSFORD BOROUGH, CARBON COUNTY, PENNSYLVANIA, JUNE 18, 1880

Gormly, (sic) Maggie	F 33			Pa.
, John	M 13	works in mine*		Pa.
, Samuel	M 11	works in mine*		Pa.
, James	M 8	at school		Pa.
, William	M 5	at school		Pa.
, Robert	M 4			Pa.
Gormly, (sic) William	M 32	laborer*	Pa.	
, Mary	F 32	keeping house		Pa.
, Emma	F 5			Pa.
, Matilda	F 2			Pa.
, Joseph	M 6/12 (Dec)			Pa.

*out of work 4 months during the census year

Just up the hill from Lansford, lived the man who would very soon become the second husband of Margaret (Glenn) Gormley. He was a bachelor named Samuel Allen who appears to have arrived in America at the Port of New York on May 11, 1839, aboard the Barque Alicia.[221] At the time of the 1850 census, he was living in Mauch Chunk Township.[222] He was naturalized

---

Pennsylvania 18940 to Kathryn C. Torpey, 5035 Domain Place, Alexandria, Virginia 22311-5066 states that James Gormley's grave was marked with a slab that had no visible engraving.

[220]1880 U.S. Census (population), Pennsylvania, Carbon County, Lansford Borough, page 332C, lines 41-50 and page 332D, line 1, National Archives Microfilm Publication T9, Roll 1107, Households of Maggie Gormley and William Gormley.

[221]Entry for Samuel Allen, Barque Alicia Passenger Manifest, May 11, 1839, Passenger Lists of Vessels Arriving at New York, 1820-1897, National Archives Microfilm Publication M237, Roll 38 says:

Allen, Samuel	16 M	laborer	Ireland	Philadelphia
Allen, Anne	14 F	spinster	Ireland	Philadelphia

[222]1850 U.S. Census (population), Pennsylvania, Carbon County, Mauch Chunk Township, page 308B, lines 3-6, National Archives Microfilm Publication M432, Roll 762, Household of Thomas Allen says:

Thomas Allen	35 M	[B-----]	Ireland
Margaret Allen	33 F		Ireland
Robert Allen	32 M	Miner	Ireland
Samuel Allen	30 M	Miner	Ireland

in the Carbon County Court of Common Pleas on October 10, 1851.[223] There is no evidence that Samuel Allen served in any capacity in the Civil War.[224]

On February 3, 1866, he purchased four contiguous lots situated on the northwardly side of Rail Road Street for $6,400.00. The total property was in breadth and depth 120 feet by 125 feet and included a double house located almost immediately across the street from one of the "Old Mines," a very steep-sided quarry where coal was once mined and hoisted to the surface in buckets.[225,226] It is at this property on Rail Road Street that Samuel Allen is thought to have lived and to have operated a general store.[227] In 1875, he bought additional property in Summit Hill from the coal company.[228]

In the 1880 census, Samuel Allen was enumerated, living alone, in Summit Hill.[229] He is presumed to have been residing at the property on Rail Road Street. The listing read as follows:

---

[223]Conversation on June 24, 1997 with Robert C. Gormley, 334 Brownsburg Road, Newtown, Pennsylvania 18940.

[224]Samuel Allen, Civil War Pension Application File, SO 271,715, SC 442,866 and Margaret Allen, Civil War Dependent Relative Pension Application File, WO 737,261, WC 825,405 (Pa), Records of the Veterans Administration, Record Group 15, National Archives, Washington, D.C., are *not* the records of the subjects of this family history, but of another soldier who served in Co. B, 119 Pennsylvania Infantry and in Co. B, 109 Pennsylvania Infantry under the name Samuel W. Lean.

[225]Deed from Daniel Bertsch, et al. to Samuel Allen, February 3, 1866 (recorded April 27, 1874), Volume 21, p. 261, Deeds, Volumes 20-21, 1872-1875, Carbon County, Pennsylvania, FHL Microfilm Roll 2209191.

[226]Conversation on June 24, 1997 with Robert C. Gormley, 334 Brownsburg Road, Newtown, Pennsylvania 18940.

[227]*Beer's Atlas of Carbon County, Pennsylvania, 1875*, shows Samuel Allen's building & store, Rail Road Street, north side, Market and westward. This street has also been known as Front Street and West Ludlow Street.

[228]Deed Index - Grantees, Carbon County, Pennsylvania, FHL Microfilm Roll 2209392 says:

   1875 Allen, Samuel from Lehigh Coal & Nav Co, Vol 63, p. 410, Jun 18, 1908, Summit Hill

[229]1880 U.S. Census (population), Pennsylvania, Carbon County, Summit Hill, page 344B, line 27, National Archives Microfilm Publication T9, Roll 1107, Household of Samuel Allen.

According to the records of the Presbyterian Church in Summit Hill, Margaret (Glenn) Gormley married Samuel Allen on December 30, 1880.[230] The groom is reported to have been 25 years older than the bride. The record of the marriage says that she was from Lansford and he was from Summit Hill.

After they were married, Margaret (Glenn) Gormley Allen and some of her sons are reported to have moved to Samuel Allen's house in Summit Hill.

ESTATE OF SAMUEL ALLEN. Samuel Allen died intestate in 1888. He and Margaret (Glenn) Gormley Allen had only one child, a daughter named Jennie Allen. Samuel Allen's widow was granted Letters of Administration to settle his estate and sell certain real estate.[231] The double house on the north side of Rail Road Street does not appear to have been sold by Margaret (Glenn) Gormley Allen, but passed by operation of law to her daughter, Jennie Allen, Samuel Allen's only child.[232,233]

---

[230]First Presbyterian Church of Panther Valley (formerly First Presbyterian Church of Summit Hill), Summit Hill, Mauch Chunk Township, Baptisms, Marriages, 1873-1928, Deaths, 1873-1903, Alphabetical List of Communicants, Historical Society of Pennsylvania, Philadelphia, Pennsylvania, Microfilm Roll XCh/362.

[231]General Index to Estates, Carbon County, Pennsylvania, FHL Microfilm Roll 1290570 contains a reference to the Estate of Samuel Allen, Summit Hill, # 1595, in which Letters of Administration were issued March 5, 1888, to Mrs. Margaret Allen, and three Orders of Sale were issued on April 17, 1888, June 22, 1889, and July 5, 1888, respectively, concerning real estate belonging to the deceased.

[232]Letter dated July 1, 1997 from Robert C. Gormley, 334 Brownsburg Road, Newtown, Pennsylvania 18940 to Kathryn C. Torpey, 5035 Domain Place, Alexandria, Virginia 22311-5066 contains a copy of a letter from J.S. Fisher, District Attorney, Mauch Chunk, dated May 9, 1895, indicating that Samuel Allen died intestate and his widow, Margaret (Glenn) Gormley Allen, was the administratrix of his estate. The letter further stated that she was desirous of raising money in a mortgage ($400.00) to put the real estate in repairs. The letter stated that she had a 1/3 interest in the real estate for and during her life. Her interest ended on death. The letter further stated that a loan of this sort would create a lien on the property so she would be required to go to court to obtain a Power to Mortgage the Estate and to secure a suitable guardian for her daughter, Jennie Allen, who was still a minor and had an interest in the estate as the only surviving child of Samuel Allen. It is unknown whether the mortgage was ever secured.

[233]Letter dated November 7, 2003 from Robert C. Gormley, 334 Brownsburg Road, Newtown, Pennsylvania 18940 to Kathryn C. Torpey, 5035 Domain Place, Alexandria, Virginia

THE LATER YEARS. In the 1900 census, Margaret (Glenn) Gormley Allen, having outlived both her first and her second husbands, was enumerated at Front Street with three of her children, the youngest being her daughter, Jennie Allen, born from her marriage to Samuel Allen.[234] The enumeration was as follows:

SUMMIT HILL BOROUGH, WARD 1, CARBON COUNTY, PENNSYLVANIA, JUNE 12 & 13, 1900

Allen, Margaret	F 52 Wd	Pa	
, Jennie P.	F 19 S	Pa	
Gormley, John	M 32 S	Pa	Brakeman
, Robert	M 24 S	Pa	Boilermaker

Major changes took place in the life of the Gormley family between 1900 and 1910. Robert Gormley married Ellen Mae Remaley on August 25, 1900 in Summit Hill.[235] Then, William B. Gormley married Hattie Lewis on February 11, 1904 in Summit Hill.[236] Their brother, James Gormley married Martha Lewis on May 16, 1905 in Germantown, and their half-sister, Jennie Allen married Wallace Tarlton in August 15, 1906 in Manhattan.[237,238] Wallace

---

22311-5066 contains the following statement concerning the double house originally owned by Samuel Allen:

> Jennie Allen owned both sides of the house... 228 W. Ludlow and 230 W. Ludlow. She sold (gave?) one share of the property to my grandfather [Robert M. Gormley] when she moved to California. As far as I know, my grandfather never lived at 230 W. Ludlow, only at 228 (where his mother [Margaret (Glenn) Gormley Allen] lived until she died in 1920). Jennie sold the other half of the property to my parents in 1934 for $4,000. Prior to that (since she was already in California) she rented the property to my grandfather's brother, James, and his family. Their brother, John, also lived there for a short while.

[234]1900 U.S. Census (population), Pennsylvania, Carbon County, Summit Hill, E.D. 23, page 9, lines 47-50, National Archives Microfilm Publication T623, Roll 1391, Household of Margaret Allen.

[235]Pennsylvania County Marriages, 1885-1950, FHL Microfilm Roll 1289273, <<www.familysearch.org>>, downloaded May 17, 2019, Robert M. Gormley to Ellen Remaley, August 25, 1900, Carbon County, Pennsylvania.

[236]Pennsylvania County Marriages, 1885-1950, FHL Microfilm Roll 1289274, <<www.familysearch.org>>, downloaded May 17, 2019, William B. Gormley to Hattie Lewis, February 11, 1904, Carbon County, Pennsylvania.

[237]Affidavit of Applicant for Marriage License, Philadelphia County, Pennsylvania, 1885-1915, FHL Microfilm Roll 1276760, downloaded May 19, 2019, James Gormley to Martha Lewis, March 16, 1905, Germantown by the Rev. William Porter Lee.

[238]New York, New York, Extracted Marriage Index, 1866-1937, <<www.ancestry.com>>,

Tarlton was from Summit Hill and a veteran of the Spanish-American War having served in Company L, 9th Infantry, with three of the Gormley brothers - John, William, and Robert - the half-brothers of his wife, Jennie Allen.[239,240]

In the 1910 census, the Gormley family was again enumerated together at Front Street. Living with Margaret (Glenn) Gormley Allen was the Tarlton family and John Gormley. Directly next door was Robert Gormley and his family.[241] The enumeration was as follows:

SUMMIT HILL BOROUGH, CARBON COUNTY, PENNSYLVANIA, APRIL 15, 1910

Gormley, Robert	H M 34 M	Pa	Boilermaker Shops
, Ellen	W F 28 M	Pa	
, Theodore	S M 9 S	Pa	
, Palmer	S M 7 S	Pa	
, Chester	S M 1-11/12 S	Pa	
Allen, Margaret	H F 62 Widow	Pa	
Tarelton (sic), Jennie	D F 29 M	Pa	
, Wallace	SIL M 38 M	Pa	Plumber Shop
, Elizabeth	GD F 2 S	Pa	
, Allan (sic)	GS M 0/12 S	Pa	
Gormley, John	S M 43 S	Pa	Laborer Coal miner

Just months before her death, Margaret (Glenn) Gormley Allen was enumerated at Rail Road Street in the 1920 census with the Tarlton family and John Gormley. Living immediately

____

downloaded May 15, 2019, Wallace Tarlton to Jennie Allen, August 15, 1906, Manhattan, Kings County, New York.

[239]U.S. Civil War & Later Pension Index, 1861-1934 contains the following information about the pension of Wallace Tarlton for service in the Spanish-American War:

Tarlton, Wallace		L 9 Pa Inf		
1923 Apr 16	SO 1,483,535	SC 1,230,910	California	
C2,413,488				

[240]Veterans Compensation Application of Wallace Tarlton, May 10, 1934, Pennsylvania, Spanish War Compensation, 1898-1934, <<www.ancestry.com>>, downloaded May 15, 2019 states that Wallace Tarlton was the son of James Tarlton and Margaret Boyd. It is unknown whether Wallace Tarlton and his family had any connection to John Boyd, the husband of Matilda (Gormley) Boyd or to Stephen Wallace, the husband of Letitia (Gormley) Wallace. Wallace Tarlton served with the Gormley brothers in the Spanish-American War.

[241]1910 U.S. Census (population), Pennsylvania, Carbon County, Summit Hill, E.D. 28, page 1B, lines 63-73, National Archives Microfilm Publication T624, Roll 1327, Households of Robert Gormley and Margaret Allen.

next door was Robert Gormley and his family.[242] The enumeration was as follows:

<pre>
SUMMIT HILL BOROUGH, CARBON COUNTY, PENNSYLVANIA, JANUARY 7, 1920
    232 (sic) RAILROAD STREET
    Tarlton, Wallace   H M 42   Pa   Miner Coal mine
        , Jennie   W F 39   Pa
        , Elizabeth   D F 11   Pa
        , Allen   S M 9   Pa
        , Reynolds   S M 4-8/12   Pa
    Allen, Margaret   MIL F 73 Wd   Pa
    Gormley, John   BIL M 53   Pa   Car Repairman Coal mine

    230 (sic) RAILROAD STREET
    Gormley, Robert   H M 43   Pa   Boilermaker Coal mine
        , Ella   W F 38   Pa
        , Palmer   S M 17   Pa   Boilermaker helper Coal mine
        , Chester   S M 11   Pa
        , Hazel   D F 7   Pa
</pre>

Wallace and Jennie (Allen) Tarlton and their three surviving children - Ruth, Wallace and Reynolds - moved to Alameda County, California, after the death of her new born son, John Tarlton on January 16, 1912 and the death of her mother, Margaret (Glenn) Gormley Allen on May 21, 1920.[243,244,245]

THE CHILDREN OF JAMES AND MARGARET (GLENN) GORMLEY. James and Margaret (Glenn) Gormley had six sons - John, Samuel, Joseph, James, William, and Robert.

According to family legend, all of the children were born in Lansford except for the

---

[242]1920 U.S. Census (population), Pennsylvania, Carbon County, Summit Hill Borough E.D. 38, page 7B, lines 58-69, National Archives Microfilm Publication T625, Roll 1534, Households of Wallace Tarlton and Robert Gormley.

[243]Death Certificate for John Tarleton (sic), January 16, 1912, # 6016 & # 5, Pennsylvania Division of Vital Statistics, New Castle, Pennsylvania 16103.

[244]Death Certificate for Margaret Allen, May 21, 1920, # 61600 & # 37, Pennsylvania Division of Vital Statistics, New Castle, Pennsylvania 16103.

[245]The California Death Index lists the following about the Tarlton family:

<pre>
Dietzler, Elizabeth Ruth   b 2/27/1908 Pa; d 8/11/1995 Alameda; mother Allen; father Tarlton
Tarlton, Wallace   b 3/13/1877 Pa; d 3/2/1953 Alameda; mother Boyd; father Tarlton
Tarlton, Jennie   b 12/22/1880 Pa; d 10/24/1964 Alameda; mother Glenn
Tarlton, Allen   b 3/28/1910 Pa; d 4/3/1976 Alameda
Tarlton, Wallace Reynolds b 5/9/1915 Pa; d 10/17/1996 Alameda; mother Allen
</pre>

youngest, Robert M. Gormley, who was born in Spring Tunnel near Summit Hill. John and Samuel, their two oldest sons, never married. Joseph died as a baby. James and William may have lived for a time at Girard College in Philadelphia after the death of their father. Later, they married sisters, Martha and Hattie Lewis.[246]

John, William, and Robert Gormley all served together in Company L of the 9th Regiment of the Pennsylvania Volunteer Infantry during the Spanish-American War.[247] A photograph was taken of the brothers sitting together in front of their tent while stationed at Camp George H. Thomas in July 1898.[248] John, William, and Robert Gormley each received Spanish-American war pensions.[249,250]

---

[246]Conversation on June 24, 1997 with Robert C. Gormley, 334 Brownsburg Road, Newtown, Pennsylvania 18940.

[247]*Record of Pennsylvania Volunteers in the Spanish-American War, 1898, Second Edition,* (Harrisburg, Pennsylvania: State Printer, 1901), 396 states:

> Gormley, John, Priv, Co. L, 9th Regt; res Summit Hill Pa; enrd July 7, 1898, MI July 9 1898, Prom to Sgt July 9 1898; MO with Co Oct 29 1898
>
> Gormley, Robert M., Priv, Co. L, 9th Regt; res Summit Hill Pa; enrd July 7, 1898, MI July 9 1898, MO with Co Oct 29 1898
>
> Gormley, William B., Priv, Co. L, 9th Regt; res Summit Hill Pa; enrd July 7, 1898, MI July 9 1898, Prom to Sgt July 9 1898; Actg 1st Sgt Aug 29 1898 to Oct 29 1898, MO as 1st Duty Sgt Oct 29 1898

[248]Thomas D. Eckhart, *The History of Carbon County,* 4 volumes, (Lehighton, Pennsylvania: TN Printing, 1992), Volume 2:463, shows photo.

[249]General Index to Pension Files, 1861-1934, National Archives Microfilm Publication T288, Roll 181 says:

> Gormley, John   L 9 Pa Inf
> 1923 Dec 15   SO 1,492,976   SC 1,267,985 Pa
> C2,380,957
>
> Gormley, William B.   L 9 Pa Inf
> 1924 Apr 21   SO 1,499,807   SC 1,249,565 Pa
> C2,400,155
>
> Gormley, Robert M.   L 9 Pa Inf
> 1905 Apr [24]   SO 1,334,878   SC 1,344,535 Pa
> C2,404,409

[250]Letter dated November 7, 2003 from Robert C. Gormley, 334 Brownsburg Road,

The Gormley brothers worked for the Lehigh Navigation Coal Company (LNC), a subsidiary of the Lehigh Coal & Navigation Company (LC&N) whose main offices were located in Mauch Chunk (now known as Jim Thorpe). Most of the miners and other employees of LNC lived and worked in the area of Summit Hill and Lansford from whence most of the coal came down the mountain. Many miners, including several of the Gormley brothers, began work with the coal company as boys picking slate and put in 50 to 60 years on the job.[251]

The first of the surviving brothers to die was **John Gormley** who passed away on December 1, 1935 in Summit Hill. His obituary read as follows:

> John Gormley Called by Death
> Pensioned Coal Company Employee was Summit Hill Resident
>
> John Gormley, resident of Summit Hill for the past 55 years, passed away last night at 6:45 o'clock at his late home, the residence of his brother James Gormley, 13 E. Ludlow street, Summit Hill, after a lingering illness of complicated ailments. He was aged 68 years.
>
> He was in failing health since 1933, and bedfast the past eleven months.
>
> Mr. Gormley was born in Coaldale, February 13, 1867, a son of the late James Gormley, Sr. He was long employed by the Lehigh Coal and Navigation company, being placed on the pension list in 1929. He started as a slate picker, and later worked as a conductor on the company's railroad, and in the Lansford shops.
>
> He was a member of Captain Klein post, Spanish-American War Veterans; the Order of Carmen and Railroad Conductors and the First Presbyterian church. He served as a sergeant in the Spanish-American war.
>
> Surviving are three brothers and one sister: James and Robert, both of Summit Hill; William, Lansford; and Mrs. Jennie Tarlton, of Oakland, California. Arrangements for the funeral have not been completed.[252]

William Gormley was the second of the brothers to die on December 12, 1937, in Coaldale, Schuylkill County. His obituary read as follows:

Newtown, Pennsylvania 18940 to Kathryn C. Torpey, 5035 Domain Place, Alexandria, Virginia 22311-5066 contains confirmation that Robert Gormley received a Spanish-American war pension.

[251]Conversation on June 24, 1997 with Robert C. Gormley, 334 Brownsburg Road, Newtown, Pennsylvania 18940.

[252]Obituary of John Gormley, *The Morning Call*, Allentown, Pennsylvania, Monday, December 2, 1935, <<www.newspapers.com>>, downloaded May 17, 2019.

William B. Gormley Dies;
Was Spanish War Veteran

William B Gormley, 63 of 133 W. (sic) Patterson St., Lansford died at 7:20
o'clock last evening in the Coaldale State hospital after he had been a patient at
the institution for the last three weeks. Death was caused by pneumonia and a
cerebral hemorrhage.

Mr. Gormley, was born and raised in Lansford. He was employed by the Lehigh
Navigation Coal Corp. at the Foster's tunnel until the time that operation shut
down in 1930. Since that time Mr. Gormley has been living retired at the home
of his son and daughter-in-law, Mr. and Mrs. Frank Gormley, 133 E. (sic)
Patterson St., Lansford.

He was a Spanish American war veteran, having served with the U.S. Army as a
sergeant in Co. L, 9th Regiment, United States Volunteers. During the war, he
was stationed at Chickamauga Park, Ga., and he served as a member of the 9th
Regiment for the duration of the war. He was a member of the First Presbyterian
Church of Lansford, the Captain George B. Klein post, Spanish-American War
Veterans of Tamaqua, and the American Hose Co. No. 1 of Lansford.

Mr. Gormley follows his wife, Hattie, in death, she having died nine years ago.
He is survived by one son, Frank of Lansford, two brothers, James and Robert of
Summit Hill, one sister, Mrs. Wallace Tarlton of Oakland, Cal. and two
grandchildren.

Funeral services will be held from his home on Wednesday afternoon at 2
o'clock, with Rev. Alexander Gilmore, pastor of the First Presbyterian Church,
officiating. Interment will be made at the G.A.R. Cemetery in Summit Hill.[253]

James Gormley died third on August 28, 1944 in Summit Hill. His obituary read as
follows:

Death of James Gormley Mourned in Valley Towns

James Gormley, of 13 East Ludlow Street, Summit Hill, died at 5:45 o'clock this
morning at his home. He had been ill for two weeks.

Deceased was a 50-year veteran of the L.N.C. Company employment and the
father of four sons in the armed service of their country. Distinguished for his
friendly attitude toward his fellow man, he was one of the most respected
members of the mining fraternity in this Valley.

Born in Lansford, he spent most of his life in Summit Hill and had been
employed as a shaftman at Lansford Colliery for many years. He was a member
of the First Presbyterian Church, Summit Hill, and a leader among its

---

[253]Obituary of William B. Gormley, *The Morning Call*, Allentown, Pennsylvania,
Monday, December 13, 1937, <<www.newspapers.com>>, downloaded May 17, 2019.

parishioners.

Surviving with his widow, the former Martha Lewis, of Lansford, are these children: Mrs. Clyde Downs, of New York City; Sgt. John M. and PFC Charles, stationed in New Guinea; Joseph, attending Officers Candidate School in Fort Benning, Ga., and Tech. Sgt. Coleman, S.C.

A granddaughter, Emma Lew Downs, a sister, Mrs. Wallace Tarleton (sic) of Oakland, Calif., and a brother, Robert, of Summit Hill, also survive.[254]

Robert Gormley, the youngest surviving son of James and Margaret (Glenn) Gormley, retired from the Lehigh Navigation Coal Company in the late 1940s after John L. Lewis negotiated a pension of $100.00 a month for the men. Over time, his pension gradually dropped off to about $40.00 a month. He died on November 16, 1954. His obituary read as follows:

Robert M. Gormley, of 228 West Ludlow Street, Summit Hill, died last night in the Gnaden Huetten Memorial Hospital, Lehighton. Born in Summit Hill, he had been a lifelong resident of that community. He was a retired inspector at the Lansford Shops and was a member of the St. Paul's Reformed Church, Summit Hill, the Knights of Malta, and a veteran of the Spanish-American War.

He is survived by his wife, the former Ellen Mae Remaley, two sons, Palmer, Summit Hill, and Chester, Harrisburg; one daughter, Mrs. Homer Mantz, Summit Hill, and one sister, Mrs. Wallace Tarleton (sic), California. Six grandchildren also survive.[255]

John, James, William, and Robert Gormley are all buried in the GAR Cemetery in Summit Hill. Samuel and Joseph Gormley were buried in the Old Presbyterian Cemetery.

WILLIAM C. GORMLEY. William C. Gormley was the great-grandson of James and Margaret (Glenn) Gormley, the grandson of William B. and Hattie (Lewis) Gormley and the son of Frank and Olivia Margaret (Creitz) Gormley. He was born in Lansford. He graduated from Lansford High School in 1949 and joined the United States Army in July of that year. He was posted to Korea in August of 1950 where he was killed in action on September 3, 1950. He was buried at Gettysburg National Cemetery on August 14, 1951.

---

[254]Letter dated July 1, 1997 from Robert C. Gormley, 334 Brownsburg Road, Newtown, Pennsylvania 18940 to Kathryn C. Torpey, 5035 Domain Place, Alexandria, Virginia 22311-5066 contains an obituary of James Gormley. published in the *Lansford Record* on August 28, 1944.

[255]Letter dated July 1, 1997 from Robert C. Gormley, 334 Brownsburg Road, Newtown, Pennsylvania 18940 to Kathryn C. Torpey, 5035 Domain Place, Alexandria, Virginia 22311-5066 contains an unsourced obituary of Robert M. Gormley.

His body was not returned to the United States until eleven months after he died.[256] The report of his burial that appeared in *The Morning Call* on August 14, 1951, read as follows:

> Lansford Vets To Attend Gormley Rite
>
> A detachment of Lansford Veterans will journey to the National Cemetery in Gettysburg today to join in paying final tribute to Pvt. William Gormley, Lansford.
>
> Pvt. Gormley, the son of Frank Gormley, W. Patterson St., Lansford, was killed in action in Korea, Sept. 3, 1950. He fell in battle less than a month after his arrival in the war zone. He will be buried in the National Cemetery.
>
> Heading the veterans who will participate in the services will be Francis Mongi, commander of the Lansford AmVets, and Atty. George Richards, commander of the Lansford American Legion.

PALMER R. GORMLEY. Palmer R. Gormley was the grandson of James and Margaret (Glenn) Gormley and the son of Robert and Ellen (Remaley) Gormley. He lived in Summit Hill. He was the father of Robert C. Gormley, the chronicler of much of the Gormley family legend as it appears in this family history.

Palmer R. Gormley continued in the footsteps of those family members who preceded him by working in the boiler shop of the Lehigh Navigation Coal Company for 36 years. Eventually he became the shop foreman. In 1954, the Lehigh Navigation Coal Company closed its doors permanently while Palmer Gormley was on leave from the company recovering from a heart attack. Thereafter, he worked at Bright's Department Store in Lansford where his wife, Thelma (Steigerwalt) Gormley, was also employed. Palmer Gormley worked for Bright's Department Store for 20 years and died on May 11, 1974, within a month of his retirement. His obituary read as follows:

> Palmer R. Gormley,
> ex-school board head
> Palmer R. Gormley of 230 W. Ludlow St., Summit Hill, president of the former Summit Hill School Board, died Saturday in Gnaden Huetten Hospital, Lehighton. He was 71. He was retired only one month from Bright's department stores. He also worked for the Lehigh Navigation Coal Co. as foremen in its Lansford shops until 1954. He was school board president from 1932 to 1938.
>
> Active in civic affairs, he was a past member of the Carbon County Boy Scout

---

[256]News Story, *The Morning Call*, Allentown, Pennsylvania, Monday, September 18, 1950, "Killed in Action," and News Story, *The Morning Call*, Allentown, Pennsylvania, Tuesday, August 14, 1951, "Lansford Vets To Attend Gormley Rite," <www.newspapers.com>, downloaded October 4, 2019.

executive committee and former secretary of the Summit Hill Fire Co.

Born in Summit Hill, he was the son of the late Robert and Ella (Remaley) Gormley.

He was a member of the Consistory of St. Paul's United Church of Christ, Summit Hill.

Surviving are his widow, the former Thelma Steigerwalt; a son, Robert of Newtown; a daughter, Mrs. Gayle Pope of Riverton, N.J.; a sister, Hazle, wife of Robert Carter of Summit Hill, and nine grandchildren.

Services will be at 11:00 a.m. Wednesday in the Henry D. Miller Funeral Home, 100 E. White St., Summit Hill. Calling hours will be 7-9 p.m., Tuesday.[257]

His widow, Thelma (Steigerwalt) Gormley, continued living in the family home at 230 West Ludlow Street in Summit Hill until her death on June 20, 2000. It was through a letter directed to her at that address by the author of this family history that the descendants of James Gormley and the descendants of Letitia (Gormley) Wallace were reunited after a separation of over 80 years.

---

[257]Letter dated July 1, 1997 from Robert C. Gormley, 334 Brownsburg Road, Newtown, Pennsylvania 18940 to Kathryn C. Torpey, 5035 Domain Place, Alexandria, Virginia 22311-5066 contains a copy of the obituary of Palmer R. Gormley that appeared on May 12, 1974 in *The Morning Call*, Allentown, Pennsylvania.

Letitia Montgomery Gormley was born c. June 22, 1827, in Magheramore, Desertoghill Parish, County Londonderry, Ireland.[258,259,260] She died October 23, 1914, at Philadelphia, Pennsylvania.[261] She was buried in Mount Moriah Cemetery in Philadelphia, Pennsylvania.[262] She married Stephen Wallace, the son of Mary Ann Wallace, on August 4, 1852 in Philadelphia, Pennsylvania.[263] He was born c. 1829 in Mullaghinch, Aghadowey Parish, County Londonderry, Ireland.[264] He probably died c. 1859 possibly in Charleston, South Carolina.[265,266,267,268]

---

[258]Baptism of Letitia Gormley, June 22, 1827, First Garvagh Presbyterian Church, Garvagh, Errigal Parish, County Londonderry, Ireland, Public Records Office of Northern Ireland, Belfast, Northern Ireland, Microfilm MIC/1P/257.

[259]Death Certificate for Letitia Wallace, October 23, 1914, # 24868 & # 104654, Pennsylvania Division of Vital Statistics, New Castle, Pennsylvania 16103 states she was born in 1827 in Ireland and she was the daughter of Joseph Gormley and Margaret Montgomery.

[260]Entry for Margaret Gormley and Children, Ship Sheridan Passenger Manifest, December 12, 1839, page 3, line 19, Passenger List of Vessels Arriving at New York, NY, 1820-1897, Records of the U.S. Customs Service, Record Group 36, National Archives Microfilm Publication M237, Roll 40 says 10, i.e. born 1829 in Ireland.

[261]Death Certificate for Letitia Wallace, October 23, 1914, # 24868 & # 104654, Pennsylvania Division of Vital Statistics, New Castle, Pennsylvania 16103.

[262]Death Certificate for Letitia Wallace, October 23, 1914, # 24868 & # 104654, Pennsylvania Division of Vital Statistics, New Castle, Pennsylvania 16103 states she was buried in Mount Moriah Cemetery.

[263]Ninth Presbyterian Church, Marriages, 1850-1908, Philadelphia, Pennsylvania, FHL Microfilm Roll 0505481 (item 1) references page 22, No. 132, 1852.

[264]Declaration of Intention of Stephen Wallace and Petition for Citizenship of Stephen Wallace, both dated October 1, 1851, District Court for the City and County of Philadelphia, Philadelphia City Archives, 401 N. Broad Street, Suite 942, Philadelphia, Pennsylvania 19108. These documents state Stephen Wallace was 22 years old in 1851.

[265]Application to Admit Child or Children to the Charleston Orphan House, Division of Archives and Records, 701 E. Bay Street, Charleston, South Carolina 29403. Application for Mary Ann Wallace and Joseph S. Wallace dated June 7, 1859 and the application for Stephen Wallace dated May 9, 1860 imply that Stephen Wallace may have died around 1859.

[266]Letter dated October 9, 1995, from Michelle Claire Harmon, Charleston County

Judging from the formal photograph of Letitia (Gormley) Wallace that appears in the *McCauley Family Album*, she was steadfast in appearance.[269]

U.S. CENSUS ENUMERATIONS. In the 1840 census, Letitia Gormley was enumerated with her parents in Mauch Chunk Township.[270]

In the 1850 census, Letitia Gormley appeared to be living in Philadelphia in South Mulberry Ward where she was working as a domestic servant in the household of Edward Matlack, a merchant.[271] Her future husband, Stephen Wallace, was enumerated in Locust Ward in Philadelphia where he was working as a painter.[272]

MARRIAGE OF LETITIA GORMLEY TO STEPHEN WALLACE. On August 4, 1852, Letitia

---

Library, 404 King Street, Charleston, South Carolina 29403 to Kathryn C. Torpey, 5035 Domain Place, Alexandria, Virginia 22311-5066 states they could not locate Stephen Wallace in the death index cards maintained by the library.

[267]Death Records, June 1854 - June 1866, Charleston, South Carolina, FHL Microfilm Roll 0023364 does not contain a death record for Stephen Wallace.

[268]Confederate Compiled Military Service Record for Stephen Wallace, Private, Co E, 19th Battalion of the South Carolina Cavalry, National Archives Microfilm Publication M267, Roll 54 does not appear to apply to the subject of this family history. This Stephen Wallace was from Marlboro, South Carolina, and appears in the census at that location after the Civil War.

[269]The photograph of Letitia (Gormley) Wallace is in the possession of Kathryn C. Torpey, 5035 Domain Place, Alexandria, Virginia 22311-5066.

[270]1840 U.S. Census (population), Pennsylvania, Northampton County, Mauch Chunk Township, page 212, line 21, National Archives Microfilm Publication M704, Roll 479, Household of Jos. Gramley (sic).

[271]1850 U.S. Census (population), Pennsylvania, Philadelphia County, City of Philadelphia, South Mulberry Ward, page 245, lines 8-17, National Archives Microfilm Publication M432, Roll 815, Household of Edward Matlack states:

Biddy (sic) Gormley   24F   Domestic, b. Ireland   enumeration: August 3, 1850

[272]1850 U.S. Census (population), Pennsylvania, Philadelphia County, City of Philadelphia, Locust Ward, page 151, lines 2-9, National Archives Microfilm Publication M432, Roll 814, Household of James Laven states:

Stephen Walland (sic)   21M   Painter, b. Ireland   enumeration: August 8, 1850

Gormley married Stephen Wallace at the Ninth Presbyterian Church in Philadelphia. The bride and the groom were both stated to be of Philadelphia. The ceremony was performed by the Reverend William Blackwood. Letitia McCormack and Anne V. Blackwood served as witnesses.[273]

The announcement of their marriage appeared in the *Philadelphia Public Ledger* on December 8, 1852, as follows:

> On the 4th of August by the Rev. W. Blackwood, Mr. Stephen Wallace to Miss Letitia Gormley, all of this city.[274]

Stephen Wallace was a painter. He appears to have been from Mullaghinch, Aghadowey Parish, County Londonderry, Ireland. His family attended the Aghadowey Presbyterian Church where his mother is buried in the church graveyard.[275,276] He arrived in New York from Liverpool on June 15, 1846, aboard the Ship Hottinguer.[277,278] His occupation was listed as a painter. He was naturalized in the District Court for the City and County of Philadelphia on

---

[273]Ninth Presbyterian Church, Marriages, 1850-1908, Philadelphia, Pennsylvania, FHL Microfilm Roll 0505481 (item 1) references page 22, No. 132, 1852.

[274]Marriage of Stephen Wallace to Letitia Gormley, *Philadelphia Public Ledger*, Wednesday, December 8, 1852, p. 2.

[275]Kathryn C. Torpey, *The McCauley Family in Philadelphia (including the Wallace & Patton Families from Mullaghinch, County Londonderry, Ireland)*, (Alexandria, Virginia: Torpey Books, 2019), Appendix I: Wallace Families in Mullaghinch says:

> Plot 201 Aghadowey Presbyterian Graveyard
> Stephen Wallace of Charlestown (sic) S.C. (sic)
> To the memory of his mother Mary Ann Wallace
> late of Mullahinch (sic) who departed this life April 10th 1852 aged 61 years.

[276]Find-A-Grave Memorial # 83747817, Mary Ann Wallace (headstone photograph), added January 20, 2012, Aghadowey Presbyterian Church Graveyard, County Londonderry, Northern Ireland, <<www.findagrave.com>>.

[277]Ira Glazier and Michael Tepper, *The Famine Immigrants: Lists of Irish Immigrants Arriving at the Port of New York, 1846-1851*, (Baltimore, Maryland: Genealogical Publishing Company, 1983), Volume I:154 says: WALLIS (sic), Stephen 17 M Painter 15 Jun 1846.

[278]Entry for Stephen Wallis (sic), Ship Hottinguer Passenger Manifest, June 15, 1846, p. 9, line 15, Passenger List of Vessels Arriving at New York, New York, 1820-1897, Records of the U.S. Customs Service, Record Group 36, National Archives Microfilm Publication M237, Roll 62. Note: The Hottinguer was a packet (or sailing ship).

October 1, 1851. He filed a minors petition because at the time of his arrival he was under the age of eighteen. His witness was Samuel Wallace, relationship, if any, unknown. He stated at the time of his naturalization that he was 22 years old.[279] A photograph of Stephen Wallace, believed to have been taken about the time of his marriage, is in the *McCauley Family Album*.[280]

SOJOURN IN SOUTH CAROLINA. For some unknown reason, Stephen and Letitia (Gormley) Wallace relocated from Philadelphia to Charleston, South Carolina, shortly after they were married.[281] In 1856, Stephen Wallace appeared in the Charleston city directory. His occupation was stated to be a painter, but no street address was listed.[282]

The whereabouts of Stephen Wallace are unknown after 1859. He did not leave a will, administration, or estate papers in Charleston, South Carolina.[283,284,285,286] Nevertheless, his wife, Letitia (Gormley) Wallace, placed their two oldest children - Mary Ann and Joseph - in the Charleston Orphan House in that year.

---

[279]Declaration of Intention of Stephen Wallace and Petition for Citizenship of Stephen Wallace, both dated October 1, 1851, District Court for the City and County of Philadelphia, Philadelphia City Archives, 401 N. Broad Street, Suite 942, Philadelphia, Pennsylvania 19108.

[280]Photograph of Stephen Wallace is in the possession of Kathryn C. Torpey, 5035 Domain Place, Alexandria, Virginia 22311-5066.

[281]Application to Admit Child or Children to the Charleston Orphan House, Division of Archives and Records, 701 E. Bay Street, Charleston, South Carolina 29403. Application for Mary Ann Wallace and Joseph S. Wallace dated June 7, 1859 states time of residence in the city or within the jurisdiction 6-1/2 years, i.e., 1852. The application for Stephen Wallace dated May 9, 1860 states time of residence in the city or within the jurisdiction 8 years, i.e., 1852/1853.

[282]1856 Charleston city directory.

[283]Index to Wills of Charleston County, South Carolina, 1671-1868, FHL Microfiche 6051308 (4 microfiches) did not contain a Stephen Wallace, Wallis, or Willis.

[284]Index to Administrations and Guardianships, Charleston, South Carolina, 1775-1869, FHL Microfilm Roll 0194626 did not contain a Stephen Wallace, Wallis, or Willis.

[285]Bonds of Administrators, v E, 1858-1869; Guardian Bonds, v E 1856-1869; Administration Bonds, v F 1859-1864, FHL Microfilm Roll 0194684.

[286]Letters of Administration, v E, 1854-1856; Letters Testamentary, v E, 1854-1857; Letters of Administration, v E 1859-1863; Letters of Guardianship, v E 1855-1869, FHL Microfilm Roll 0194698.

THE CHARLESTON ORPHAN HOUSE. The Charleston Orphan House stood on the corner of Calhoun and St. Philip Streets. Children were admitted to the house by a church or city warden, parent or guardian after a short investigation by a Visiting Commissioner. When admitted, the children were indentured to the house which retained the legal right to bind the child out at a later date. This apprenticeship was a legal and binding document whereby the parent or guardian lost all control over the child. The boys were bound out at age 14 and the girls at age 12. A master agreed to train, house, clothe, and oversee the moral and religious development of the apprentice. Boys were apprenticed until 21 and girls until 18.[287]

According to the Application to Admit the children into the Charleston Orphan House, Mary Ann Wallace and Joseph S. Wallace were 5½ and 4½ years old, respectively, when their mother submitted an application for their admission on June 7, 1859 and their brother Stephen Wallace was 2 years old when she submitted an application for his admission on May 9, 1860. They are all believed to have been born in Charleston even though the word is crossed out in the first application and Ireland is handwritten in its place.[288]

The Indentures and the Commissioners Minutes of the Charleston Orphan House state that Mary Ann Wallace, aged 5½ years and Joseph S. Wallace, aged 4½ years, were formally admitted on June 16, 1859. The records state the indentures of Mary Ann Wallace would expire on December 16, 1871, about a month after her 18th birthday if she was born in 1853 and the indentures of Joseph S. Wallace would expire on December 16, 1875, one day after his 21st birthday.[289,290,291] The Indentures and the Commissioners Minutes of the Charleston Orphan

---

[287]Susan King, *History and Records of the Charleston Orphans House, 1790-1860,* (Easley, South Carolina: Southern Historical Press, 1984), 16.

[288]*Application to Admit a Child or Children into the ORPHAN HOUSE* for Mary Ann Wallace and Joseph S. Wallace dated June 7, 1859 and *Application to Admit a Child or Children into the ORPHAN HOUSE* for Stephen Wallace dated May 9, 1860, Archives and Records Division, 701 East Bay Street, Suite 348, Charleston, South Carolina 29403.

[289]Charleston Orphan House, Commissioners Minutes, Charleston, South Carolina, FHL Microfilm Roll 0023351 says:

> Thursday, June 9, 1859
> Read applications from ... Also from Mrs. Letitia Wallace for the admission of her two children, Mary Ann, aged 5-1/2 yrs and Joseph S. Wallace, aged 4-1/2 yrs which were severally referred to the V.C.

> Thursday, June 16, 1859
> He reported favorably on the application of Mrs. Letitia Wallace for the admission of her two children, Mary Ann, aged 5-1/2 years and Joseph S, aged 4-1/2 years. Ordered that they be received upon being bound according to law.

House state their brother, George Stephen Wallace, aged 2 years, was formally admitted on May 17, 1860, with an indenture expiration date of May 17, 1879, the day of his 21st birthday.[292,293,294]

Register of Boys

Name:	Wallace, Joseph S.
Age:	4-1/2
Indenture Book:	T-175
Bound out:	–
To Whom Bound:	To his mother
Exp of Indenture:	16 December 1875

[290]Indentures, Charleston, Charleston County, South Carolina, FHL DGS 100665041, images 335-338 (sic), Volume T, items 175 & 176 dated June 16, 1859, expiring December 16, 1875, regarding Joseph Wallace and FHL DGS 100665042, images 383-384, Volume U, item 200 dated June 16, 1859, expiring December 16, 1871, regarding Mary Ann Wallace.

[291]Susan King, *History and Records of the Charleston Orphans House, 1860 - 1899,* (Easley, South Carolina: Southern Historical Press, 1984), 164, states, erroneously, that the indentures of Mary Ann Wallace would expire on June (sic) 16, 1871, and the indentures of Joseph Wallace would expire on June (sic) 16, 1875. The correct expiration month of their indentures was December [see fn 290].

[292]Charleston Orphan House, Commissioners Minutes, Charleston, South Carolina, FHL Microfilm Roll 0023351 says:

Thursday, May 10, 1860
Read an application from Mrs. Lucretia (sic) Wallace for the admission of her son Stephen aged 2 years. Referred to the V.C.

Thursday, May 17, 1860
He also reported favorably on the application of Mrs. Lucretia (sic) Wallace for the admission of her son Stephen aged 2 years. Ordered that the child be admitted on being bound according to law.

Register of Boys

Name:	Wallace, Stephen
Age:	2
Indenture Book:	T-218
Bound out:	–
To Whom Bound:	Left
Exp of Indenture:	17 May 1879

[293]Indentures, Charleston, Charleston County, South Carolina, FHL DGS 100665041, images 407-408, Volume T, item 218 dated May 17, 1860 regarding Stephen Wallace.

[294]Susan King, *History and Records of the Charleston Orphans House, 1860 - 1899,* (Easley, South Carolina: Southern Historical Press, 1984), 117, says the indentures of Stephen

In both Applications to Admit the children into the Charleston Orphan House, Letitia (Gormley) Wallace indicated that she was living at Hyams Court/Alley, 331 King Street, between George and Calhoun Streets, in the rear of Mr. Dinant's hat store. In 1860, this address was in Ward 4 of the City of Charleston.

The two boys, but not their sister, were enumerated at the Charleston Orphan House in the 1860 census as follows:

CHARLESTON, CHARLESTON TOWNSHIP, SOUTH CAROLINA JUNE 9 1860

| Joseph S. Wallace | 5 M | orphan | b. South Carolina |
| Stephen Wallace | 2 M | orphan | b. South Carolina[295] |

RETURN TO PHILADELPHIA. Exactly what happened after Letitia Wallace placed the children in the Charleston Orphan House in unclear. No record of her has been found in the 1860 census. According to the Register of Boys, Joseph S. Wallace was "Bound to his Mother," but no date was provided. Stephen Wallace was stated in the Register of Boys to have "Left," but no date was provided. The Register of Girls could not be located for information about Mary Ann Wallace and her date of departure.[296]

In the 1870 census (second enumeration), Letitia (Gormley) Wallace was enumerated in Philadelphia as a domestic servant in the household of Mary Johnson who lived at 1722 Chestnut Street.[297] Mary Johnson was a very wealthy woman who was born in Maryland.[298]

Wallace were recorded in book T-218. The entry states *Episcopal* followed by the abbreviation (AtoA), but the word *Episcopal* was not found on the original application. An inquiry dated January 17, 1997, was sent to the Archives and Records Division in Charleston which elicited the following one line reply on January 22, 1997: "The person who served you, Ms. Susan King, gave you all the information that we have in our files."

[295]1860 U.S. Census (population), South Carolina, Charleston County, Charleston, Ward 6, page 427, lines 4-5, National Archives Microfilm Publication M653, Roll 1216, Charleston Orphan House.

[296]Charleston Orphan House, Commissioners Minutes, Charleston, South Carolina, FHL Microfilm Roll 0023351.

[297]1870 U.S. Census (population), Second Enumeration, Pennsylvania, Philadelphia County, Philadelphia, Ward 8, page 145B, lines 22-25, National Archives Microfilm Publication M593, Roll 1421, Household of Mary Johnson. Enumerated as: Letitia Wallace 36y.

[298]1870 U.S. Census (population), First Enumeration, Pennsylvania, Philadelphia County, Philadelphia, Ward 8, page 143A, lines 5-10, National Archives Microfilm Publication M593, Roll 1393, Household of Mary Johnson does not include the enumeration of Letitia (Gormley)

In the 1880 census, Letitia (Gormley) Wallace was again enumerated as a domestic servant in the household of Mary Johnson who still lived at 1722 Chestnut Street.[299]

On June 29, 1888, Letitia (Gormley) Wallace joined Tabor Presbyterian Church.[300] This is the same church that her daughter, Mary Ann (Wallace) McCauley joined on June 30 1880, and her son-in-law, Thomas McCauley, joined on October 20, 1878.[301]

In the 1900 census, Letitia (Gormley) Wallace was living in Philadelphia at 1818 Montrose Street with her daughter and son-in-law, Thomas and Mary Ann (Wallace) McCauley, and their four children and Stephen McCauley, the father of Thomas McCauley.[302] The enumeration was as follows:

PHILADELPHIA WARD 30, PHILADELPHIA, PENNSYLVANIA, JUNE 4-5, 1900

McCauley, Thomas	Head Feb 1854 46y M 21y	PA IRE IRE	Brickmaker
McCauley, Mary A.	Wife Nov 1856 (sic) 44y M 21y 6-4	SC IRE IRE	
McCauley, Margaret	Dau Oct 1883 16y S	PA PA SC	Oper. Telephone
McCauley, Letitia	Dau July 1885 14y S	PA PA SC	Labels In Lab.
McCauley, Mary A.	Dau July 1892 7y S	PA PA SC	At school
McCauley, Willis S.	Son Sep 1896 3y S	PA PA SC	
McCauley, Stephen	Father May 1830 (sic) 70y M 50y	IRE IRE IRE	Laborer
Wallace, Letitia	MIL July1834 (sic) 65y Wd 48y 3-3	IRE IRE IRE	

Letitia (Gormley) Wallace executed her Last Will and Testament on July 13, 1903, just ten days after the death of her brother, William Gormley. In her will, she named her brother-in-law, Henry Erwin, of the Borough of West Bethlehem, Lehigh County, Pennsylvania, as her

---

Wallace.

[299]1880 U.S. Census (population), Pennsylvania, Philadelphia County, Philadelphia, E.D. 148, page 465B, lines 41-44, National Archives Microfilm Publication T9, Roll 1171, Household of Mary Johnson. Enumerated as: Letitia Wallace 50y servant Ireland

[300]Tabor Presbyterian Church, Session Minutes, 1881-1896, Presbyterian Historical Society, Philadelphia, Pennsylvania, V, MI46, P5383, Volume 2, p 45.

[301]Tabor Presbyterian Church, Session Minutes, 1863-1880, Presbyterian Historical Society, Philadelphia, Pennsylvania, V, MI46, P5383, Volume 1, p. 167 & 176.

[302]1900 U.S. Census (population), Pennsylvania, Philadelphia County, City of Philadelphia, E.D. 758, page 4A, lines 46-50, and page 5A, lines 51-53, National Archives Microfilm Publication T623, Roll 1472, Household of Thomas McCauley, states Letitia Wallace was born July 1834 which is in error in that she was baptized on June 22, 1927. Note: There is a page 4B erroneously inserted between pages 4A and 5A that breaks the McCauley enumeration into two households and adds unrelated people to the separated households.

executor. Her niece, Margaret M. Erwin, signed the will as a witness. This may indicate that Letitia (Gormley) Wallace was present in West Bethlehem, Lehigh County, Pennsylvania, for her brother's funeral and burial. In her will, she directed that her entire estate be converted to cash as soon as convenient after her death and distributed evenly among her ten grandchildren whom she mentioned by name.[303]

Less than two months later, on September 4, 1903, she signed a document renouncing her right to serve as administratrix of her brother's estate in favor of her sister, Jane (Gormley) Erwin, regarding the sale of property in Summit Hill in which her brother, William Gormley, had a life estate under the terms of the will of their mother, Margaret (Montgomery) Gormley.[304] The renunciation document was witnessed by Letitia (Gormley) Wallace's son-in-law and daughter, Thomas and Mary Ann (Wallace) McCauley.

According to family legend, Letitia (Gormley) Wallace spent her final years living in the home of her daughter and son-in-law, Thomas and Mary Ann (Wallace) McCauley.[305] This is partially confirmed by the following listings in the Philadelphia city directories:

1901	Wallace, Letitia, wid Stephen	1818 Montrose
1903	Wallace, Letitia, wid Stephen	921 S. 19th Street[306]
1908	Wallace, Letitia, wid Stephen	1818 Montrose
1909	Wallace, Letitia, wid Stephen	1818 Montrose
1910	Wallace, Letitia, wid Stephen	1818 Montrose

Letitia (Gormley) Wallace has not been found in the 1910 census. She also dropped out of the Philadelphia city directories after 1910 which roughly coincides with the McCauley family moving from 1818 Montrose Street in South Philadelphia to 1606 S. 53rd Street in West Philadelphia. According to family legend, Letitia (Gormley) Wallace did not entirely approve of her son-in-law, Thomas McCauley, because of his lack of a formal education.[307] It is, therefore,

---

[303]Estate of Letitia Wallace, Philadelphia, # 19, 1915, Register of Wills, Philadelphia, Philadelphia County, Pennsylvania.

[304]Estate of Margaret Gormley, Summit Hill, # 1309, Carbon County Courthouse, Jim Thorpe, Pennsylvania.

[305]Conversation (date unknown) with Mary Ann (McCauley) Chambers, daughter of Mary Ann (Wallace) McCauley in which she stated that her grandmother moved with them when she was growing up at 1818 Montrose Street.

[306]This address is about one block away from 1818 Montrose Street.

[307]Conversation (date unknown) with Mary Ann (McCauley) Chambers, daughter of Mary Ann (Wallace) McCauley, in which she stated that her grandmother, Letitia (Gormley) Wallace believed that her daughter, Mary Ann (Wallace) McCauley had married beneath her social status

entirely possible that when her daughter, Mary Ann (Wallace) McCauley, died, unexpectedly, on December 31, 1909, Letitia (Gormley) Wallace may have moved elsewhere. Eventually, she is believed to have rejoined the McCauley family in West Philadelphia as their street address is specified as her usual residence on her death certificate.

DEATH OF LETITIA (GORMLEY) WALLACE. Letitia (Gormley) Wallace died on October 23, 1914, at 6:30 PM at the American Oncologic Hospital located at S.E. 33rd and Powelton Avenue in Philadelphia. She died from epithelioma of the face.[308]

Her obituary appeared in the *Philadelphia Inquirer* on Saturday, October 24, 1914.[309] It read as follows:

> Wallace - October 23, 1914, Letitia Wallace, aged 87 years. Relatives and friends of the family are invited to attend funeral services Tuesday 2 P.M. from the residence of her son-in-law, Thomas McCauley, 1606 S. 53rd Street. Interment at Mount Moriah Cemetery.

She was buried at Mount Moriah Cemetery alongside her daughter, Mary Ann (Wallace) McCauley, and some of her grandchildren in a plot belonging to her son-in-law, Thomas McCauley.[310]

THE WILL OF LETITIA (GORMLEY) WALLACE. Letitia (Gormley) Wallace executed her Last Will and Testament on July 13, 1903.[311] In her will, Letitia (Gormley) Wallace directed that her entire estate be converted to cash as soon as convenient after her death and distributed evenly among her ten grandchildren whom she mentioned by name as follows:

---

when she married Thomas McCauley.

[308]Death Certificate for Letitia Wallace, October 23, 1914, # 24868 & # 104654, Pennsylvania Division of Vital Statistics, New Castle, Pennsylvania 16103 states she died of epithelioma of the face (i.e., cancer of the face).

[309]Obituary of Letitia Wallace, *Philadelphia Inquirer*, Saturday, October 24, 1914, p. 14 and Sunday, October 25, 1914, p. 15.

[310]Letter dated December 18, 1985, from Horatio C. Jones, Jr., Mount Moriah Cemetery, 62nd Street and Kingsessing Avenue, Philadelphia, Pennsylvania 19142 to Bernard Erl, 820 Mason Avenue, Drexell Hill, Pennsylvania 19026 concerning burials in Section 123, Lot 53 purchased by Thomas McCauley on January 8, 1883.

[311]Will of Letitia Wallace, July 13, 1903, January 4, 1915, Will Book 361, page 311, Philadelphia County, Pennsylvania, FHL Microfilm Roll 1311230.

Joseph Wallace, Jr.
Margaret McCauley
Letitia McCauley
Mary W. (sic) McCauley
Willis McCauley
George S. Wallace
Robert Wallace
Letitia Wallace
Verna (sic) Wallace
Mary L. Wallace.[312]

She died on October 23, 1914. In her will, she named her brother-in-law, Henry Erwin, of the Borough of West Bethlehem, Lehigh County, Pennsylvania, as her executor, but he had died on February 12, 1912, making it necessary to appoint an administrator to execute the will. The two adult granddaughters with whom she was living in Philadelphia at the time of her death were Margaret McCauley and Mary A. McCauley. Mary A. McCauley renounced her right to serve as administratrix on January 4, 1915 in favor of her sister, Margaret McCauley, who was appointed by the Register of Wills for the City and County of Pennsylvania to administer the estate of their grandmother.

THE CHILDREN OF STEPHEN AND LETITIA (GORMLEY) WALLACE. Stephen and Letitia (Gormley) Wallace had three children - Mary Ann, Joseph S., and George Stephen.

Mary Ann Wallace was the oldest child. According to Mary Ann (McCauley) Chambers, her mother, Mary Ann Wallace, was educated to be a teacher, but where she may have received that education is unknown.[313,314]

In the 1870 census, Mary Ann Wallace was enumerated as a domestic servant in the household of Levi Harrison, but there is no indication of the nature of her position such as that of

---

[312]Estate of Letitia Wallace, Philadelphia, # 19, 1915, Register of Wills, Philadelphia, Philadelphia County, Pennsylvania Wills and Probate Records, 1683-1993, <<www.ancestry.com>>, downloaded May 25, 2019.

[313]Conversation (date unknown) with Mary Ann (McCauley) Chambers, daughter of Mary Ann (Wallace) McCauley in which she stated that her mother was college educated to be a teacher.

[314]Letter dated February 2, 1996 from Barbara B. Hoeft, Administrative Assistant, Alumnae & Alumni of Vassar College, Alumnae House, 61 Raymond Avenue, Poughkeepsie, New York 12601-6199 to Kathryn C. Torpey, 5035 Domain Place, Alexandria, Virginia 22311-5066 states that there is no record of Mary Ann Wallace having attended or graduated from that institution despite family legend to the contrary.

a nannie or governess versus a maid.[315]

On December 15, 1871, she wrote a letter to her uncle, James Gormley, who was probably living in Lansford, Carbon County, Pennsylvania, next door to his brother, William Gormley. The letter was well written in terms of grammar, syntax, and handwriting indicating that the author was fairly well educated. The letter read as follows:

Phila. Dec 15 1871

Dear Uncle

I am almost ashamed to write to you now after waiting so long but had nothing to say and I was waiting for mother to come from the country. I received your letter and I was very glad to hear that the baby was better but sorry to hear that Johney was sick but hope he is better by this time. Jimmy Boyd has been sick with the Typhoid fever. They did not expect him to live. Aunt Tilly had to go up to nurse him. She was gone four weeks but he is better now he was able to come down stairs when she came home wich (sic) was three weeks ago. The city has been in the greatess (sic) excitement about the Grand Duke from Russia, We have had quite a spell of cold weather, it has been cold for the last two weeks but we have had very little snow yet. Mother is right well and she says she will write to you soon. Aunt Tilly is also well and sends her love to you all. I would like very much for you to send the children's pictures also yours and Aunt Margaret's and will send one of mine when I get them taken. Maggie Boyd would like to have them too if you can spare them. Remember me to Willie and all the rest. I hope you will excuse this short letter but I having nothing to say. Mother the Boys and all send their love. I remain your affectionate niece Mary Wallace[316]

She joined Tabor Presbyterian Church on July 4, 1879.[317] On November 20, 1879, she

---

[315] 1870 U.S. Census (population), First Enumeration, Pennsylvania, Philadelphia County, Philadelphia, Ward 23, page 145A, lines 18-25, National Archives Microfilm Publication M593, Roll 1421, Household of Levi Harrison, says:

Wallace, Mary   16 F   domestic   b S. Carolina   (August 6, 1870)

[316] The original letter was in the possession of Robert C. Gormley, 334 Brownsburg Road, Newtown, Pennsylvania 18940, until March 1, 1997, when he gave it to Kathryn C. Torpey, 5035 Domain Place, Alexandria, Virginia 22311-5066. Robert C. Gormley is the great-grandson of James Gormley, the recipient of the letter, and Kathryn C. Torpey is the great-granddaughter of Mary Ann (Wallace) McCauley, the author of the letter.

[317] Presbyterian Historical Society; Philadelphia, Pennsylvania; U.S., Presbyterian Church Records, 1701-1907; Book Title: Communicant Roll 1878-1919; Accession Number: V MI46 P5383c v.3, <<www.ancestry.com>>, downloaded May 25, 2019.

married Thomas McCauley, the son of Stephen and Margaret (Wallace) McCauley.[318] They had six children - Letitia, Margaret, Letitia (2nd), Thomas, Mary Ann, and Willis. An account of their married life together is contained in *The McCauley Family in Philadelphia*.[319]

Mary Ann (Wallace) McCauley died of heart disease on December 31, 1909, the month after their 30th wedding anniversary.[320] She was only 56 years old. Her obituary appeared in the *Philadelphia Inquirer* on Monday, January 3, 1910. It read as follows:

> McCauley - Entered into rest, Mary A., wife of Thomas McCauley. Relatives and friends are invited to attend the funeral on Thursday at 2 P.M., from her late residence 1818 Montrose Street. Interment at Mount Moriah Cemetery.[321]

She left a very brief will that was entirely handwritten and dated three days before she died. Her witnesses were her husband's first cousin, William Patton, and his second wife, Ella (Stewart) Patton. The will read as follows:

Dec 28th, 1909

> I, Mary A. McCauley, of sound mind, desire to leave all my possessions, both personal and all moneys which are invested in my name entirely and absolutely to my husband Thomas McCauley knowing he will make good use of it and will do all right with the children.

Mary A. McCauley

Witnessed by:
Ella S. Patton

---

[318]Marriage Certificate of Thomas McCauley and Mary Ann Wallace, Tabor Presbyterian Church, Philadelphia, Pennsylvania, November 20, 1879, original in the possession of Kathryn C. Torpey, 5035 Domain Place, Alexandria, Virginia 22311.

[319]Kathryn C. Torpey, *The McCauley Family in Philadelphia (including the Wallace & Patton Families from Mullaghinch, County Londonderry, Ireland)*, (Alexandria, Virginia: Torpey Books, 2019).

[320]Death Certificate of Mary A. McCauley, Pennsylvania Death Certificates,1906-1966, Philadelphia, Philadelphia County, Pennsylvania, <<www.ancestry.com>>, downloaded August 25, 2018, says: b. November 25, 1854 in South Carolina, d. December 31, 1909 in Philadelphia, Father: Stephen Wallace, Mother: Letitia Gormley.

[321]Obituary of Mary A. McCauley, *Philadelphia Inquirer*, Monday, January 3, 1910, p. 10, Philadelphia Free Library, Philadelphia, Pennsylvania.

No executor was named in the will of Mary Ann (Wallace) McCauley so her husband, Thomas McCauley, petitioned the court and was appointed by the Register of Wills for the City and County of Pennsylvania to administer the estate of his late wife.[323]

Joseph S. Wallace was the middle child of Stephen and Letitia (Gormley) Wallace. Judging from his photograph which appears in the *McCauley Family Album*, Joseph S. Wallace was a handsome man.[324] According to family legend, he worked for Robinson and Crawford, the founders of the American Store (aka Acme) in Philadelphia.[325] He married Elizabeth Urwiler about 1878, but where they met or where they were married is unknown.

In the 1880 census, Joseph S. Wallace and his family were enumerated in Philadelphia. He was working as a clerk and living with the family of Charles D. Tyson, a grocer, at 300 Cumberland Street.[326] The enumeration was as follows:

PHILADELPHIA, PENNSYLVANIA, WARD 31, JUNE 4, 1880
Wallace, Joseph S.   M 25   Clerk   Pa (sic)

Meanwhile, his wife and their only child, Joseph Wallace, Jr., were enumerated with the family of Margaret (Boyd) Strawbridge, the daughter of Matilda (Gormley) Boyd at 1924 Latona

---

[322]Will of Mary A. McCauley, December 28, 1909, January 8, 1910, Will Book 312, page 215, Philadelphia County, Pennsylvania, FHL Microfilm Roll 1311088.

[323]Estate of Mary A. McCauley, Philadelphia, # 43, 1910, Register of Wills, Philadelphia, Philadelphia County, Pennsylvania Wills and Probate Records, 1683-1993, <<www.ancestry.com>>, downloaded May 25, 2019.

[324]The photograph of Joseph S. Wallace is in the possession of Kathryn C. Torpey, 5035 Domain Place, Alexandria, Virginia, 22311-5066.

[325]E-mail dated August 17, 1999 from William S. Chambers, 9221 West Broward Boulevard, # 2510, Plantation, Florida 33324 stating that he recalled his mother, Mary Ann (McCauley) Chambers, saying she had an uncle who worked for the founders of the American stores and that he had a chance to go into business with them, but he didn't take advantage of the opportunity.

[326]1880 U.S. Census (population), Pennsylvania, Philadelphia County, Philadelphia, E.D. 684, page 579A, lines 1-5, National Archives Microfilm Publication T9, Roll 1190, Household of Charles D. Tyson. Note: Joseph Wallace is stated to have been born in Pennsylvania not South Carolina.

Street.[327] The enumeration was as follows:

PHILADELPHIA, PENNSYLVANIA, WARD 26, JUNE 7, 1880

Strawbridge, John	M 30	Wire Worker	Ireland
, Margaret	F 25	Keeping Home	Pa
, Margaret	F 4		Pa
, Tillie	F 3		Pa
Wallace, Lizzie	F 21		Pa
, Joseph	M 8/12		Pa

In the 1900 census, Joseph S. Wallace, his wife, and son were enumerated together at 2518 Myrtlewood Street in Philadelphia.[328] His occupation was listed as a grocer and his son was listed as a salesman. Four years later, Joseph S. Wallace, Jr., married Letitia "Lettie" Kennedy at the West York Street Methodist Episcopal Church.[329,330] Life moved on with both father and son working in the grocery business.

At the time of the 1910 census, Joseph S. Wallace was enumerated with his wife, Elizabeth (Urwiler) Wallace, at 2604 Hollywood Street. He was then working as a grocery broker.[331] His son, Joseph Wallace, Jr., a butter and eggs salesman, was enumerated with his wife, Letitia (Kennedy) Wallace, at 3751 Percy Street.[332]

----

[327]1880 U.S. Census (population), Pennsylvania, Philadelphia County, Philadelphia, E.D. 563, page 704D, lines 14-19, National Archives Microfilm Publication T9, Roll 1185, Household of John Strawbridge.

[328]1900 U.S. Census (population), Pennsylvania, Philadelphia County, Philadelphia, E.D. 698, page 10A, lines 37-39, National Archives Microfilm Publication T623, Roll 1470. Note: Joseph Wallace is stated to have been born in Pennsylvania not South Carolina.

[329]Affidavit of Applicant for Marriage License # 172069, April 9, 1904, (Joseph Wallace, Jr., to Lettie Kennedy), City of Philadelphia, Philadelphia City Archives, Philadelphia, Pennsylvania.

[330]Marriage of Joseph Wallace to Lettie Kennedy, April 1, 1904, West York Street Methodist Episcopal Church, Pennsylvania and New Jersey Church and Town Records, 1169-2013, <<www.ancestry.com>>, downloaded May 26, 2019.

[331]1910 U.S. Census (population), Pennsylvania, Philadelphia County, Philadelphia, E.D. 654, Family Number 149, line 37-39, National Archives Microfilm Publication T624, Roll 1402. Note: Joseph Wallace is stated to have been born in Pennsylvania not South Carolina.

[332]1910 U.S. Census (population), Pennsylvania, Philadelphia County, Philadelphia, E.D. 1091, Family Number 362, lines 68-69, National Archives Microfilm Publication T624, Roll 1411, Household of Joseph Wallace, Jr. Note: Joseph Wallace Jr.'s father is stated to have been

Tragically, Joseph S. Wallace died on May 28, 1915, from a fractured skull.[333,334] Apparently, he sustained a fatal head injury from having fallen in the street after an attack of apoplexy, i.e., a hemorrhage or a stroke.[335] His obituary appeared in the *Philadelphia Inquirer*.[336] It read as follows:

> WALLACE - Suddenly on May 28, 1915, JOSEPH S. WALLACE. Relatives and friends are invited to attend the funeral services Tuesday 2 P.M. at his late residence 2604 North Hollywood st. Interment Ardsley Burial Park.

Soon thereafter, his son, Joseph Wallace, Jr., moved with his wife and his mother to New Jersey. They were all enumerated in the 1920 census at 103 Haveland Avenue, in the Borough of Audubon, Camden County, New Jersey.[337] The enumeration was as follows:

---

born in Pennsylvania not South Carolina.

[333]Death Certificate for Joseph S. Wallace, May 28, 1915, $54606 & # 12586, Pennsylvania Department of Vital Statistics, New Castle, Pennsylvania 16103 erroneously says his occupation was barber (sic) not broker.

[334]Oliver Bair Funeral Home Record for J. Wallace, May 28, 1915, June 1, 1915, Oliver Bair Funeral Home Records, Pennsylvania and New Jersey Church and Town Records, 1669-2013, <<www.ancestry.com>>, downloaded May 22, 2019, wherein he was described as having been born in Philadelphia, not South Carolina, on December 15, 1855, the son of Stephen Wallace and Letitia Gormley. He was further described as a broker by occupation, 5' 8-1/2" tall, 165 pounds, gray hair, and blue eyes. His minister was identified as the Rev. Mr. Turnbull.

[335]News Story, *Philadelphia Public Ledger*, Friday, May 28, 1915, Philadelphia, Pennsylvania, <<www.newspapers.com>>, downloaded May 25, 2019, states:

MAN FATALLY STRICKEN ON STREET

Joseph Wallace, 58 years old, a salesman living at 2604 Hollywood street, fell and struck his head on the curb at Front and Market streets this morning and died five minutes after being admitted to the Jefferson Hospital. Wallace was standing at the depot talking to the car dispatcher, when he suddenly fell backwards. Physicians at the hospital said he suffered apoplexy. The police are looking for his relatives.

[336]Obituary of Joseph S. Wallace, *Philadelphia Inquirer*, Sunday, May 30, 1915, p. 9 and Monday, May 31, 1915, p. 9, Library of Congress, Newspaper and Periodical Reading Room, Washington, D.C.

[337]1920 U.S. Census (population), New Jersey, Camden County, Borough of Audubon, E.D. 186, page 26A, lines 28-30, National Archives Microfilm Publication T625, Roll 1024, Household of Joseph Wallace. Note: Joseph Wallace Jr.'s father is stated to have been born in

Wallace, Joseph, Jr.	M 40	Pa	Salesman, Butter & Eggs
, Letitia	F 45	Pa	
, Elizabeth	F 61 (widow)	Pa	

Joseph Wallace, Jr., was active in local politics and served as a borough councilman in Audubon. He worked for J. Barnett & Company, a Philadelphia butter and eggs business. He was killed instantly in a horrific accident on May 10, 1934, at the Pennsylvania Railroad crossing in West Berlin, Camden County, New Jersey, when a train struck the truck in which he was riding. The driver, Sidney H. Sobel, had stopped at the railroad crossing to yield to a northbound train, but apparently unaware of the southbound train, had started onto the tracks when the accident occurred that killed both men. The accident ended a long day during which Joseph Wallace, Jr., had spent most of his time introducing Sidney Sobel to his customers in preparation for the younger man taking over the route.[338,339]

An account of the accident appeared in at least five newspapers. Two of the news stories appeared in New Jersey newspapers including one in *The Evening Courier* that said Joseph Wallace, Jr., was survived by his wife and his mother.[340,341] Two accounts appeared in

----

Pennsylvania not South Carolina.

[338]Death Certificate for Joseph Wallace, May 10, 1934, Camden County, Berlin Township, Borough of West Berlin, New Jersey State Archives, Trenton, New Jersey.

[339]Obituary of Joseph Wallace, *Courier-Post*, Camden, New Jersey, Saturday, May 12, 1934, p. 18 read as follows:

> WALLACE - Suddenly, on May 10, 1934, Joseph Wallace, Jr., beloved husband
> of Lettie Wallace, of 10 S. Haveland Ave., Audubon N.J. Relatives and friends,
> also Washington Camp, No. 127, P.O.S. of A., are invited to attend the funeral
> services on Monday afternoon, at 1 o'clock, D.S.T., at Foster's Funeral Home,
> 250 White Horse Pike, Audubon, N.J. Interment at Ardsley Burial Park.
> Friends may call Sunday evening after 7 o'clock.

[340]News Story, *The Morning Post*, Camden, New Jersey, Friday, May 11, 1934, p. 1, "2 Killed As A Train Hits Truck At Berlin," New Jersey State Library, Trenton, New Jersey.

[341]News Story, *The Evening Courier*, Camden, New Jersey, Friday, May 11, 1934, p. 1, "2 Instantly Killed As Train Hits Truck At Grade Crossing," New Jersey State Library, Trenton, New Jersey.

Philadelphia newspapers and another account appeared in *The New York Times*.[342,343,344]

Joseph Wallace, Jr., bequeathed his entire estate to his wife, Letitia "Lettie" (Kennedy) Wallace.[345] His mother, Elizabeth (Urwiler) Wallace, died five years later on August 27, 1939, at the Old Ladies Home in Philadelphia, Pennsylvania.[346,347] His widow, Letitia "Lettie" (Kennedy) Wallace, died on April 12, 1952.[348,349] She and Joseph S. Wallace, Jr., had no children.

––––––––––––––––––––

[342]News Story, *The Philadelphia Record*, Philadelphia, Pennsylvania, Friday, May 11, 1934, p. 1, "2 Die As Train Smashes Truck," Library of Congress, Newspaper and Periodical Reading Room, Washington, D.C.

[343]News Story, *Philadelphia Inquirer*, Philadelphia, Pennsylvania, Friday, May 11, 1934, p. 5, "2 In Truck Killed By Shore Express," Library of Congress, Newspaper and Periodical Reading Room, Washington, D.C.

[344]News Story, *The New York Times*, New York City, New York, Friday, May 11, 1934, p. 13, "Train Kills Two on Truck," Library of Congress, Newspaper and Periodical Reading Room, Washington, D.C.

[345]Will of Joseph Wallace, Jr., February 12, 1921, June 29, 1934, Will Book 87, p. 181, Petition for Probate, Vol. 24, p. 173, Camden County Surrogate's Office, Hall of Justice, Camden, New Jersey, left his entire estate to his wife, Lettie Wallace. There is no record in Camden County of a will for Lettie Wallace.

[346]Death Certificate of Elizabeth Wallace, August 27, 1939, Philadelphia, Pennsylvania, Pennsylvania Death Certificates, 1906-1966, <<www.ancestry.com>>, downloaded May 24, 2019, says: Hillside Cemetery, Montgomery County, Pennsylvania, August 30, 1939.

[347]Obituary of Elizabeth Wallace, *Philadelphia Inquirer*, Philadelphia, Pennsylvania, Tuesday, August 29, 1939, Tuesday, p. 29.

WALLACE - Aug 27 1939, ELIZABETH M., widow of Joseph S. Wallace.
Relatives and friends are invited to the service, Wed., 2 P.M. at the Oliver H.
Bair Bldg., 1820 Chestnut st. Int private. Viewing Tues. evening.

[348]Death Certificate for Letitia (Kennedy) Wallace, April 12, 1952, Camden County, Audubon Borough, New Jersey State Department of Health, Bureau of Vital Statistics, Trenton, New Jersey 08625.

[349]Obituary of Lettie Wallace, *Courier-Post*, Camden, New Jersey, April 15, 1952, p. 2.

WALLACE, On April 12th, 1952, Lettie, beloved wife of the late Joseph
Wallace, Jr., of 24 N. Logan Ave., Audubon, N.J., age 78 years. Relatives and
friends of the family are invited to attend the funeral services on Thursday at 11

Concerning their final resting place, Joseph S. Wallace is buried at Ardsley Memorial Park, now part of Hillside Cemetery, in Roslyn, Montgomery County, Pennsylvania, in the same plot as his son, Joseph S. Wallace, Jr., and his daughter-in-law, Letitia "Lettie" (Kennedy) Wallace.[350] The Hillside Cemetery could not confirm the burial location of his widow, Elizabeth (Urwiler) Wallace, despite ample evidence in her death certificate, her retirement home record, her church burial record, and her funeral home record that she was buried in that cemetery in the same plot with her husband, her son, and her daughter-in-law.[351,352,353,354]

George Stephen Wallace was the youngest child of Stephen and Letitia (Gormley) Wallace. He married Louise E. Hartman, the daughter of Ambrose Hartman and Elizabeth

---

a.m., at Foster's Funeral Home, 250 White Horse Pike, Audubon, N.J. Interment at Ardsley Burial Park. Friends may call Wednesday evening.

[350]Letter dated August 18, 1999 from Debra S. Baxter, Administrative Assistant, Hillside Cemetery, Susquehanna & Bradfield Roads, P.O. Box 1177, Roslyn, Pennsylvania 19001 to Kathryn C. Torpey, 5035 Domain Place, Alexandria, Virginia 22311-5066 concerning burials in the Birch Section, Lot 234. A site visit to the cemetery reveals that a large tree has grown immediately in front of the Wallace headstone making it hard to read.

[351]Death Certificate of Elizabeth Wallace, August 27, 1939, Philadelphia, Pennsylvania, Pennsylvania Death Certificates, 1906-1966, <<www.ancestry.com>>, downloaded May 24, 2019, says: Hillside Cemetery, Montgomery County, Pennsylvania, August 30, 1939.

[352]Old Ladies Home of Philadelphia Ledger, ACC. 855, Records, 1890-1952, Urban Archives, Samuel Paley Library, Temple University, Philadelphia, Pennsylvania, states the following with respect to Elizabeth M. Wallace:

Name: Wallace, Elizabeth M.; Age: 71 July 10, 1859; Nationality: Pennsylvania, Philadelphia; Church: Presbyterian; Entrance Date: July 30, 1929; Place of Burial: Hillside Cemetery; Name of Relative: Mrs. Mattie G. Hamill 6218 Wayne Ave - letter attached. In case of Mrs. Hamell's death, Grace Hamell will attend the burial.

[353]Register of Deaths, Session Register, 1930-1955, Ninth Presbyterian Church, Philadelphia, Pennsylvania, Presbyterian Historical Society, U.S. Presbyterian Church Records, 1701-1970, <<www.ancestry.com>>, downloaded May 22, 2019 says:

Elizabeth M. Wallace; Res: Wissinoming, Pa; Death: 8-30-30; Burial: Hillside Cemetery

[354]Oliver Bair Funeral Home Records Indexes, 1920-1980, Billing Information for Elizabeth M. Wallace, Hillside Cemetery, August 30, 1939, <<www.ancestry.com>>, downloaded May 24, 2019.

Bontley (sic), about 1885, but where they met and where they married is unknown.[355,356,357,358]
After their marriage. they lived in the vicinity of Montgomery, Alabama, but when they arrived
there is unknown.

All five of the known children of George Stephen and Louise (Hartman) Wallace were
stated by their mother, Louise (Hartman) Wallace, in a sworn deposition included in the passport
application of her daughter-in-law, Jean (Tait) Wallace, to have been born in Edgewood, Elmore
County, Alabama.[359,360] A possible sixth child identified only as "Master Wallace" may have
been born in Weatherly, Carbon County, Pennsylvania, on February 19, 1895. He lived only 2

---

[355]Louise E. Hartman's mother, Elisabeth Hartmann (sic), predeceased her husband,
Ambrose Hartman, in March 1871 after a miscarriage. She was buried in Poughkeepsie Rural
Cemetery, Lot 52, Section B, in the plot of Emil Greiner. Louise E. Hartman's father, Ambrose
"Ambrosius" Hartman, died in Poughkeepsie, Dutchess County, New York, on September 26,
1885, at the age of 62. He was buried in Saint Peter's Cemetery in Poughkeepsie, Dutchess
County, New York. The second wife of Ambrose Hartman, Catharine, died November 5, 1889,
in Poughkeepsie, Dutchess County, New York. Her burial location is unknown.

[356]1900 U.S. Census (population), Alabama, Autauga County, Prattville, E.D. 0002, page
13, lines 13-18, National Archives Microfilm Publication T623, Roll 1, Household of George
Walace (sic) says they were married for 15 years. i.e., 1885.

[357]Larry W. Nobles, *Autauga County, Alabama, Index to Marriage Records*, (Prattville,
Alabama: Autauga Genealogical Society, n.d.), does not contain a reference to the marriage of
George S. Wallace to Louise Hartman.

[358]Letter dated January 31, 1997 from the Department of Archives and History, State of
Alabama, 624 Washington Avenue, Montgomery, Alabama 36130-0100 to Kathryn C. Torpey,
5035 Domain Place, Alexandria, Virginia 22311-5066 stating that they were unable to find a
record of the marriage of George S. Wallace to Louise E. Hartman in Montgomery County or
Autauga County, Alabama.

[359]U.S. Passport Application of Mrs. Jean Wallace, Certificate # 331536, August 11,
1923, National Archives and Records Administration (NARA); Washington, D.C., U.S. Passport
Applications, 1795-1925, <<www.ancestry.com>>, downloaded June 6, 2019, contains a sworn
statement by Mrs. Louise Wallace, widow of George S. Wallace, Sr., dated July 9, 1923 that
states ALL HER CHILDREN were born in Edgewood, Elmore County, Alabama, but she has not
been able to obtain proof of their birth place due to poor record keeping in said county.

[360]World War I Draft Registration Cards, New York, Poughkeepsie City, 5th Ward, 1st
District, S-Z, FHL Microfilm Roll 1818711 says George Stephen Wallace was born in
Montgomery (sic), Alabama, September 12, 1888 and Robert Earl Wallace was born in
Edgewood, Alabama, September (sic) 4, 1891.

days dying on February 21, 1895. He was buried in Weatherly in an unknown cemetery.[361]

Regarding the residence of the Wallace family, there is an inconclusive listing for a George S. Wallace that appeared in the 1887 Montgomery city directory living at South end Union Street. Recognizable listings appeared in the Montgomery city directories as follows:

1897	Wallace, George (Mrs. Louisa) supt Ala Fert Co., res Prattville rd bey limits
1898	Wallace, George S., supt Ala Fert Co., res Prattville rd bey lim
1899	Wallace, George S., wks Ala Fert Co., res Vesavius
1901	Wallace, George S., supt Ala Fert Co., r Riverside Park
1902	Wallace, George S., supt Ala Fert Co
1903	Wallace, George S., (Louisa) sup h 608 Columbus

At the time of the 1900 census, the Wallace family was enumerated just outside Montgomery, Alabama, in Prattville.[362] The enumeration was follows:

PRATTVILLE, AUTAUGA COUNTY, ALABAMA, JUNE 8, 1900

Walace (sic), George, Sr.	M 42	South Carolina	Manufacturer of [?] Farmer
, Louisa	F 32	New York	7 children 4 living
, George, Jr.	M 11	Alabama	
, Robert E.	M 9	Alabama	
, Vera T.	F 6	Alabama	
, Lettie M.	F 2	Alabama	

---

[361]Registration of Deaths, Borough of Weatherly, Ward 3, Carbon County, Pennsylvania, Filed April 11, 1895, FHL Microfilm Roll 1290569 (item 1), contains a death record for a child who was two days old which may refer to another child of George Stephen and Louise E. (Hartman) Wallace. An inquiry concerning this child was made of Jack Koehler, 108 Hudsondale Street, Weatherly, Pennsylvania 18255, a historian in Weatherly. In a letter dated October 23, 1999, Jack Koehler reported that he is the clerk of the Presbyterian Church in Weatherly, but there is no record of this family or this child in that church or in the records of the Evangelical Lutheran Church to which he also has access. There is also no record of the burial of the child in Union Cemetery or any other cemetery checked by Jack Koehler so this burial could not be confirmed. Furthermore, the birth of this child is less than 30 days after the birth of Vera Matilda Wallace which is a problem except that according to the 1900 & 1910 censuses Vera Matilda Butler may have been born about 1894 not 1985. The Weatherly Registration of Death entry is as follows:

Master Wallace, W M 2 days b. Weatherly, d. Feb 21 1895 in Weatherly of unknown causes, buried in Weatherly Feb 22, 1895, parents, George Wallace, Louisa Wallace

[362]1900 U.S. Census (population), Alabama, Autauga County, Prattville, E.D. 0002, page 13, lines 13-18, National Archives Microfilm Publication T623, Roll 1, Household of George Walace (sic).

Unfortunately, George Stephen Wallace died unexpectedly, on November 26, 1902, of bronchitis.[363] Although no death certificate or will has been found, his obituary appeared in the *Montgomery Advertiser* on November 27, 1902.[364,365] It read as follows:

DEATH OF MR. WALLACE

Respected Citizen Passed Away at Home on Columbus Street.

Mr. George S. Wallace, aged 54 (sic) years, died Wednesday morning at 2 o'clock at his home, 608 Columbia Street.

He was a highly respected citizen and his death was a shock to his friends. He will be buried at Oakwood Cemetery.

After the death of George Stephen Wallace, his widow, Louise E. (Hartman) Wallace, and the children removed to Poughkeepsie, Dutchess County, New York, where she was born. When the Wallace family left Alabama, Louise E. (Hartman) Wallace made arrangements for her late husband's body to be disinterred and removed to Poughkeepsie where she had him re-interred in Poughkeepsie Rural Cemetery.[366] She is buried in the same plot.[367,368]

---

[363]Letter dated January 19, 1996 from Charles H. Fells, Superintendent, Poughkeepsie Rural Cemetery, P.O. Box 977, 342 South Avenue, Poughkeepsie, New York 12602-0977 to Kathryn C. Torpey, 5035 Domain Place, Alexandria, Virginia 22311-5066 regarding burials in Lot 33, Section 19 belonging to Louise (Hartman) Wallace. The letter transmitted a 3x5 card stating he died in Montgomery, Alabama, on November 26, 1902, of bronchitis.

[364]Letter dated January 31, 1997 from the Department of Archives and History, State of Alabama, 624 Washington Avenue, Montgomery, Alabama 36130-0100 to Kathryn C. Torpey, 5035 Domain Place, Alexandria, Virginia 22311-5066 stating that they were unable to find a record of the death of George S. Wallace in the form of a death certificate or a will in Montgomery County, Alabama.

[365]Obituary of George S. Wallace, *Montgomery Advertiser*, Thursday, November 27, 1902, p. unknown.

[366]Letter dated August 14, 1996, from Phillip Taunton, II, Sexton, Oakwood Cemetery, 829 Columbus Street, Montgomery, Alabama 36104 to Kathryn C. Torpey, 5035 Domain Place, Alexandria, Virginia 22311-5066 states that George S. Wallace, aged 45, was interred on November 28, 1902, in Square 11 of Scott's Free Burying Ground in Oakwood Cemetery and later disinterred and re-interred in New York.

[367]Obituary of Louise E. Wallace, *Poughkeepsie New Yorker*, Monday, October 14, 1946, p. 12, says:

After Louise E. (Hartman) Wallace returned to Poughkeepsie, she resided in the same neighborhood for the rest of her life, usually, with one or more of her children. Her addresses as they appeared in the Poughkeepsie city directories were:

1907 - 1910	145 Cannon Street
1910 - 1920	22 Crannell Street[369,370]
1920 - 1934	61 Catherine Street [371]
1935 +	21 Conklin Street[372]

George Stephen and Louise (Hartman) Wallace had five surviving children - two sons and three daughters. Their oldest son, George Stephen Wallace, Jr., first married Minnie Albertina Switzer.[373] They removed to Chicago, Cook County, Illinois, where they divorced on

---

WALLACE - At Poughkeepsie, New York, October 12, 1946, Louise E. Wallace. Services at the Miller Funeral Home, 310 Mill Street, Tuesday at 2 p.m. Relatives and friends invited. Interment Poughkeepsie Rural Cemetery. Arrangements in charge of William G. Miller.

[368]Registration of Death of Louise E. Wallace, # 439, d. October 12, 1946, in Poughkeepsie, 77y, 11m, 29d, birthplace Poughkeepsie, widow of George S. Wallace, daughter of Ambrose Hartman and Elizabeth Bontley (sic), Register of Deaths in the City of Poughkeepsie, County of Dutchess, State of New York.

[369]1910 U.S. Census (population), New York, Dutchess County, Poughkeepsie City, E.D. 69, Family Number 174, page 7A, lines 46-50, National Archives Microfilm Publication T624, Roll 936, Household of Louise Wallace.

[370]1920 U.S. Census (population), New York, Dutchess County, Poughkeepsie City, E.D. 49, sheet 7B, line 56-59, National Archives Microfilm Publication T625, Roll 1098, Household of Wallace Louise (sic).

[371]1930 U.S. Census (population), New York, Dutchess County, Poughkeepsie City, E.D. 52, page 11B, lines 77-81, National Archives Microfilm Publication T626, Roll 1120, Household of Louise Wallace.

[372]1940 U.S. Census (population), New York, Dutchess County, Poughkeepsie City, E.D. 14-66, page 12B, lines 68-74, National Archives Microfilm Publication T267, Roll 2524, Household of Harry Ackert says 21 Conklin Street. Louise Wallace and her daughter, Vera (Wallace) Butler, were not enumerated at this address and could not be located in the 1940 Federal census in New York or New Jersey.

[373]Helen Wilkinson Reynolds, editor, *Records of Christ Church (Episcopal Church), Poughkeepsie, New York*, (Zephyrhills, Florida: Jean D. Woodson, 1994), Volume II:189 states "Wallace, George Stephen a 22 of Poughkeepsie son of George S. and Louisa H. Wallace of

April 8, 1920.[374] After his divorce, George Stephen Wallace, Jr., appears to have relocated to Detroit, Wayne County, Michigan for work.[375] Two years later, on August 26, 1922, he married Jean Tait, a Scottish immigrant, in Newark, Essex County, New Jersey.[376] They made their home in Newark where they raised two sons, George and Robert.[377,378] George Stephen Wallace, Jr., died in Newark, Essex County, New Jersey on March 15, 1955 from an unknown accident. His remains were cremated at Rosedale Crematory.[379,380] His second wife, Jean (Tait) Wallace, died

---

Poughkeepsie and Minnie Albertina Switzer a 25 of Poughkeepsie daughter of Joseph and Caroline K. Switzer of Poughkeepsie, October 8, 1910, witnesses John Edward Herr, Vera Fogg."

[374]Minnie Wallace v George Wallace, Gen, No. 348175, December 24, 1919, April 8, 1920, Superior Court of Cook County, Chicago, Illinois.

[375]1920 U.S. Census (population), Michigan, Wayne County, Detroit, E.D. 183, page 11A, line 31, National Archives Microfilm Publication T625, Roll 806, Household of Orra Winslow, which states:

Wallace, George S. W M 31; married; roomer; born in Alabama; parents born U.S.; iron worker in iron works

[376]Marriage of George S. Wallace and Jean Tait, August 26, 1922, Second Reformed Church, Newark, New Jersey, Archives of the Dutch Reformed Church in America, New Brunswick, New Jersey, <<www.ancestry.com>>, downloaded June 8, 2019.

[377]1930 U.S. Census (population), New Jersey, Essex County, Newark, E.D. 653, page 10B, lines 56-59, National Archives Microfilm Publication T626, Roll 1336, Household of George Wallace.

[378]1940 U.S. Census (population), New Jersey, Essex County, Newark, E.D. 25-41, page 10A, lines 10-13, National Archives Microfilm Publication T627, Roll 2412, Household of George Wallace.

[379]Social Security Applications and Claims Index for George S. Wallace, <<www.ancestry.com>>, downloaded June 8, 2019, says: George S Wallace; SSN: 137-09-6328; Birth Date: 12 Sep 1888; Death Date: 12 Mar 1955; Claim Date: 17 Mar 1955; Type of Claim: Death Claim.

[380]Death Certificate for George Stephen Wallace, March 13, 1955, # 10602, New Jersey Department of Health, Trenton, New Jersey 08625 -0370 says he died at St. Michael's Hospital.

in Lyndhurst Bergen County, New Jersey on May 11, 1982.[381,382] Her burial place is unknown.

The former wife of George Stephen Wallace, Jr., Minnie Albertina (Switzer) Wallace, returned to Poughkeepsie where she married her former husband's brother, Robert Earl Wallace, a World War I veteran.[383] They lived their entire married life in Poughkeepsie, Dutchess County, New York. They had no children. He died on January 2, 1948.[384,385] He was buried in Poughkeepsie Rural Cemetery in the plot belonging to his mother, Louise (Hartman) Wallace.[386]

---

[381]Social Security Death Index for Jean Wallace, <<www.ancestry.com>>, downloaded June 8, 2019, says: Jean Wallace; SSN: 146-28-5596; Birth Date: 12 Feb 1894; Death Date: May 1982; Last Residence: 07071 Lyndhurst, Bergen, New Jersey, USA.

[382]New Jersey Death Index, <<www.newjerseydeathindex.com>>, downloaded June 8, 2019, says: Jean Wallace; 5/11/1982; Lyndhurst, Bergen County, New Jersey.

[383]Affidavit for License to Marry # 4519, & # 21919, September 21, 1922, (Robert Earl Wallace to Minnie Albertina Wallace), City of Poughkeepsie, Dutchess County, New York, New York State Archives, Albany, New York.

[384]Death Certificate for Robert Earl Wallace, January 2, 1948, #1148, City of Poughkeepsie, Dutchess County, New York, New York State Archives, Albany, New York.

[385]Obituary Robert E. Wallace, *Poughkeepsie New Yorker*, Friday, January 2, 1948, Dutchess County Historical Society, P.O. Box 88, Poughkeepsie, New York 12602-0088, read as follows:

> WALLACE - At Poughkeepsie, N.Y., January 2 1947 *(sic)*, Robert E., beloved husband of Minnie Surtzer (sic). Services at the Miller Funeral Home, 310 Mill St., Monday at 2 P.M. Relatives and friends invited. Interment Poughkeepsie Rural Cemetery. Friends may call Saturday after 7 P.M. Arrangements in charge of William G. Miller.

[386]Letter dated November 20, 1995 from Charles H. Fells, Superintendent, Poughkeepsie Rural Cemetery, P.O. Box 977, 342 South Avenue, Poughkeepsie, New York 12602-0977 to Kathryn C. Torpey, 5035 Domain Place, Alexandria, Virginia 22311-5066 regarding the burials in Lot 33, Section 19 belonging to Louise (Hartman) Wallace states the headstone for her son reads:

Robert E. Wallace
New Jersey
Mess Sgt 310 Inf
78 Div
World War I
August 4 1891
January 2 1948

A lengthy obituary for him appeared in the *Poughkeepsie New Yorker*. It read as follows:

> Robert E. Wallace
> Dies in 57th Year
>
> Robert E. Wallace, 56 died at his home, 143 Mansion street, early this morning. He had been ill the last week.
>
> A veteran of the World War, Mr. Wallace served overseas for 14 months. He had been employed as a laundryman for Courtney's laundry until a year ago, when he retired.
>
> Born in Montgomery, Ala., Mr. Wallace was the son of the late George S. and Louise E. Hartman Wallace. He had resided here the last 40 years.
>
> Surviving are his wife, Mrs. Minnie Switzer Wallace; three sisters, Mrs. John Butler, and Mrs. William Witzenbocker, here, and Mrs. Edward Buckalew, South Amboy, N.J., and several nieces and nephews.
>
> Funeral services will be conducted at the Miller funeral home, 310 Mill street, at 2 o'clock Monday. The Rev. Roland J. Bunten, rector of St. Paul's Episcopal church will officiate. Military rights will be offered by Lafayette post American Legion. Burial will be in the Poughkeepsie Rural cemetery. Friends may call at the funeral home after 7 o'clock tomorrow night.[387]

His widow, Minnie Albertina (Switzer) Wallace died on December 31, 1948.[388] Her obituary read as follows:

> Mrs. Wallace Dies
>
> Mrs. Minnie Wallace, widow of Robert Wallace, 143 Mansion street, died at St. Francis' hospital Friday night. In her 63rd year, she suffered a heart seizure, having been a patient at the hospital on Friday only.
>
> Mrs. Wallace was the daughter of the late Joseph and Caroline Kessler Switzer. She was a native of this city and made her home here all her life. Her husband died a year ago yesterday.
>
> Survivors include a brother, Albert J Switzer Sr., this city; two sisters, Mrs. Matthew McCabe, and Mrs. Anna Clackner, also of Poughkeepsie.
>
> Mrs. Wallace was a member of Lafayette post, American Legion, auxiliary.
>
> Funeral services will be held at the Mueller Funeral home, 310 Mill street, Tuesday

---

[387]Obituary of Robert E. Wallace, *Poughkeepsie New Yorker*, Friday, January 2, 1948, Dutchess County Historical Society, P.O. Box 88, Poughkeepsie, New York 12602-0088.

[388]Death Certificate for Minnie Wallace, December 31, 1948, #70830, City of Poughkeepsie, Dutchess County, New York, New York State Archives, Albany, New York.

afternoon at 2 o'clock. The Rev. Roland J. Bunten, rector of St. Paul's Episcopal Church,
of which Mrs. Wallace was a member, will officiate. Burial will be in Poughkeepsie
Rural cemetery. Friends may call at the funeral home tomorrow afternoon and evening.[389]

She was buried in a separate plot in Poughkeepsie Rural Cemetery belonging to her sister,
Mrs. Anna Clackner.[390]

The oldest of the three daughters of George Stephen and Louise (Hartman) Wallace was
Vera Matilda Wallace who married John Joseph Butler.[391] They had twin boys, Robert Earl
Butler, and John Joseph Butler, Jr., the father of Linda L. Butler and Kandee S. Butler. It was
through a letter directed to Linda L. Butler, in 1997 by the author of this family history that the
descendants of George Stephen Wallace, Sr., and the descendants of his sister, Mary Ann
(Wallace) McCauley, were reunited after a separation of almost 30 years.

Vera (Wallace) Butler died on September 28, 1948 in Poughkeepsie.[392] Her obituary read
as follows:

> Mrs. Vera Butler
>
> Mrs. Vera M Butler, 53, wife of John J Butler, Sr., 12 Conklin street, died at her home,
> this morning. She had been ill the last month.
>
> Funeral services will be conducted at the William G Miller Funeral home, 310 Mill street,
> at 2 o'clock, Friday. The Rev. Roland J Bunten, rector of St. Paul's Episcopal church,
> will officiate. Burial will be in the Poughkeepsie Rural cemetery. Friends may call after 7
> o'clock tomorrow night.
>
> Born in Montgomery, Ala., Mrs. Butler had attended schools there and in this city. She

------

[389]Obituary of Minnie (Switzer) Wallace, *Poughkeepsie New Yorker*, Sunday, January 2,
1949, p. 14, Dutchess County Historical Society, P.O. Box 88, Poughkeepsie, New York 12602-
0088.

[390]Letter dated May 6, 1999 from Charles H. Fells, Superintendent, Poughkeepsie Rural
Cemetery, P.O. Box 977, 342 South Avenue, Poughkeepsie, New York 12602-0977 to Kathryn
C. Torpey, 5035 Domain Place, Alexandria, Virginia 22311-5066 regarding the burial location of
Minnie Albertina (Switzer) Wallace, widow of Robert E. Wallace, indicates that she died on
December 31, 1948 and was buried in January 1949 in Lot 226, Section 15 (Anna Clackner plot).

[391]Affidavit for License to Marry # 2529, & # 26628, October 24, 1816, (John Joseph
Butler to Vera Matilda Wallace), City of Poughkeepsie, Dutchess County, New York, New York
State Archives, Albany, New York.

[392]Death Certificate for Vera Butler, September 28, 1948, #52710, City of Poughkeepsie,
Dutchess County, New York, New York State Archives, Albany, New York.

had resided here for a number of years.

The daughter of the late George S. and Louise Hartman Wallace, Mrs. Butler is survived in addition to her husband, by two sons, Robert Earl and John Joseph Butler, Jr., here; three grandchildren, Linda Lou, Kandee Sue and Robert Earl Butler; two sisters, Mrs. William Witzenbocker, here and Mrs. Edward Buckalew, South Amboy, N.J., a brother, George S Wallace, Newark, and several nieces and nephews.[393,394]

Her husband, John Joseph Butler, Sr., died on October 30, 1943 in Poughkeepsie.[395] They are both buried in Poughkeepsie Rural Cemetery.[396]

The middle daughter of George Stephen and Louise (Hartman) Wallace was Lettie May Wallace who married Edward Buckalew.[397] The Buckalew family removed to South Amboy, Middlesex County, New Jersey, where Lettie May (Wallace) Buckalew raised a family while her husband worked for the railroad.[398] Lettie Mae (Wallace) Buckalew died on October 29, 1962 in

---

[393]Obituary of Vera (Wallace) Butler, *Poughkeepsie Journal,* Tuesday, September 28, 1948, <<www.newspapers.com>>, downloaded May 29, 2019.

[394]Obituary of Vera (Wallace) Butler, *Poughkeepsie New Yorker,* Wednesday, September 29, 1948, Dutchess County Historical Society, P.O. Box 88, Poughkeepsie, New York 12602-0088, read as follows:

> BUTLER - At Poughkeepsie, N.Y., September 28, 1948, Vera M. Butler, wife of John J. Butler, Sr. Services at the Miller Funeral Home, 310 Mills Street, Friday, at 2 p.m. Relatives and friends invited. Interment Poughkeepsie Rural Cemetery. Friends may call Wednesday after 7 p.m. Arrangements in charge of William G. Miller.

[395]New York State Death Index, New York Department of Health, Albany, New York, <<www.ancestry.com>>, downloaded June 11, 2019, says: John Butler, age: 63, death date: October 30, 1953, death place: Poughkeepsie, New York; Certificate Number: 62491.

[396]Letter dated November 20, 1995 from Charles H. Fells, Superintendent, Poughkeepsie Rural Cemetery, P.O. Box 977, 342 South Avenue, Poughkeepsie, New York 12602-0977 to Kathryn C. Torpey, 5035 Domain Place, Alexandria, Virginia 22311-5066 regarding burials in Lot 71-A, Section 25 belonging to William H. and Mary Witzenbocker and John J. Butler, Sr.

[397]Affidavit for License to Marry # 1053, & # 2316, March 16, 1816, (Edward Buckalew to Lettie May Wallace), City of Poughkeepsie, Dutchess County, New York, New York State Archives, Albany, New York.

[398]Letter dated November 1, 1999 from Bill Poulos, Director of Public Affairs, Railroad Retirement Board, 844 North Rush Street, Chicago, Illinois 60611-2092 to Kathryn C. Torpey, 5035 Domain Place, Alexandria, Virginia 22311-5066 transmitting the retirement papers of Edward Buckalew, 147-03-8398.

South Amboy, Middlesex County, New Jersey. Her obituary appeared in the *Central New Jersey Home News*, on Tuesday, October 30, 1962. It read as follows:

Mrs. Edward Buckalew

SOUTH AMBOY - Mrs. Lettie M. Buckalew, 133 Augusta St., died Monday in South Amboy Memorial Hospital after a brief illness.

Born in Montgomery, Ala., she was a daughter of the late Mr. And Mrs. George Wallace. She lived here 47 years, moving here from Poughkeepsie, N.Y.

She was a communicant of Christ Church.

Surviving are her husband, Edward; five daughters, Mrs. Louise Keelyn and Mrs. Phyllis Stamm, both of South Amboy, Mrs. Edith Bang and Mrs. Joan Olshaskey, both of Edison, and Mrs. Vera Twardos of Sayreville; two sons, Edward G. and John F., both of South Amboy; 19 grandchildren; three great-grandchildren; and a sister, Mrs. Mary Witzenbocker of Poughkeepsie, N.Y.

Funeral services will be held Thursday at 10:30 am from Home for Funerals, the Gundrum Service, 237 Bordentown Ave., to Christ Church 11 am where a requiem eucharist will be offered with the Rev. Ronald G. Albury officiating. Interment will be in Clover Leaf Park Cemetery, Woodbridge.[399]

Edward and Lettie May (Wallace) Buckalew are both buried in Clover Leaf Cemetery in Woodbridge, New Jersey.[400]

The youngest daughter of George Stephen and Louise (Hartman) Wallace was Mary Louise Wallace. She married William H. Witzenbocker on June 18, 1922.[401] They resided in Poughkeepsie during their entire married life. They had no children. Mary Louise (Wallace) Witzenbocker was the last of the Wallace children to die.[402] A copy of her obituary was found in

---

[399]Obituary of Lettie M. (Wallace) Buckalew, *Central New Jersey Home News,* Tuesday, October 30, 1962, <<www.newspapers.com>>, downloaded June 11, 2019.

[400]Note dated September 20, 1999 from Clover Leaf Cemetery, U.S. Highway 1 S, Woodbridge New Jersey 07095-2553 to Kathryn C. Torpey, 5035 Domain Place, Alexandria, Virginia 22311-5066 stating Edward and Lettie Buckalew are buried in the Lake Section, Plot 278, graves 1 & 2.

[401]Affidavit for License to Marry # 4409, & # 12753, June 12, 1922, (William Henry Witzenbocker to Mary Louise Wallace), City of Poughkeepsie, Dutchess County, New York, New York State Archives, Albany, New York.

[402]Estate of Mary L. (Wallace) Witzenbocker, File Box 63448, 1972, Surrogate Court of the County of Dutchess, Poughkeepsie, New York.

the *McCauley Family Album*.[403] Her husband, William Witzenbocker died October 8, 1986.[404,405] They are both buried in Poughkeepsie Rural Cemetery in the same plot as her sister and brother-in-law, John Joseph and Vera (Wallace) Butler.[406]

---

[403]Obituary of Mary (Wallace) Witzenbocker. unknown newspaper, Poughkeepsie, New York, c. March 18, 1970, read as follows:

> Mrs. William Witzenbocker, 69 of 21 Thompson St., died Tuesday at Vassar Hospital.
>
> The former Mary Wallace, she was born in Montgomery, Ala., the daughter of George and Louise (Hartman) Wallace. Mrs. Witzenbocker retired in 1967 as office manager of Courtney's laundry.
>
> She was a member of Ladies Society and Parish Aid Society of St. Paul's Episcopal Church. She also was a member of the Chapel Corners Grange and the National Grange.
>
> Mrs. Witzenbocker is survived by her husband and several nieces and nephews.
>
> Friends may call at the William G. Miller and Son Funeral Home, 310 Mill St., tonight, 7 to 9 o'clock and Thursday 2 to 4 and 7 to 9 p.m.
>
> Funeral services will be Friday at 2 p.m. at the funeral home. Burial will be in the Poughkeepsie Rural Cemetery.

[404]Will of William Witzenbocker, March 13, 1986, probate date unknown, 139W-28, Surrogate Court of the County of Dutchess, Poughkeepsie, New York.

[405]Estate of William Witzenbocker, File Box 77673, 1986, Surrogate Court of the County of Dutchess, Poughkeepsie, New York.

[406]Letter dated November 20, 1995 from Charles H. Fells, Superintendent, Poughkeepsie Rural Cemetery, P.O. Box 977, 342 South Avenue, Poughkeepsie, New York 12602-0977 to Kathryn C. Torpey, 5035 Domain Place, Alexandria, Virginia 22311-5066 transmitted a copy of an obituary for William H. Witzenbocker from a local newspaper in Poughkeepsie saying that although he was born on Newburgh, he was a local resident of Poughkeepsie for 65 years.

Matilda Montgomery Gormley was born c. June 1831 in County Londonderry, Ireland.[407,408,409] She died August 15, 1905, at Philadelphia, Pennsylvania.[410,411] She was buried in Mount Moriah Cemetery in Philadelphia, Pennsylvania.[412] She married John Boyd on April 5, 1851 in Philadelphia, Pennsylvania.[413] He died c. 1874 probably in Placer County, California.[414]

Judging from the formal photograph of Matilda (Gormley) Boyd that appears in the

---

[407]There is no baptismal entry for Matilda Montgomery Gormley in the records of the First Garvagh Presbyterian Church, Errigal Parish, County Londonderry, Ireland.

[408]Entry for Margaret Gormley and Children, Ship Sheridan Passenger Manifest, December 12, 1839, page 3, line 19, Passenger List of Vessels Arriving at New York, NY, 1820-1897, Records of the U.S. Customs Service, Record Group 36, National Archives Microfilm Publication M237, Roll 40 says 8, i.e. born 1831 in Ireland.

[409]1900 U.S. Census (population), Pennsylvania, Philadelphia County, Philadelphia, E.D. 812, page 1, lines 60-65, National Archives Microfilm Publication T623, Roll 1473, Household of John Strawbridge says b. June 1832 which is probably incorrect because the ship passenger manifest for the Ship Sheridan indicates she was older than her brother, Robert Montgomery Gormley, who was baptized on January 9, 1832.

[410]Death Certificate for Matilda Boyd, August 15, 1905, # 19026, Philadelphia, Pennsylvania, Pennsylvania, Philadelphia City Death Certificates, 1803-1915, FHL Microfilm 1022636, <<www.familysearch.org>>, downloaded July 15, 2019 erroneously says Matilda Boyd was born in Philadelphia and her parents were born in the U.S.

[411]Obituary of Matilda Boyd, *Philadelphia Public Ledger*, Wednesday, August 16, 1905, p. 7; Thursday, August 17, 1905, p. 7; and Friday, August 18, 1905, p. 7.

[412]Mount Moriah Cemetery, Burials 2 June 1869-June 1885 (M-Z); June 1885-March 1898 (A-Z); March 1898-August 1911 (A-S), Genealogical Society of Pennsylvania, Philadelphia, Pennsylvania, Microfilm Roll XX826:2 says:

    7653   Boyd, Matilda   74   August 18 1905, Section 150, Lot 277, 2 fr S Line New

[413]Ninth Presbyterian Church, Marriages, 1850-1908, Philadelphia, Pennsylvania, FHL Microfilm Roll 0505481 (item 1), page 8, No. 42, 1851.

[414]Estate of John Boyd, Placer County, California, # 0848, Carbon County Courthouse, Jim Thorpe, Pennsylvania, contains papers dated 1874 describing John Boyd as deceased.

McCauley Family Album, she was a very attractive woman.[415]

    U.S. CENSUS ENUMERATIONS. Matilda (Gormley) Boyd was enumerated in the following census schedules:

    In the 1840 census, Matilda Gormley was enumerated with her parents in Mauch Chunk Township.[416]

    In the 1850 census, Matilda Gormley appears to have been enumerated in the household of Pierre V Duffon, a merchant, where she was probably working as a servant.[417]

NORTH WARD, PHILADELPHIA, PHILADELPHIA COUNTY, PENNSYLVANIA
Matilda Gornly (sic)   18 F   Ireland

    In the 1860 census, Matilda Boyd was enumerated as a servant in the household of her employer, William Dulles.[418]

WARD 8, PHILADELPHIA, PHILADELPHIA COUNTY, PENNSYLVANIA
Tillie Boyd   28 F   Domestic servant   Ireland

    In the 1870 census, Matilda Boyd was enumerated again in the household of her employer, William Dulles.[419,420]

---

    [415]The photograph of Matilda (Gormley) Boyd is in the possession of Kathryn C. Torpey, 5035 Domain Place, Alexandria, Virginia, 22311-5066.

    [416]1840 U.S. Census (population), Pennsylvania, Northampton County, Mauch Chunk Township, page 212, line 21, National Archives Microfilm Publication M704, Roll 479, Household of Jos. Gramley (sic).

    [417]1850 U.S. Census (population), Pennsylvania, Philadelphia County, City of Philadelphia, North Ward, page 327B, lines 8-16, National Archives Microfilm Publication M432, Roll 817, Household of Pierre V. Duffon.

    [418]1860 U.S. Census (population), Pennsylvania, Philadelphia County, City of Philadelphia, Ward 8, page 453, lines 28-34, National Archives Microfilm Publication M653, Roll 1158, Household of William Dulles. Note: William Dulles was from a prominent family that originated in Charleston, South Carolina, but relocated to Philadelphia after the War of 1812. William Dulles had a brother named John Welsh Dulles who was the grandfather of John Foster Dulles and Allen Dulles both of whom were highly respected and influential political figures in mid-20th Century America.

    [419]1870 U.S. Census (population), First Enumeration, Pennsylvania, Philadelphia County,

WARD 8, PHILADELPHIA, PHILADELPHIA COUNTY, PENNSYLVANIA
Boyd, Matilda   34 F   Domestic servant   Ireland

In the 1880 census, Matilda Boyd was enumerated as follows at 262 South 16th Street in the household of her employer, William Dulles.[421,422]

WARD 8, PHILADELPHIA, PHILADELPHIA COUNTY, PENNSYLVANIA, JUNE 1, 1880
Boyd, Matilda   40 F   Servant   Ireland

In the 1900 census, Matilda Boyd, whose daughter, Margaret had died on March 28, 1900, was enumerated in the household of her son-in-law, John Strawbridge, 2135 18th Street.[423,424]

PHILADELPHIA, PENNSYLVANIA, JUNE 1, 1900
Boyd, Matilda   67 F   Ireland

MARRIAGE OF MATILDA GORMLEY TO JOHN BOYD. On April 5, 1851, Matilda Gormley married John Boyd at the Ninth Presbyterian Church in Philadelphia. The bride was stated to be of Philadelphia and the groom was stated to be of Conshohocken. The ceremony was performed by the Reverend William Blackwood. Mary Mooney and Mary Jane Neely

---

City of Philadelphia, Ward 8, page 137A, lines 5-14, National Archives Microfilm Publication M593, Roll 1393, Household of William Dulles.

[420]1870 U.S. Census (population), Second Enumeration, Pennsylvania, Philadelphia County, City of Philadelphia, Ward 8, page 174B, lines 31-36, National Archives Microfilm Publication M593, Roll 1421, Household of William Dulles.

[421]1880 U.S. Census (population), Pennsylvania, Philadelphia County, City of Philadelphia, E.D. 150, page 478A, lines 22-27, National Archives Microfilm Publication T9, Roll 1171, Household of William Dulles.

[422]1881 Philadelphia City Directory confirms the 1880 census entry.

1881   Boyd, Matilda, widow John, h 262 S 16th.

[423]1900 U.S. Census (population), Pennsylvania, Philadelphia County, Philadelphia, E.D. 812, page 1, lines 60-65, National Archives Microfilm Publication T623, Roll 1473, Household of John Strawbridge.

[424]Death Certificate for Margaret A. Strawbridge, March 28, 1900, # 20499, Philadelphia, Pennsylvania, Pennsylvania, Philadelphia City Death Certificates, 1803-1915, FHL Microfilm 1838856, <<www.familysearch.org>>, downloaded July 15, 2019.

served as witnesses.[425]

LIFE AND DEATH OF JOHN BOYD. It is speculated that John Boyd may have gone west with his brother-in-law, James Gormley.[426]

Nothing further is known about his life in the west.[427,428,429,430] He appears to have died

---

[425]Ninth Presbyterian Church, Marriages, 1850-1908, Philadelphia, Pennsylvania, FHL Microfilm Roll 0505481 (item 1) references page 8, No. 42, 1851.

[426]Letter dated May 17, 1997 from Robert C. Gormley, 334 Brownsburg Road, Newtown, Pennsylvania 18940 to Kathryn C. Torpey, 5035 Domain Place, Alexandria, Virginia 22311-5066 states that John Boyd and James Gormley may have traveled together to California possibly in search of gold.

[427]1860 U.S. Census (population), California, Placer County, Township No. 6, page 831, lines 34-36, National Archives Microfilm Publication M593, Roll 62, Household of Samuel Salis, contains the following unlikely enumeration for a man named John Boyd who appears to be too young to be the subject of this family history.

TOWNSHIP NO. 6, PLACER COUNTY, CALIFORNIA, JUNE 20, 1860
Boyd, John   24 (sic) M   Steward   Mich (sic)

[428]Jim W. Faulkinbury's index to the "Foreign-Born Voters of California in 1872" extracted from the county level Great Registers of Voters for California in 1872, <<www.jwfgenresearch.com/GR1872Home.htm>>, downloaded April 6, 1997, contains a listing for three men named John Boyd who were born in Ireland. On December 19, 2003 an examination was made of the full database entries as provided by Jim W. Faulkinbury, CGRS, P.O. Box 60727, Sacramento, California 95860-0727 to Kathryn C. Torpey, 5035 Domain Place, Alexandria, Virginia 22311-5066. The examination failed to reveal whether any of the three men is the subject of this family history.

[429]Letter dated June 13, 1997 from Jim McCauley, County Clerk-Recorder-Registrar, Placer County Clerk-Recorder's Office, 11960 Hertigate Oaks Place, Suite 15, P.O. Box 5228, Auburn, California 95604-5228 to Kathryn C. Torpey, 5035 Domain Place, Alexandria, Virginia 22311-5066 states that a search of their indexes for the period 1872 to 1892 indicates that they have no record of the death of John Boyd. According to the letter, their death records do not begin until 1873.

[430]The Bureau of Land Management Government Land Office database of Land Patents, <<www.glorecords.blm.gov/>>, downloaded November 16, 2003, contains a listing for a Patentee named John Boyd who was issued a title for 160 acres in Placer County, California, on October 3, 1873. The patent says "State In Favor Of: Texas." It is unknown whether this record

around 1874 probably in Placer County, California.[431] His place of burial could not be ascertained.[432]

On October 6, 1874, Matilda (Gormley) Boyd, renounced her right to Letters of Administration to settle the estate of her deceased husband, John Boyd, late of Placer County, California, in favor of her brother, William B. Gormley. The renunciation was witnessed by William Dulles, the employer of Matilda (Gormley) Boyd. A Bond on the Estate of John Boyd, late of Placer County, California, was filed by William B. Gormley with the Register of Wills in Carbon County, Pennsylvania, on October, 17, 1874. On October 19, 1874, Matilda (Gormley) Boyd executed a document notifying William B. Gormley that she elected to retain real property belonging to the deceased to the value of $300.00 for the use of herself and her family and she requested that William B. Gormley have the property appraised. These documents were filed with the court on October 21, 1874. The inventory of John Boyd's real and personal property was accomplished and a widow's appraisement was secured. The value of the estate was determined not to exceed $300.00. On February 10, 1875, William B. Gormley filed a memorandum with the Register of Wills stating that the whole of the real estate belonging to the deceased was elected and retained by Matilda (Gormley) Boyd, widow of the deceased, for the use of herself and family according to the Act of Assembly in such case made and provided and that there was no personal property for which reason no general inventory was filed in said estate.[433]

REAL ESTATE OF JOHN BOYD. The real estate of John Boyd in Carbon County, Pennsylvania, consisted of a single parcel of land containing 50 acres and 55 perches in Mahoning Township bounded by the property of Robert Neal, James Sinyard, Caleb Lownes, and Oliver Musselman. The property was almost immediately adjacent to the property purchased by John Boyd's mother-in-law, Margaret (Montgomery) Gormley, in 1859. For some reason, John

---

pertains to the subject of this family history.

[431]Estate of John Boyd, Placer County, California, # 0848, Carbon County Courthouse, Jim Thorpe, Pennsylvania, contains papers dated 1874 describing John Boyd as deceased.

[432]Find-A-Grave Memorial # 122319896, unknown Boyd (no headstone photograph), added December 28, 2013, Trails End Cemetery, Tahoe City, Placer County, California, <<www.findagrave.com>>. This burial could not be eliminated.

[433]Estate of John Boyd, late of Placer County, California, # 0848, Carbon County Courthouse, Jim Thorpe, Pennsylvania. Note: This estate file contains documents related to the estate of another John Boyd who died on April 18, 1895, at the age of 25 years and 9 months. The second John Boyd was buried in Section 2, Lot 164 of Mauch Chuck Cemetery. At this time, there does not appear to be any connection between these two men.

Boyd bought this property twice from Henry Williamson.[434] The first time the property was conveyed was on June 22, 1852, when John Boyd purchased it for $197.50.[435] The second time the exact same property was conveyed was on April 1, 1865, when John Boyd bought it for $200.00.[436] There is no record that John Boyd sold the property back to Henry Williamson in between these two conveyances. On February 4, 1875, the property was sold to Nathan Wagamen by Matilda (Gormley) Boyd, widow of John Boyd.[437]

DEATH OF MATILDA (GORMLEY) BOYD. Matilda (Gormley) Boyd died on August 15, 1905. Her obituary, which appeared in the *Philadelphia Public Ledger*.[438] It read as follows:

> BOYD - On August 15, 1905, Matilda, widow of John Boyd, aged 74 years. Relatives and friends are invited to attend the funeral services today (Friday) at 2 P.M. at the residence of her son-in-law, John Strawbridge, 2629 North 29th Street. Interment private.

------

[434]Letter dated August 28, 2000 from Ted Dombroski, 81st PVI, Co. K, 768 McNair Street, Hazelton, Pennsylvania 18201-2639 to Kathryn C. Torpey, 5035 Domain Place, Alexandria, Virginia 22311-5066 states that his group is in possession of a letter from a Sergeant John Williamson, Co. K, to his wife in which he mentioned the death of a Sergeant John Boyd of Co. H who enlisted with John Gormley, the subject of this family history. It is unknown whether the Sergeant John Williamson who wrote the letter is related to the Henry Williamson who sold 50 acres of land in Mahoning Township to John Boyd, the husband of Matilda (Gormley) Boyd. Sergeant John Williamson was killed on June 29, 1862 at Charles City Cross Roads. His letter states, in part:

> Sergeant John Boyd of Company H died on Wednesday night and his company buried him at the forte on Friday. I believe he is only to be buried there till they find where his friends are and then he will be sent home.

[435]Deed from Henry Williamson to John Boyd, June 22, 1852, (recorded October 22, 1852), Volume 5, p. 275, Deeds, Volumes 4-7, 1851-1855, Carbon County, Pennsylvania, FHL Microfilm Roll 2208974.

[436]Deed from Henry Williamson & Wife to John Boyd, April 1, 1865, (recorded June 21, 1865), Volume 13, p. 471, Deeds, Volumes 12-15, 1864-1867, Carbon County, Pennsylvania, FHL Microfilm Roll 2208977.

[437]Deed, Matilda Boyd to Nathan Wagamen, February 4, 1875, (recorded April 2, 1875), Volume 22, p. 205, Deeds, Volumes 22-23, 1875-1877, Carbon County, Pennsylvania, FHL Microfilm Roll 2209192.

[438]Obituary of Matilda Boyd, *Philadelphia Public Ledger*, Wednesday, August 16, 1905, p. 7; Thursday, August 17, 1905, p. 7; and Friday, August 18, 1905, p. 7.

Matilda (Gormley) Boyd was buried in the Boyd family plot at Mount Moriah Cemetery in Philadelphia.[439]

ESTATE OF MATILDA (GORMLEY) BOYD. The following announcement appeared in the *Philadelphia Public Ledger* shortly after the death of Matilda (Gormley) Boyd:

> Estate of Matilda Boyd, Deceased. Letters testamentary on the above estate have been granted to the undersigned, all parties indebted to the said estate are requested to make payment and those having claims to present the same without delay to John Strawbridge, 2629 North 29th Street, or to his attorney, William T. Wheeler, 1228-29 Stephen Girard Building.[440]

The estate papers of Matilda (Gormley) Boyd reveal that she left a will which she executed on May 22, 1905. John Strawbridge, her son-in-law, was the executor of her estate and the inventory and appraisal were accomplished by Sydney Morris Snyder and Jessie M. Bircks, who were married to two of Matilda (Gormley) Boyd's granddaughters. She left an estate of approximately $17,000.00 in cash and bonds and a house located at 2135 N. 18th Street valued at $5,000.00. According to her will, her estate was to be divided into two equal shares for the benefit of her grandchildren, i.e., the children of James Boyd and the children of Margaret Ann (Boyd) Strawbridge. The income from the first share was to be paid to her son, James Boyd, during the term of his natural life, and thereafter the income and principal was to be paid to his seven children. The principal and income from the second share was to be paid to the five children of her daughter, Margaret Ann (Boyd) Strawbridge. Final payments were to be made to each child when he or she reached the age of thirty-five.[441]

THE CHILDREN OF JOHN AND MATILDA (GORMLEY) BOYD. John and Matilda (Gormley) Boyd had two children - James and Margaret.[442] In the 1860 census, James Boyd and

---

[439]Mount Moriah Cemetery, Burials 2 June 1869-June 1885 (M-Z); June 1885-March 1898 (A-Z); March 1898-August 1911 (A-S), Genealogical Society of Pennsylvania, Philadelphia, Pennsylvania, Microfilm Roll XX826:2 says: "7653 Boyd, Matilda 74 August 18 1905, Section 150, Lot 277, 2 fr S Line New."

[440]Estate of Matilda Boyd, *Philadelphia Public Ledger*, Monday, August 28, 1905, p. 13.

[441]Estate of Matilda Boyd, Philadelphia, # 1590, 1905, Register of Wills, Philadelphia, Philadelphia County, Pennsylvania.

[442]1900 U.S. Census (population), Pennsylvania, Philadelphia County, Philadelphia, E.D. 812, sheet 1, lines 60-65, National Archives Microfilm Publication T623, Roll 1473, Household of John Strawbridge, states that Matilda (Gormley) Boyd had three children, but only one was living at the time of the 1900 census. Nothing is known about the third child of Matilda (Gormley) Boyd.

Margaret Boyd, the children of Matilda (Gormley) Boyd, were enumerated in her parents' household on their property in Mahoning Township.[443]

Margaret Ann Boyd was the youngest child of John and Matilda (Gormley) Boyd. In the 1870 census, she was enumerated in the household of her aunt and uncle, Henry and Jennie (Gormley) Erwin. The enumeration was as follows:

SOUTH BETHLEHEM, NORTHAMPTON COUNTY, PENNSYLVANIA, AUGUST 5, 1870
Boyd, Maggie   15 F   Dressmaker   Pa[444]

On August 1, 1871, Margaret Ann Boyd was listed in the Register of the Philadelphia General Hospital. The listing was as follows:

Mary (sic) Boyd, varioloid, born Pa, age 17, 262 South 16th Street
Dressmaker, 22 days in hospital, discharged 9-2-71,
Good vaccine mark, very mild attack, not sure if paid or free[445]

Margaret Ann Boyd married John Strawbridge on August 17, 1874, at the United Presbyterian Church located at 705 South 16th Street in Philadelphia. The Reverend W.W. Barr officiated.[446] John Strawbridge was in the wire manufacturing business with William Chase.

The Strawbridge family was enumerated in the 1880 census at 1924 Latona Street in Philadelphia in the same household with the wife and son of Joseph S. Wallace, one of the sons of Letitia (Gormley) Wallace. The enumeration was as follows:

PHILADELPHIA, PENNSYLVANIA, WARD 26, JUNE 7, 1880
Strawbridge, John   M 30   Wire Worker   Ireland
, Margaret   F 25   Keeping Home   Pa
, Margaret   F 4   Pa
, Tillie   F 3   Pa

---

[443]1860 U.S. Census (population), Pennsylvania, Carbon County, Mahoning Township, page 972, lines 11-20, National Archives Microfilm Publication M653, Roll 1089, Household of Joseph Gomly (sic).

[444]1870 U.S. Census (population), Pennsylvania, Northampton County, South Bethlehem, page 335, lines 5-11, National Archives Microfilm Publication M593, Roll 1381, Household of Henry Erwin.

[445]Philadelphia City Hospital Register, 1865-1896, FHL Microfilm Roll 0976944 (item 3). Note: varioloid means "resembling smallpox."

[446]Return of Marriages, 1874, Second Quarter (Sisty) to Fourth Quarter (Yarnell), City of Philadelphia, Pennsylvania, FHL Microfilm Roll 1769060.

| Wallace, Lizzie | F 21 | Pa |
| , Joseph | M 8/12 | Pa [447] |

Margaret (Boyd) Strawbridge died on March 28, 1900. Her obituary appeared in the *Philadelphia Public Ledger*. It read as follows:

> Strawbridge - On the 28th inst., Margaret A., wife of John Strawbridge. The relatives and friends of the family are invited to attend services, Saturday afternoon at 2 o'clock at her late residence 2135 N. 15th (sic) St. Interment private.[448]

She was buried in the plot belonging to her mother, Matilda (Gormley) Boyd, at Mount Moriah Cemetery on March 31, 1900.[449] Possibly due to the death of her daughter, Matilda (Gormley) Boyd retired from her job as a domestic servant to the Dulles family and went to live with her son-in-law, John Strawbridge, and her grandchildren where she was enumerated with them in the 1900 census.[450] John Strawbridge, the widower of Margaret Ann (Boyd) Strawbridge, and some of their children were still enumerated together in Philadelphia in the 1910 census and in the 1920 census.[451,452] In the 1910 census, John Strawbridge was listed as the foreman of a wire works. In the 1920 census, at the age of 75, he was stated to be the superintendent of a grocery store.

John Strawbridge died on September 21, 1923. His obituary appeared in the *Philadelphia*

---

[447]1880 U.S. Census (population), Pennsylvania, Philadelphia County, Philadelphia, E.D. 563, page 704D, lines 14-19, National Archives Microfilm Publication T9, Roll 1185, Household of John Strawbridge.

[448]Obituary of Margaret Strawbridge, *Philadelphia Public Ledger*, Friday, March 30, 1900, p. 9, and Saturday, March 31, 1900, p. 9.

[449]Mount Moriah Cemetery, Burials, Genealogical Society of Pennsylvania, Philadelphia, Pennsylvania, Microfilm Roll XX826:3 says: 3-31-00 Mgt. Strawbridge, age 45, Sec 150, 277.

[450]1900 U.S. Census (population), Pennsylvania, Philadelphia County, Philadelphia, E.D. 812, page 1, lines 60-65, National Archives Microfilm Publication T623, Roll 1473, Household of John Strawbridge.

[451]1910 U.S. Census (population), Pennsylvania, Philadelphia County, Philadelphia, E.D. 845, Family Number 123, lines 27-33, National Archives Microfilm Publication T624, Roll 1406, Household of John Strawbridge.

[452]1920 U.S. Census (population), Pennsylvania, Philadelphia County, Philadelphia, E.D. 1848, page 9A, lines 10-11, National Archives Microfilm Publication T625, Roll 1647, Household of John Strawbridge.

Public Ledger.[453] It read as follows:

> Strawbridge - Sept 21 John Strawbridge husband of the late Margaret Boyd, aged 80.
> Funeral services Mon., 2 P.M. at his late residence 430 S. 63rd *(sic)* St. Int private.
> Friends may call Sun eve.

He was buried in the plot belonging to his mother-in-law, Matilda (Gormley) Boyd, at Mount Moriah Cemetery on September 24, 1923.[454] In his will, he left his entire estate including his two story brick home at 430 S. 62nd Street, to his five daughters.[455] His executor was his son-in-law, Sidney Morris Snyder.

James Boyd was the oldest child of John and Matilda (Gormley) Boyd. He married Ellen Sinyard, the daughter of William Sinyard and Margaret McMichael.[456] In the 1880 census, James and Ellen (Sinyard) Boyd were enumerated as follows:

RAHN TOWNSHIP, SCHUYLKILL COUNTY, PENNSYLVANIA, JUNE 17, 1880

Boyd, James	M 27	Laborer	Pa
, Ellen	F 28	Keeping House	Pa
, William	M 4		Pa
, Robert	M 2		Pa[457]

In 1900, James and Ellen (Sinyard) Boyd were enumerated on White Street in Summit Hill with 6 of their 7 living children - Robert, Mary M., Matthew, Letitia Jane, and twins James and Lizzie.[458]

----

[453]Obituary of John Strawbridge, *Philadelphia Public Ledger*, Saturday, September 22, 1923, p. 9, Sunday, September 23, 1923, p. 13, and Monday, September 24, 1923, p. 24.

[454]Mount Moriah Cemetery, Burials, Genealogical Society of Pennsylvania, Philadelphia, Pennsylvania, Microfilm Roll XX826:3 says: 9-24-23 John Strawbridge, age 80, Sec 150, 277.

[455]Estate of John Strawbridge, Philadelphia, # 2835, Yr 1923, Register of Wills, Philadelphia, Philadelphia County, Pennsylvania.

[456]Death Certificate of Ellen Boyd, December 1, 1916, Summit Hill, Carbon County, Pennsylvania, Pennsylvania Death Certificates, 1906-1966, <<www.ancestry.com>>, downloaded August 7, 2019. Note: The 1850 and 1860 censuses say her mother's name was Mary Ann Sinyard and Mary Sinyard, respectively.

[457]1880 U.S. Census (population), Pennsylvania, Schuylkill County, Rahn Township, E.D. 229, page 19C, lines 15-18, National Archives Microfilm Publication T9, Roll 1193, Household of James Boyd..

[458]1900 U.S. Census (population), Pennsylvania, Carbon County, Summit Hill, E.D. 24,

Ten year later, in 1910, they were again enumerated on White Street in Summit Hill this time with 5 of their children, Robert, Matthew, Lettie J., and twins, James and Lizzie.[459] The census states that James Boyd was living on his "own income" possibly inherited from the estate of his mother, Matilda (Gormley) Boyd.

Ellen (Sinyard) Boyd died on December 1, 1916.[460] Her estate was submitted for probate on December 12, 1916.[461] In 1920, James Boyd, widower, was enumerated at 109 East White Street with 3 of his children, Lettie, and twins Lizzie, and James; and a lodger named Joseph Vermillion. James Boyd's occupation was listed as a miner in a coal mine.[462]

In 1930, James Boyd was enumerated in the household of his son, James G. Boyd, Jr., and his family at 109 East White Street.[463] Also enumerated in the same household were 3 of the sisters of James G. Boyd, Jr., namely Elizabeth and Letitia, both single and his married sister Matilda M. Lewis and her family; as well as Joseph Vermillion, a boarder.

James Boyd died on August 13, 1930.[464] No estate was submitted for probate. James and

---

page 7, lines 89-95, National Archives Microfilm Publication T623, Roll 1391, Household of James Boyd.

[459] 1910 U.S. Census (population), Pennsylvania, Carbon County, Summit Hill, Ward 3, E.D. 29, page 13B, Family Number 263, lines 66-72, National Archives Microfilm Publication T624, Roll 1327, Household of James Boyd.

[460] Death Certificate of Ellen Boyd, December 1, 1916, Summit Hill, Carbon County, Pennsylvania, Pennsylvania Death Certificates, 1906-1966, <<www.ancestry.com>>, downloaded August 7, 2019.

[461] Estate of Ellen Boyd, # 4982, Carbon County Courthouse, Jim Thorpe, Pennsylvania. The estate file index states Will Book 8, Page 622, residence, Summit Hill, James G. Boyd, executor. Note: James G. Boyd may be her son.

[462] 1920 U.S. Census (population), Pennsylvania, Carbon County, Summit Hill Borough, E.D. 43, page 1A, lines 8-12, National Archives Microfilm Publication T625, Roll 1534, Household of James Boyd.

[463] 1930 U.S. Census (population), Pennsylvania, Carbon County, Summit Hill, E.D. 40, lines 82-91, National Archives Microfilm Publication T626, Roll 2015, Household of James G. Boyd, Jr.

[464] Death Certificate of James Boyd, August 13, 1930, Summit Hill, Carbon County, Pennsylvania, Pennsylvania Death Certificates, 1906-1966, <<www.ancestry.com>>, downloaded August 7, 2019.

Ellen (Sinyard) Boyd were both buried in the GAR Cemetery in Summit Hill.[465,466,467] Some of their descendants still live in the surrounding area today.

---

[465]Letter dated August 12, 1999 from Charles F. Seng, P.O. Box 4012, Jim Thorpe, Pennsylvania, 18229-4012 to Kathryn C. Torpey, 5035 Domain Place, Alexandria, Virginia 22311-5066 provided the birth and death years and burial locations for James and Ellen Boyd. No estate record was found for James Boyd.

[466]Find-A-Grave Memorial # 113733511, James M. Boyd (headstone photograph), added July 13, 2013, GAR Cemetery, Summit Hill, Carbon County, Pennsylvania, <<www.findagrave.com>>.

[467]Find-A-Grave Memorial # 113733508, Ellen S. Sinyard Boyd (headstone photograph), added July 13, 2013, GAR Cemetery, Summit Hill, Carbon County, Pennsylvania, <<www.findagrave.com>>.

Robert Montgomery Gormley was born c. January 3, 1832 in Mullinabrone, Aghadowey Parish, Ireland.[468,469] He died on August 2, 1875 in Fountain Hill (then part of South Bethlehem), Lehigh County, Pennsylvania.[470,471] He married Hannah Jane Johnson, the daughter of Andrew and Mary (Gilmore) Johnson.[472,473] She was born on March 21, 1842 in Nesquehoning, Mauch

---

[468]Baptism of Robert Gormley, January 3, 1832, First Garvagh Presbyterian Church, Garvagh, Errigal Parish, County Londonderry, Ireland, Public Records Office of Northern Ireland, Belfast, Northern Ireland, Microfilm MIC/1P/257.

[469]Entry for Margaret Gormley and Children, Ship Sheridan Passenger Manifest, December 12, 1839, page 3, line 19, Passenger List of Vessels Arriving at New York, NY, 1820-1897, Records of the U.S. Customs Service, Record Group 36, National Archives Microfilm Publication M237, Roll 40 says 7, i.e. born 1832 in Ireland.

[470]Obituary of Robert Gormley, *Bethlehem Globe Times*, Tuesday, August 3, 1875, p. 2., Bethlehem Area Public Library, 11 West Church Street, Bethlehem, Pennsylvania, 18018-5888.

[471]Edward J. Redding, *The History of Fountain Hill, Pennsylvania*, (n.p., Edward J. Redding, 1996), p. unk., states that in 1892 there was a concerted effort to unite the three Bethlehems - Bethlehem, South Bethlehem, and West Bethlehem, but the residents of the Lehigh County portion of South Bethlehem resisted this effort. Fountain Hill was then located in that portion of South Bethlehem that was in Lehigh County. The next year, on November 7, 1893, the residents of Fountain Hill voted to become the Borough of Fountain Hill in Lehigh County.

[472]Death Certificate for Hannah Jane Gormley, January 22, 1926, # 10478 & # 6, Pennsylvania Division of Vital Statistics, New Castle, Pennsylvania 16103 states that her parents were Andrew Johnson and Mary Gilmore.

[473]Marriage of Andrew Johnston (sic) to Mary Gilmore, July 22, 1836, First Garvagh Presbyterian Church, Garvagh, Errigal Parish, County Londonderry, Ireland, Public Records Office of Northern Ireland, Belfast, Northern Ireland, Microfilm MIC/1P/257.

Chunk Township, Carbon County, Pennsylvania.[474,475,476] She died January 22, 1926, in Summit Hill, Carbon County, Pennsylvania.[477,478] They were both buried in the GAR Cemetery, Summit Hill, Carbon County, Pennsylvania.[479,480]

U.S. CENSUS ENUMERATIONS. Robert Gormley was enumerated with his parents in the 1840 census in Mauch Chunk Township.[481] In the 1850 census, he appears to be enumerated in Lausanne Township with his brother, Smith Gormley, and another person with the same last name whose first name is unrecognizable.[482] They were living with the family of William

---

[474]Death Certificate for Hannah Jane Gormley, January 22, 1926, # [10458] & # 6, Pennsylvania Division of Vital Statistics, New Castle, Pennsylvania 16103 states she was born March 21, 1842 in Nesquehoning, Pennsylvania.

[475]1900 U.S. Census (population), Pennsylvania, Carbon County, Summit Hill, E.D. 23, page 8, lines 74-79, National Archives Microfilm Publication T623, Roll 1391, Household of Jennie Gormley says March 1843 (sic).

[476]Notes and documents provided on October 27, 1999 by Robert C. Gormley, 334 Brownsburg Road, Newtown, Pennsylvania 18940 to Kathryn C. Torpey, 5035 Domain Place, Alexandria, Virginia 22311-5066 contains a copy of the memorial piece concerning Joseph Gormley that says his mother, Hannah Jane (Johnson) Gormley was a native of Nesquehoning.

[477]Death Certificate for Hannah Jane Gormley, January 22, 1926, # 10478 & # 6, Pennsylvania Division of Vital Statistics, New Castle, Pennsylvania 16103 states she died January 22, 1926, at 2 (sic) P.M. at Summit Hill.

[478]Estate of Hannah Jane Gormley, # 7829, Carbon County Courthouse, Jim Thorpe, Pennsylvania. The estate file contains a petition signed by Margaret M. Gormley, her executor, stating that Hannah Jane Gormley died January 22, 1926, at 3 (sic) P.M. at Summit Hill.

[479]Letter dated October 8, 1996 from Robert C. Gormley, 334 Brownsburg Road, Newtown, Pennsylvania 18940 to Kathryn C. Torpey, 5035 Domain Place, Alexandria, Virginia 22311-5066.

[480]Site visit on June 24, 1997 to the GAR Cemetery, Summit Hill, Carbon County, Pennsylvania, in the company of Robert C. Gormley, great-grandson of James and Margaret (Glenn) Gormley, revealed a headstone for Robert Gormley, his wife, Hannah Jane (Johnson) Gormley, and all five of their children.

[481]1840 U.S. Census (population), Pennsylvania, Northampton County, Mauch Chunk Township, page 212, line 21, National Archives Publication M704, Roll 479, Household of Jos. Gramley (sic).

[482]1850 U.S. Census (population), Pennsylvania, Carbon County, Lausanne Township,

Cambell (sic) and next door to the family of James Boyd. The entry is very difficult to discern because the spelling of the surname is terrible and the gender of the second person on the list may be either male or a female. The entry is as follows:

LAUSANNE TOWNSHIP, CARBON COUNTY, PENNSYLVANIA, AUGUST 24, 1850

Smith Gaennely (sic)	28 M	Hosler	Ireland
Maldusia "	28 M or F	Miner	Ireland
Robert Garmeny (sic)	20 M	Laborer	Ireland

In the 1860 census, Robert Gormley was enumerated in his parents' household on their property in Mahoning Township.[483]

SERVICE IN THE CIVIL WAR. During the Civil War, Robert Gormley enlisted in Company D of the 34th Regiment of the Pennsylvania Volunteer Militia. Apparently, he and his brother, Smith Gormley, enlisted together. Robert Gormley was mustered in on June 30, 1863 at Reading, Pennsylvania, and mustered out on August 19, 1863. He was stated to be 25 (sic) years old at the time.[484,485]

There is no evidence that Robert M. Gormley or his widow, Hannah Jane (Johnson) Gormley, received a Civil War pension for his service. To the contrary, it is reported that Hannah Jane (Johnson) Gormley would not apply for a widow's pension because she would not accept any charity from the government. She was a proud woman.[486]

---

page 233, lines 24-35, National Archives Microfilm Publication M432, Roll 762, Household of William Cambell (sic).

[483] 1860 U.S. Census (population), Pennsylvania, Carbon County, Mahoning Township, page 972, lines 11-20, National Archives Microfilm Publication M653, Roll 1089, Household of Joseph Gomly (sic).

[484] Letter dated September 2, 1996 from Robert C. Gormley, 334 Brownsburg Road, Newtown, Pennsylvania 18940 to Kathryn C. Torpey, 5035 Domain Place, Alexandria, Virginia 22311-5066 in which he reported on Robert Gormley's Civil War service record and age which appears to be incorrect given that he was baptized on January 3, 1832.

[485] Samuel P. Bates, *History of the Pennsylvania Volunteers - 1861-1865*, (Harrisburg, Pennsylvania: B. Singlerly, State Printer, 1871). Volume X:1253, says:

> Robert M. Gormley, 34th Regiment, Co. D. mustered in June 3, 1863, mustered out August 24, 1863

[486] Letter dated November 23, 2003 from Robert C. Gormley, 334 Brownsburg Road, Newtown, Pennsylvania 18940 to Kathryn C. Torpey, 5035 Domain Place, Alexandria, Virginia 22311-5066 which provided a copy of a letter postmarked April 30, 1973, from his cousin, John

MARRIAGE TO HANNAH JANE JOHNSON. Although no record of the date and place of Robert Gormley's marriage to Hannah Jane Johnson has ever been found, the obituary of Hannah Jane (Johnson) Gormley that was published on January 25, 1926 in *The Morning Call* says the couple was married in Bethlehem.

Hannah Jane Johnson was from Mauch Chunk Township. She appears to have been nicknamed *Jennie*.[487,488,489] Her father was Andrew Johnson who is said to have arrived in Summit Hill at about the same time as Joseph Gormley.[490] Her mother was Mary (Gilmore) Johnson who arrived at the Port of New York on December 2, 1839, aboard the Ship Franconia with her oldest child, Andrew Johnson, aged 2.[491]

Hannah Jane Johnson had at least seven siblings. Her older brother, Andrew Johnson, served in the Civil War.[492,493] Her others siblings included Nancy, Ellen, Mary, David, John, and

---

M. Gormley, in which he explained why Hannah Jane (Johnson) Gormley did not receive a widow's pension for her late husband's service in the Civil War.

[487]1900 U.S. Census (population), Pennsylvania, Carbon County, Summit Hill, E.D. 23, page 8, lines 74-79, National Archives Microfilm Publication T623, Roll 1391, Household of Jennie Gormley.

[488]1910 U.S. Census (population), Pennsylvania, Carbon County, Summit Hill, Ward 1, E.D. 28, page 3B, lines 62-67, National Archives Microfilm Publication T624, Roll 1624, Household of Hannah Gormley.

[489]1920 U.S. Census (population), Pennsylvania, Carbon County, Summit Hill, Ward 1, E.D. 38, page 1A, lines 25-29, National Archives Microfilm Publication T625, Roll 1534, Household of Jennie Gormley.

[490]Fred Brenckman, *History of Carbon County, Pennsylvania*, (Harrisburg, Pennsylvania: James J. Nungesser, Publisher, 1913), 324.

[491]Entry for Mary Johnson and child, Andrew Johnson, Ship Franconia Passenger Manifest, December 2, 1839, New York, Passenger and Crew Lists (including Castle Garden and Ellis Island), 1820-1957), <<www.ancestry.com>>, downloaded August 10, 2019.

[492]Baptism of Andrew son of Andrew Johnston (sic) of Moneycarrie, September 3, 1837, First Garvagh Presbyterian Church, Garvagh, Errigal Parish, County Londonderry, Ireland, Public Records Office of Northern Ireland, Belfast, Northern Ireland, Microfilm MIC/1P/257. Note: Moneycarrie is located adjacent to Mullinabrone where the Gormley family was enumerated in the 1831 Census of County Londonderry.

[493]Letter dated October 8, 1996 from Robert C. Gormley, 334 Brownsburg Road, Newtown, Pennsylvania 18940 to Kathryn C. Torpey, 5035 Domain Place, Alexandria, Virginia

Matthew all of whom were born in Pennsylvania.[494,495]

Hannah Jane Johnson's father, Andrew Johnson, appears to have died before 1860.[496] After the death of Andrew Johnson, his widow, Mary (Gilmore) Johnson married a man named William Boyd.[497,498] Mary (Gilmore) Johnson Boyd left a will dated June 22, 1900. In her will, she named her grandson, Joseph Gormley, the son of Robert and Hannah Jane (Johnson) Gormley as her executor. Her will was witnessed by another grandson, Robert M. Gormley, also the son of Robert and Hannah Jane (Johnson) Gormley and it mentions Mary Boyd's son, Matthew Johnson.[499] Mary Boyd also left behind a large family *Bible* which bears the imprint of William and Mary Boyd.[500]

22311-5066 states that Hannah Jane (Johnson) Gormley had a brother named Andrew Johnson, who served in the Union Army during the Civil War. Robert C. Gormley has in his possession some of the letters that Andrew Johnson wrote to his sister, Hannah Jane (Johnson) Gormley, while he was in the Army. He also has in his possession a picture of Andrew Johnson, in uniform, and detailed records of his military service during the Civil War.

[494]1850 U.S. Census (population), Pennsylvania, Carbon County, Mauch Chunk Township, page 313B, lines 25-33, National Archives Microfilm Publication M432, Roll 762, Household of Andrew Johnson.

[495]1860 U.S. Census (population), Pennsylvania, Carbon County, Mauch Chunk Township, page 187, lines 31-38, National Archives Microfilm Publication M653, Roll 1089, Household of Mary Johnston (sic).

[496]1860 U.S. Census (population), Pennsylvania, Carbon County, Mauch Chunk Township, page 187, lines 31-38, National Archives Microfilm Publication M653, Roll 1089, Household of Mary Johnston (sic), enumerates Mary Johnson with seven Johnson children.

[497]1860 U.S. Census (population), Pennsylvania, Carbon County, Mauch Chunk Township, page 184, line 40 & page 185, lines 1-3, National Archives Microfilm Publication M653, Roll 1089, Household of Wm Boyd, enumerates William Boyd with three Boyd children, Wm, Henry and James.

[498]1870 U.S. Census (population), Pennsylvania, Carbon County, Mauch Chunk Township, page 235, lines 7-15, National Archives Microfilm Publication M593, Roll 1320, Household of William Boyd, enumerates William and Mary Boyd with five Johnston (sic) children and two Boyd children.

[499]Estate of Mary Boyd, # 2949, Carbon County Courthouse, Jim Thorpe, Pennsylvania. The estate file contains the will of Mary Boyd dated June 22, 1900.

[500]Letter dated June 30, 1998, and conversation on June 24, 1997 with Robert C. Gormley, 334 Brownsburg Road, Newtown, Pennsylvania 18940 in which he reported that his

REMOVAL TO SOUTH BETHLEHEM. After they were married, Robert and Hannah Jane (Johnson) Gormley removed to South Bethlehem, Northampton County, Pennsylvania, where Robert Gormley bought land on September 11, 1866 from Tinsley and Mary Jeter.[501,502]

According to the baptismal records of the Church of the Nativity, their two oldest children, Joseph and Mary, were born and baptized in Bethlehem.[503,504] Although no baptismal records have been found for the younger three children, the obituaries of Margaret, Robert and William all state they were born in Bethlehem.

It is unclear exactly how Robert Gormley earned a living after he moved to South Bethlehem. His sister, Margaret (Gormley) Brashear made the following comments about his work in two of her letters from Shanghai.[505]

---

cousin, Coleman "Pete" Gormley, had in his possession a large family *Bible* that bears the imprint of William and Mary Boyd, the mother and step-father of Hannah Jane (Johnson) Gormley. The *Bible* came from the home of Hannah Jane (Johnson) Gormley on Holland Street.

[501]Notes and documents provided on October 27, 1999 by Robert C. Gormley, 334 Brownsburg Road, Newtown, Pennsylvania 18940 to Kathryn C. Torpey, 5035 Domain Place, Alexandria, Virginia 22311-5066 contains information concerning property purchased by Robert M. Gormley and his wife's family.

[502]Deed Index - Grantees, Northampton County, Pennsylvania, FHL Microfilm Roll 0954012 says:

> Gormley, Robert M. from Tinsley Jeter & wf, Book G-11, p. 44, Sep 11 1866, Dec 19 1866, S. Beth

[503]Church of the Nativity (Episcopal), Bethlehem, Northampton County, Pennsylvania, 1862-1912, FHL Microfilm Roll 1671329 (item 3) says:

> 1867, June 21 # 48 Joseph Gormley b. Dec 20 1866, Bethlehem to Robert M. & Hannah J. Gormley
> 1869, May 28 # 85 Mary Gormley b. Bethlehem, January 12 1869 to Robert Gormley & Jane

[504]Notes and documents provided on October 27, 1999 by Robert C. Gormley, 334 Brownsburg Road, Newtown, Pennsylvania 18940 to Kathryn C. Torpey, 5035 Domain Place, Alexandria, Virginia 22311-5066 contains a copy of the original baptismal certificate of Joseph Gormley.

[505]Letter dated May 17, 1997 from Robert C. Gormley, 334 Brownsburg Road, Newtown, Pennsylvania 18940 to Kathryn C. Torpey, 5035 Domain Place, Alexandria, Virginia 22311-5066 provided copies of these letters for transcription.

The letter dated July 11, 1870, says:

> ...after I shall not forget you my dear brother, you say your wages are small but I
> know your work is not hard you are now getting to have a little family and it will
> be [necessary] to have a little more if you have a horse and a dray could you do
> well do you think if so let me know what it will cost and I will try what I can do
> for you Robert if you think you can do better, but do not undertake it unless you
> think you can do well...

The letter dated March 12, 1871, says:

> ...I am writing this in such a hurry I do hardly know what to write I am only so
> anxious you shall have the money but am so afraid it is too late should it be so
> and you have no horses and Dray then give one hundred dollars to father and
> mother but if you require it all now give a trifle to them and by the time I receive
> an answer to your letter I may be able to send them some but I hope my dear
> brother and sister [it] is not too late...

DEATH AND BURIAL OF ROBERT GORMLEY. Robert Gormley died on August 2, 1875 in
Fountain Hill which was then part of South Bethlehem, Lehigh County, Pennsylvania.[506] On
August 3, 1875, his obituary appeared in the *Bethlehem Globe Times*. It read as follows:

> DIED - After an illness of nearly nine months' duration, Robert Gormley died at
> his residence on Fountain Hill about 8 o'clock last evening. His disease was
> ulceration of the stomach and liver, from which he suffered greatly. He leaves a
> wife and five children. Mr. Gormley was a member of the South Bethlehem
> Division, Sons of Temperance, which organization will attend his funeral in
> body.[507]

On August 16, 1875, his estate was billed $54.50 by Edward Shafer, General Undertaker,
for expenses related to his funeral including:

one large coffin	$38.00
ice and labor	6.50
out site box & catage (sic)	5.00

---

[506]Edward J. Redding, *The History of Fountain Hill, Pennsylvania*, (n.p., Edward J.
Redding, 1996), p. unk, states that in 1892 there was a concerted effort to unite the three
Bethlehems - Bethlehem, South Bethlehem, and West Bethlehem, but the residents of the Lehigh
County portion of South Bethlehem resisted this effort. Fountain Hill was then located in that
portion of South Bethlehem that was in Lehigh County. The next year, on November 7, 1893,
the residents of Fountain Hill voted to become the Borough of Fountain Hill in Lehigh County.

[507]Obituary of Robert Gormley, *Bethlehem Globe Times*, Tuesday, August 3, 1875, p. 2.,
Bethlehem Area Public Library, 11 West Church Street, Bethlehem, Pennsylvania, 18018-5888.

Hearse & attending funerall (sic)   5.00[508]

The bill appears to itemize services related to the transportation of Robert Gormley's remains to Summit Hill for burial in the GAR Cemetery.

RETURN TO SUMMIT HILL. After the death of Robert Gormley in 1875, his widow, Hannah Jane (Johnson) Gormley, removed to Summit Hill where she was admitted to the Presbyterian Church on January 13, 1877.[509] At the time of the 1880 census, she and her children were enumerated with her mother-in-law, Margaret (Montgomery) Gormley.[510]

THE FAMILY HOME IN SUMMIT HILL.   At some point, Hannah Jane (Johnson) Gormley and her five children moved to a house located on Holland Street in Summit Hill.

The property consisted of two halves of a double home. The first half of the property, then known as Lot 26, was purchased by her mother, Mary (Gilmore) Johnson Boyd, on April 1,1873, from the coal company.[511] The other half of the property, then known as Lot 25, was purchased by Hannah Jane (Johnson) Gormley's step-father, William Boyd, on October 19, 1875 from the coal company.[512] When William Boyd died on or about January 23, 1876, he left a will

---

[508]Notes and documents provided on October 27, 1999 by Robert C. Gormley, 334 Brownsburg Road, Newtown, Pennsylvania 18940 to Kathryn C. Torpey, 5035 Domain Place, Alexandria, Virginia 22311-5066 contains a copy of the bill from Edward Shafer, General Undertaker.

[509]Letter dated June 12, 1997 from Robert C. Gormley, 334 Brownsburg Road, Newtown, Pennsylvania 18940 to Kathryn C. Torpey, 5035 Domain Place, Alexandria, Virginia 22311-5066 contains extracts from the Records of the First Presbyterian Church of Summit Hill and Tamaqua as prepared by an elderly member of the church which state:

VOLUME II (1873-1903)
REGISTER OF MEMBERS:
Mrs. Joseph Gormley   DIED 11/4/1883
Hanna (sic) Gormley   ADMISSION 1/13/1877

[510]1880 U.S. Census (population), Pennsylvania, Carbon County, Summit Hill, page 349D, Lines 22-28, National Archives Microfilm Publication T9, Roll 1107, Household of Margaret Gormley.

[511]Deed from the Lehigh Coal & Navigation Company to Mrs. Mary Boyd, April 1, 1873 (recorded August 26, 1873), Volume 20, p. 547, Deeds, Volumes 20-21, 1872-1875, Carbon County, Pennsylvania, FHL Microfilm Roll 2209191.

[512]Deed from the Lehigh Coal & Navigation Company to William Boyd, October 19, 1875 (recorded November 5, 1885), Volume 30, p. 672, Deeds, Volumes 28-31, 1884-1886,

that bequeathed his property, i.e., Lot 25 on Holland Street, to his wife, Mary (Gilmore) Johnson Boyd.[513]

On December 20, 1894, Mary (Gilmore) Johnson Boyd sold both halves of the property on Holland Street to her daughter, Hannah Jane (Johnson) Gormley.[514] Hannah Jane (Johnson) Gormley conveyed the property to her daughter, Margaret M. Gormley, just before her death in 1926.[515]

The Holland Street property remained in the hands of Hannah Jane (Johnson) Gormley's children until the death of Robert M. Gormley in 1964.[516,517] The house and property are clearly marked on *Beer's 1875 Atlas of Carbon County* as being on the south side of Rail Road Street,

---

Carbon County, Pennsylvania, FHL Microfilm Roll 2209195.

[513]Will of William Boyd, January 23, 1876, April 18, 1876, Will Book 1, page 222, Carbon County, Pennsylvania, FHL Microfilm Roll 1290573 read, in its entirety as follows:

> January 23rd 1876 I mean the House and 1 Lot on which the house is built or stands and what is in it to go to my wife except such things as belongs to any son Williams Mather and the Building and loan. William and James to keep up the payments if possible and two shares in savings bank to go to my sons William and James to be divided between them that is the Building and loan and Bank the lot alongside to go to my wife she to pay all the Burial and other expenses William Boyd Witness John B. Kolb John Johnson Robert Steward

[514]Deed from Mary Boyd, widow, to Hannah Jane Gormley, widow, December 20, 1894, (recorded December 31, 1894), Volume 41, p. 185, Deeds, Volumes 39-41, 1893-1895, Carbon County, Pennsylvania, FHL Microfilm Roll 2209199.

[515]Deed Index - Grantors, Carbon County, Pennsylvania, FHL Microfilm Roll 2209390 says:

> 1926 Gormley, Hannah to Margaret Gormley Vol 99, p. 598, Feb. 2, 1826, Summit Hill

[516]Letter dated June 30, 1998 from Robert C. Gormley, 334 Brownsburg Road, Newtown, Pennsylvania 18940 to Kathryn C. Torpey, 5035 Domain Place, Alexandria, Virginia 22311-5066 stating that he located the deeds to the property belonging to Hannah Jane (Johnson) Gormley and summarizing their content.

[517]Notes and documents provided on October 27, 1999 by Robert C. Gormley, 334 Brownsburg Road, Newtown, Pennsylvania 18940 to Kathryn C. Torpey, 5035 Domain Place, Alexandria, Virginia 22311-5066 contains information concerning property purchased by Robert M. Gormley and his wife's family, i.e., "April 1, 1873 - Mary Boyd purchased land on Holland Street, Summit Hill from LC&N. October 19, 1875 - William Boyd purchased land on Holland Street from LC&N Co. William Boyd died 1/23/1876."

west of Market Street.[518] Today, the property is known as 213/215 Holland Street.[519]

HANNAH JANE (JOHNSON) GORMLEY, WIDOW OF ROBERT. Hannah Jane (Johnson) Gormley and her five children appear to have lived continuously at their home on Holland Street for most of the rest of their lives.

At the time of the 1900 census, Hannah Jane (Johnson) Gormley and her five children were living together on Holland Street in Summit Hill. They were enumerated as follows:

SUMMIT HILL, CARBON COUNTY, PENNSYLVANIA

Gormley, Jennie (sic)	F 57 Wd	Pa	
, Joseph	M 32 S	Pa	Office clerk
, Mary	F 30 S	Pa	Seamstress
, Robert M.	M 27 S	Pa	Pump man
, Margaret	F 26 S	Pa	Seamstress
, William	M 24 S	Pa	Compositor[520]

Hannah Jane (Johnson) Gormley's mother, Mary (Gilmore) Johnson Boyd, was enumerated nearby on Front Street, living alone, as follows:

SUMMIT HILL, CARBON COUNTY, PENNSYLVANIA

Boyd, Mary	F 88 Wd	Ire	(year of immigration 1839)[521]

At the time of the 1910 census, Hannah Jane (Johnson) Gormley and all five of her children were still living together on Holland Street. The entry contained the following information:

SUMMIT HILL, CARBON COUNTY, PENNSYLVANIA

Gormley, Hannah	F 67 Wd	Pa	
, Joseph	M 41 S	Pa	Coal office

---

[518]*Beer's Atlas of Carbon County, 1875*, "Property of Mrs. William Boyd, building, Rail Road Street, Market & westward, South Side."

[519]Letter dated November 7, 2003 from Robert C. Gormley, 334 Brownsburg Road, Newtown, Pennsylvania 18940 to Kathryn C. Torpey, 5035 Domain Place, Alexandria, Virginia 22311-5066 states that when he was a boy the entire family lived at 213 West Holland Street.

[520]1900 U.S. Census (population), Pennsylvania, Carbon County, Summit Hill, E.D. 23, page 8, lines 74-79, National Archives Microfilm Publication T623, Roll 1391, Household of Jennie (sic) Gormley.

[521]1900 U.S. Census (population), Pennsylvania, Carbon County, Summit Hill, E.D. 23, page 9, line 2, National Archives Microfilm Publication T623, Roll 1391, Household of Mary Boyd.

111

, Mary	F 49 S	Pa	Private Family
, Margaret	F 37 S	Pa	--
, Robert	M 34 S	Pa	Stationary
, William	M 32 S	Pa	Weekly Paper[522]

At the time of the 1920 census, Hannah Jane (Johnson) Gormley and four of her children were enumerated living together at 215 (sic) Holland Street. The entry contained the following information:

SUMMIT HILL, CARBON COUNTY, PENNSYLVANIA, JANUARY 2, 1920
215 (sic) HOLLAND STREET

Gormley, Jennie (sic)	F 76 Wd	Pa	
, Joseph	M 53 S	Pa	Assistant, Coal Mine Co.
, Robert M.	M 49 S	Pa	Stationary Engr, Coal Mine
, Margaret	F 42 S	Pa	none
, William	M 39 S	Pa	Printer, Newspaper[523]

THE DEATH OF HANNAH JANE (JOHNSON) GORMLEY. An influenza epidemic that was more than ordinarily severe began in the late winter of 1925. It reached its peak in the last week of March 1926 having caused about 100,000 deaths in the United States. Two of its victims were Hannah Jane (Johnson) Gormley and her daughter, Mary E. Gormley, who succumbed six days apart in January 1926 from pneumonia that probably resulted from catching the flu during the influenza epidemic.[524,525]

The obituary of Hannah Jane (Johnson) Gormley appeared in *The Morning Call* on Monday, January 25, 1926. It read as follows:

MRS. HANNAH J. GORMLEY

Mrs. Hannah Jane (Johnson) Gormley, widow of Robert Gormley, died of pneumonia at 3 o'clock Friday afternoon at her home on Holland street, Summit Hill, age 83 years and 10 months. She had been ill just a few days. Her

---

[522]1910 U.S. Census (population), Pennsylvania, Carbon County, Summit Hill, E.D. 28, page 3B, lines 62-67, Family Number 54, National Archives Microfilm Publication T624, Roll 1327, Household of Hannah (sic) Gormley.

[523]1920 U.S. Census (population), Pennsylvania, Carbon County, Summit Hill Borough, E.D. 38, page 1A, lines 25-29, National Archives Microfilm Publication T625, Roll 1534, Household of Jennie (sic) Gormley.

[524]Death Certificate for Hannah Jane Gormley, January 22, 1926, # 10478 & # 6, Pennsylvania Division of Vital Statistics, New Castle, Pennsylvania 16103.

[525]Death Certificate for Mary E. Gormley, January 16, 1926, # 10476 & # 4, Pennsylvania Division of Vital Statistics, New Castle, Pennsylvania 16103.

daughter, Mary, also died of pneumonia within the past week.

Mrs. Gormley was a most highly respected and charitable resident of Summit Hill. She was born in Nesquehoning on March 21, 1842. During her early life, she moved to Bethlehem, where she was married to Robert Gormley. They resided there until the death of Mr. Gormley, who was a veteran of the civil war. Subsequently, she moved to Summit Hill, where she maintained her residence until her death. She was a lifelong member of the Presbyterian church.

There survive three sons and one daughter, Joseph, Robert, William and Margaret, all at home; three brothers and two sisters: John, David and Matthew Johnson, of Philadelphia; Mrs. Ellen Nicholas, of Camden, and Mrs. Nancy Walker, of Lansford.

Funeral services will be held at the family residence at 2 o'clock Tuesday afternoon, and burial will follow in the Grand Army cemetery at Summit Hill.[526]

Hannah Jane (Johnson) Gormley executed her will on her death bed at home in Summit Hill. She signed it with her mark undoubtedly because she was too sick to sign her name. She left her entire estate, real, personal, and mixed, to her daughter, Margaret M. Gormley whom she also appointed as her sole executor. Her estate papers say she died possessed of $830.61 in personal property and no real estate.[527]

THE CHILDREN OF ROBERT AND HANNAH JANE (JOHNSON) GORMLEY. Robert M. and Hannah Jane (Johnson) Gormley had five children. All five of the children survived their father.

Mary E. Gormley, predeceased her mother by six days.[528] She died of pneumonia on January 16, 1926, during a particularly harsh influenza epidemic that ravaged the country that year. She died at home in Summit Hill but seems to have worked for a time as a nurse whose duties may have taken her to Philadelphia and possibly elsewhere which might have exposed her to the fatal virus.[529]

––––––––––––––––––––

[526]Obituary of Hannah J. Gormley, *The Morning Call*, Monday, January 25, 1926, Allentown, Pennsylvania, <<www.newspapers.com>>, downloaded, August 10, 2019.

[527]Estate of Hannah Jane Gormley, # 7829, Carbon County Courthouse, Jim Thorpe, Pennsylvania.

[528]Death Certificate for Mary E. Gormley, January 16, 1926, # 10476 & # 4, Pennsylvania Division of Vital Statistics, New Castle, Pennsylvania 16103 says she was born January 12, 1869 in Bethlehem, Pennsylvania.

[529]Letter dated June 12, 1997 from Robert C. Gormley, 334 Brownsburg Road, Newtown, Pennsylvania 18940 to Kathryn C. Torpey, 5035 Domain Place, Alexandria, Virginia 22311-5066 contains extracts from the Records of the First Presbyterian Church of Summit Hill and Tamaqua as prepared by an elderly member of the church which state:

The obituary of Mary E. Gormley appeared in *The Morning Call* on Thursday, January 21, 1926. It read as follows:

> The death of Mary Gormley has caused quite a gloom of sorrow among her
> legion of friends, death coming so suddenly at the family home while she had
> been sick only a week with a cold which later developed into pneumonia, her
> condition not being considered serious until Friday when there was a sudden
> change which continued until early morning when she entered into her last sleep.
> Deceased was a young woman with many accomplishments and possessed
> talents that made her popular. In her home life she was ideal in its conception of
> duty and her filial devotion was most marked, in this circle she will be sorely
> missed while her absence from the legion of friends formed during life will be
> more regretfully noted with the passing of time. Besides her mother, Mrs. Jane
> Gormley, one sister, Marget (sic), and three brothers, Joseph, Robert and
> William, survive.[530]

Mary E. Gormley died intestate possessed of personal property valued at $3,403.57 and no real estate. Intestate papers were filed by her brother, Joseph Gormley, in which he stated her date of death as January 16, 1826 at 2:30 A.M. He also named her mother and her four surviving siblings in the intestate papers.[531]

The four remaining children of Robert M. and Hannah Jane (Johnson) Gormley - Joseph, Robert (Jr.), Margaret, and William - all continued to live in the old homestead in Summit Hill. None of them married. The last of the children, Robert Gormley (Jr.), died in 1964 at the age of 93.

Robert C. Gormley, the chronicler of much of the family legend as told in this family history, knew all four of the surviving children of Robert M. Gormley. According to his recollection, they were fine people and well respected in the community.

Joseph Gormley and Robert Gormley (Jr.) worked for the coal company. William Gormley was an editor and typesetter for the local newspaper. It was through them that the letters written by Margaret (Gormley) Brashear from Shanghai and other family memorabilia survived.

VOLUME II (1873 - 1903)
REGISTER OF MEMBERS:
Mary E. Gormley
Received in Membership 1/5/1895
DISMISSED PHILA -NURSE

[530]Obituary of Mary Gormley, *The Morning Call*, Thursday, January 21, 1926, Allentown, Pennsylvania, <<www.newspapers.com>>, downloaded, August 10, 2019.

[531]Estate of Mary Gormley, # 7793, Carbon County Courthouse, Jim Thorpe, Pennsylvania.

On August 9, 1948, Robert Gormley (Jr.) and Joseph Gormley were interviewed for an article that appeared in a Tamaqua newspaper. The article read, in part, as follows:

> Robert M. and Joseph Gormley, brothers, who reside at 213 West Holland Street, Summit Hill, each have over 66 years of service [with the Lehigh Navigation Coal Company]. Robert began work with the LNC as a slate picker at the old No. 6 operation in March 1880 and retired on February 1, 1947. He was a hoist operating engineer at the No. 8 shaft when he retired, and his service in that capacity totals 47 years. Previously he held various positions about and in the mines. He is a member of the Board of Trustees of the Coaldale State Hospital.
>
> Joseph Gormley began his career with the LNC as a slate picker at No. 9[532]. He was a time keeper at No. 8 before he joined the company's main office force. At the time of his retirement in September 1945, he was in the auditing department. His service in the office totaled 55 years. In his younger days Mr. Gormley was well known as a pitcher[533]. He played with Lansford, Tamaqua, Summit Hill, and Mauch Chunk teams and at one time was given a try-out by the Phillies.[534]

Joseph Gormley died on July 2, 1950, at his home in Summit Hill.[535] Both his obituary and the report of his funeral describe him as a well known baseball pitcher in the 1890s and an outstanding baseball player.[536,537] The following memorial was also published in *The Coaldale Observer* about his life:

DEATH CLAIMS JOSEPH GORMLEY, OLD TIME BASEBALL PITCHER

Joseph Gormley died at his home in Summit Hill, Sunday, July 2. His funeral took place

---

[532]Site visit on June 24, 1997 to the No. 9 tunnel in Lansford, Carbon County, Pennsylvania, in the company of Robert C. Gormley, great-grandson of James and Margaret (Glenn) Gormley, revealed that it runs all the way from Lansford to Summit Hill.

[533]*Encyclopedia of Baseball*, Pitcher Register, p. 1836, contains the record Joseph Gormley, b. December 20, 1866, Summit Hill (sic), PA d. July 2, 1950, Summit Hill, PA.

[534]Letter dated July 1, 1997 from Robert C. Gormley, 334 Brownsburg Road, Newtown, Pennsylvania 18940 to Kathryn C. Torpey, 5035 Domain Place, Alexandria, Virginia 22311-5066 contains a copy of the original article.

[535]Death Certificate for Joseph Gormley, July 2, 1950, Summit Hill, Carbon County, Pennsylvania, Pennsylvania Death Certificates, 1906-1966, <<www.ancestry.com>>, downloaded August 12, 2019 says he was born December 20, 1866 in Pennsylvania.

[536]Obituary of Joseph Gormley, *The Morning Call*, Wednesday, July 5, 1950, Allentown, Pennsylvania, <<www.newspapers.com>>, downloaded, August 10, 2019.

[537]Funeral of Joseph Gormley, *Mauch Chunk Times-News*, Wednesday, July 5, 1950, Mauch Chunk, Pennsylvania, <<www.newspapers.com>>, downloaded, August 10, 2019.

Thursday afternoon with services conducted by Rev. Henry Maue, of the Presbyterian Church, officiating. Interment was made in the G.A.R. Cemetery, Summit Hill.

Joe Gormley in early life was teamed up with Chris Fulmer, Tamaqua's big league catcher, as the outstanding battery of the period in the Panther Valley. Fulmer came back to Tamaqua after playing on championship ballclubs and helped develop Gormley who later had a tryout with the Phillies.

He played the game of life with the same quiet persistence he played baseball and was respected and admired by later day ball players trying to break into the game. He always took an interest in Summit Hill's town teams and the words he liked best in recreation periods were: "The batteries for today..."

Being a keen student of baseball as well as a star player in his youth he never missed the opportunity to see a game and never passed up the chance to tell youngsters breaking in to play it fair and square.

Deceased was the son of Mr. and Mrs. Robert Gormley. His father was born in Ireland and his mother, the former Hannah Johnson, was a native of Nesquehoning. Survivors are a sister, Margaret and two brothers, Robert and William.

He was employed until his retirement in 1945 in the main office of the Lehigh Navigation Coal Company and leaves to mourn his death a multitude of close friends.[538]

William A. Gormley died on November 24, 1955 at his home in Summit Hill.[539,540,541] Four years earlier, he was honored on the occasion of his retirement by the following article that appeared in *The Evening Record*, Lansford, Pennsylvania, on March 9, 1951:

> William A. Gormley, of Summit Hill, was presented a Certificate of Honorable Retirement last night during a testimonial dinner given for him in the Old Company's Club, Edgemont, by members of The Evening Record staff.

---

[538]Notes and documents provided on October 27, 1999 by Robert C. Gormley, 334 Brownsburg Road, Newtown, Pennsylvania 18940 to Kathryn C. Torpey, 5035 Domain Place, Alexandria, Virginia 22311-5066 contains a copy of the memorial piece concerning Joseph Gormley.

[539]Death Certificate for William A. Gormley, November 24, 1955, Summit Hill, Carbon County, Pennsylvania, Pennsylvania Death Certificates, 1906-1966, <<www.ancestry.com>>, downloaded August 12, 2019 says he was born July 30 1877 (sic) which is more than a year after his father died.

[540]Obituary of William A. Gormley, *The Morning Call*, Friday, November 25, 1955, Allentown, Pennsylvania, <<www.newspapers.com>>, downloaded, August 10, 2019.

[541]Obituary of William Gormley, *Pottsville Republican*, Friday, November 25, 1955, Pottsville, Pennsylvania, <<www.newspapers.com>>, downloaded, August 10, 2019.

Mr. Gormley is the oldest member of the International Typographical Union in Schuylkill and Carbon Counties and has been in Evening Record service more than 40 years before he decided some time ago to "take some of that good Summit Hill air and take it easy". He was shown by his workers last night that his unfailing kindness, his courtesy and his trade abilities had earned for him their lasting respect.

Mr. Gormley, member of one of Summit Hill's oldest families, learned the printing trade in the original Summit Hill and Lansford Record, a weekly newspaper.[542] He continued in the newspaper's service when it was converted into a daily by the late David G. Watkins and subsequently was operated by a partnership comprised of the children of Mr. Watkins. "Old Bill" stayed on under the stewardship of Patrick J. McCall when he purchased the newspaper in 1948. But around the turn of the year he elected to go into retirement. His certificate of retirement was signed by Mr. McCall, for McCall Publications, Inc. and by Luther J. Nochton, president, for the Pottsville Local of the International Typographical Union. It reads:

"This is inscribed in grateful respect and tribute to Mr. William A. Gormley, in recognition of more than forty years of loyal and capable service to the publishers of The Evening Record. His fellowship with several generations of printers and reporters was an inspiration. His honest aptitude added new credit to his craft. The examples he set will be an incentive to those who succeed him in the honored field of typography."

Mr. Gormley also received a purchase certificate, representing a cash tribute from his fellow workers and entitling him to "pick his own gift".

Miss Jean Henninger, Lansford soloist, provided dinner music with accompaniment by her mother. Dancing and impromptu entertainment continued in the club's rumpus room.

Mr. Nochton was toastmaster for the occasion and presentation of the certificate and gift was done by Russell Thomas, managing editor of the newspaper.[543]

Margaret M. Gormley died on August 18, 1956 at the Coaldale Hospital.[544] Much of her time was spent keeping house for the family. She was also a member of the First Presbyterian Church of Summit Hill and the Lansford Chapter of the Order of Eastern Star.

---

[542]Fred Brenckman, *History of Carbon County, Pennsylvania*, (Harrisburg, Pennsylvania: James J. Nungesser, Publisher, 1913), 217, says that when J.W. Malloy, editor of the Summit Hill and Lansford Record, died in 1910 active management of the newspaper devolved upon William Gormley.

[543]Letter dated July 1, 1997 from Robert C. Gormley, 334 Brownsburg Road, Newtown, Pennsylvania 18940 to Kathryn C. Torpey, 5035 Domain Place, Alexandria, Virginia 22311-5066 contains a copy of the original article.

[544]Death Certificate for Margaret M. Gormley, August 18, 1956, Coaldale, Schuylkill County, Pennsylvania, Pennsylvania Death Certificates, 1906-1966, <<www.ancestry.com>>, downloaded August 12, 2019.

Her obituary was published in *The Morning Call* on Tuesday, August 21, 1956. It read as follows:

> MISS MARGARET GORMLEY
>
> Miss Margaret M Gormley, 213 W. Holland St., Summit Hill, died Sunday in Coaldale Hospital, where she had been a patient the last 10 days.
>
> She had been ill the last three months.
>
> Born in Bethlehem, a daughter of Robert and Hannah Johnson Gormley, she was a member of the First Presbyterian Church, Summit Hill, and Lansford Chapter, Order of Eastern Star.
>
> Surviving are a brother, Robert M., at home.
>
> Services will be at 2 p.m. Wednesday in Walker Funeral Home, 120 W. White St., Summit Hill.[545]

Robert M. Gormley (Jr.) died on January 24, 1964 at the Coaldale Hospital.[546,547] He retired from the Lehigh Navigation Coal Company in 1947 after 65 years of service. He was a former member of the Summit Hill Borough Council, a member of the Board of Health, and at one time served as a constable in that borough. He was a charter member of the Summit Hill Diligent Fire Company, a member of the Rod and Gun Club, and the oldest member of the First Presbyterian Church of Summit Hill, serving as a trustee for many years. In 1959, the Young Republicans of Carbon County awarded him its first Lincoln Day Award. Before that, in February 1953, he was given a citation by the Carbon County Republican Party in honor of his outstanding service and loyalty to the party as a veteran county committeeman. An article concerning the award contained his biography that read, in part, as follows:

> Born in Bethlehem July 12, 1870, he is the son of the late Robert and Hannah (Johnson) Gormley, former residents of Summit Hill. Upon the early death of his father, Mr. Gormley came to Summit Hill with his mother and four small brothers. He was five years old at the time.
>
> For the last 83 years he has been a resident of the hilltop town.

---

[545]Obituary of Margaret Gormley, *The Morning Call*, Tuesday, August 21, 1956, Allentown, Pennsylvania, <<www.newspapers.com>>, downloaded, August 10, 2019.

[546]Death Certificate for Robert M. Gormley, January 24, 1964, Coaldale, Schuylkill County, Pennsylvania, Pennsylvania Death Certificates, 1906-1966, <<www.ancestry.com>>, downloaded August 12, 2019 says he was born July 12, 1870 (sic).

[547]Obituary of Robert Gormley, *Jim Thorpe Times News*, Friday, January 24, 1964, Jim Thorpe, Pennsylvania, <<www.newspapers.com>>, downloaded, August 10, 2019.

He attended the Summit Hill schools in his early years, but left school at the age of nine to start work at the Lehigh Navigation Coal Company, walking many miles each day through what was then a densely wooded area to the breaker.

He often recalls now that payday then was his most happy day when he turned his pay over to his widowed mother. His pay was the sole support of his family.

In his spare time, he picked coal for his family and planted and weeded the family garden.

"Robbie" can recall labor activities from the days of the old Knights of Labor to the present United Mine Workers, of which he is a member.

In 1947 he retired after working for 66 years and 10 months for the Lehigh Navigation Coal Company, starting out as a slate picker and mule-driver and retiring as a hoisting engineer.

His political career started at an early age. Before he was 21 he worked for the Republican Party, helping to get out the GOP vote in Summit Hill.

He first voted at the age of 21 and has never missed voting in a primary or general election since 1891.[548]

All the members of the family were buried in the same plot in the GAR Cemetery in Summit Hill. The plot contains a large memorial stone and individual headstones for Robert Gormley, his wife, Hannah Jane (Johnson) Gormley, and each of their five of children.[549]

---

[548]Letter dated July 1, 1997 from Robert C. Gormley, 334 Brownsburg Road, Newtown, Pennsylvania 18940 to Kathryn C. Torpey, 5035 Domain Place, Alexandria, Virginia 22311-5066 contains a copy of the original article.

[549]Site visit on June 24, 1997 to the GAR Cemetery, Summit Hill, Carbon County, Pennsylvania, in the company of Robert C. Gormley, great-grandson of James and Margaret (Glenn) Gormley, revealed a headstone for Robert Gormley, his wife, Hannah Jane (Johnson) Gormley, and all five of their children.

Margaret Gormley was born c. March 27, 1834, in Mullinabrone, Aghadowey Parish, County Londonderry, Ireland.[550,551] She died between 1871 and 1915.[552,553,554] She married Mr. Brashear between 1850 and 1864.[555,556] No reliable information was found regarding the identity of Mr. Brashear.

U.S. CENSUS ENUMERATIONS. Margaret Gormley was enumerated with her parents in the 1840 census in Mauch Chunk Township then in Northampton County, Pennsylvania.[557] In

---

[550]Baptism of Margaret Gormley, March 27, 1834, First Garvagh Presbyterian Church, Garvagh, Errigal Parish, County Londonderry, Ireland, Public Records Office of Northern Ireland, Belfast, Northern Ireland, Microfilm MIC/1P/257.

[551]Entry for Margaret Gormley and Children, Ship Sheridan Passenger Manifest, December 12, 1839, page 3, line 19, Passenger List of Vessels Arriving at New York, NY, 1820-1897, Records of the U.S. Customs Service, Record Group 36, National Archives Microfilm Publication M237, Roll 40 says 5, i.e. born 1834 in Ireland.

[552]The year of Margaret (Gormley) Brashear's last surviving letter from Shanghai was 1871. Her three letters from Shanghai are in the possession of her great-grand nephew, Robert C. Gormley, 334 Brownsburg Road, Newtown, Pennsylvania 18940

[553]Obituary of Mrs. Henry Erwin, *Bethlehem Globe Times*, Friday, May 7, 1915, p. 12, Bethlehem Area Public Library, 11 West Church Street, Bethlehem, Pennsylvania, 18018-5888 states Jane (Gormley) Erwin, the sister of Margaret (Gormley) Brashear was the last surviving of the children of Joseph and Margaret (Montgomery) Gormley.

[554]Letter dated August 8, 1996 from Robert C. Gormley, 334 Brownsburg Road, Newtown, Pennsylvania 18940 to Kathryn C. Torpey, 5035 Domain Place, Alexandria, Virginia 22311-5066 says Margaret (Gormley) Beaslear (sic) may have perished in China during the Boxer Rebellion in 1900.

[555]1850 U.S. Census (population), Pennsylvania, Carbon County, Mahoning Township, page 388, lines 11-18, National Archives Microfilm Publication M432, Roll 762, Household of Joseph Gormley is the last United States Federal census in which she was reliably enumerated.

[556]Entry for Mrs. M. Brashear, Ship Ocean Queen Passenger Manifest, November 15, 1864, p. 1, line 4, Passenger Lists of Vessels Arriving at New York, New York, 1820-1897, Records of the U.S. Customs Service, Records Group 36, National Archives Microfilm Publication M237, Roll 247 states that the point of departure was Aspinwall, Panama.

[557]1840 U.S. Census (population), Pennsylvania, Northampton County, Mauch Chunk Township, page 212, line 21, National Archives Microfilm Publication M704, Roll 479,

the 1850 census she was enumerated with her parents in Mahoning Township, Carbon County, Pennsylvania.[558] Thereafter, she has not been found in any census enumerations.

MARRIAGE OF MARGARET GORMLEY TO MR. BRASHEAR. Unfortunately, Margaret Gormley's husband's full name and the date and place of their marriage are unknown.

According to family legend, Margaret Gormley was a beautiful woman who left Summit Hill and married a man named Beasler (sic) who was either a sea captain or a tea merchant that she met while living in Philadelphia.[559,560] Although her husband's last name is reported to have been Beasler, her letter from Shanghai dated March 12, 1871, seems to indicate that she spelled her name Brashear After her marriage, she and her husband appear to have moved to California.[561]

Furthermore, there is a reference in a ship passenger manifest dated November 15, 1864, to a Mrs. M. Brashear, aged 31, arriving at the Port of New York from Aspinwall, Panama, aboard the S.S. Ocean Queen.[562] Since the subject of this family history would have been 31

Household of Jos. Gramley (sic).

[558]1850 U.S. Census (population), Pennsylvania, Carbon County, Mahoning Township, page 388, lines 11-18, National Archives Microfilm Publication M432, Roll 762, Household of Joseph Gormley.

[559]Letter dated February 25, 2004 from Robert C. Gormley, 334 Brownsburg Road, Newtown, Pennsylvania 18940 to Kathryn C. Torpey, 5035 Domain Place, Alexandria, Virginia 22311-5066 contains a copy of notes made by his mother on the back of a flyer from the Men's Department at Bright's Department Store stating that Margaret Gormley was a beautiful woman who married a sea captain and was lost at sea possibly in 1870. This information may have come from John M. Gormley, great-grandson of Joseph and Margaret (Montgomery) Gormley, who worked in the Men's Department of Bright's Department Store.

[560]Letter dated November 7, 2003 from Robert C. Gormley, 334 Brownsburg Road, Newtown, Pennsylvania 18940 to Kathryn C. Torpey, 5035 Domain Place, Alexandria, Virginia 22311-5066 contains a copy of an article by Ed Gildea entitled "Summit Hill Woman Murdered in China" that appeared in a June 1973 issue of *The Valley Gazette* in which John M. Gormley, great-grandson of Joseph and Margaret (Montgomery) Gormley, relates the family legend concerning the marriage of Margaret Gormley to a tea merchant named Beasler (sic).

[561]Letter of March 12, 1871 says, in part, "...Billy made a mistake while I was in California in the number of my Box at the Post Office..."

[562]Entry for Mrs. M. Brashear, Ship Ocean Queen Passenger Manifest, November 15, 1864, p. 1, line 4, Passenger Lists of Vessels Arriving at New York, New York, 1820-1897,

years old in 1864, a review was undertaken of the shipping news reported in the *New York Times* to determine whether additional information was available about Mrs. M. Brashear and the nature of her voyage. An article appeared in the *New York Times* stating that the S.S. Ocean Queen arrived at the Port of New York with mail, passengers, cargo, and $476,654 in cash. The bulk of the cash ($469,634.00) was from businesses operating out of San Francisco and the remainder was from businesses operating out of Aspinwall.[563] The S.S. Ocean Queen made the 10 day voyage from Aspinwall, Panama, to the Port of New York in convoy with the United States Gunboat Grand Gulf. The passenger list, as published in the *New York Times*, included a Mrs. Margaret Bradshear (sic), who is probably the subject of this family history.[564] In both the passenger manifest and the arrival notice published in the *New York Times*, she appeared to have been traveling alone.

SOJOURN IN SHANGHAI. After Margaret (Gormley) Brashear's marriage, her husband's business is reported to have taken them to Shanghai where they lived for some part of their married life.

Shanghai was (and still is) a port city located on the East China Sea. The Huangpu River, which runs through the city, is a tributary of the Yangtze River which served as the central gateway to the interior of China. Initially, Shanghai exported tea and silk to the outside world. It did not begin to grow commercially until the middle of the 19th Century when westerners, scrambling for an economic foothold in China, chose this city as their primary port for the importation of opium into the interior of the country. The Manchu dynasty objected to the foreign importation of opium into China which resulted in two Opium Wars both of which China lost. In defeat, China was forced to accept port and trade treaties with the west that converted Shanghai into a boomtown for foreign business.

When Margaret (Gormley) Brashear arrived in Shanghai, the central business district was known as the Bund (an Anglo-American word meaning embankment). It was in the Bund that foreign businessmen built their trading houses, offices, banks, and hotels. The British, French, and Americans leased land in Shanghai in perpetuity in the area extending north and west of the Bund. The British settlement merged with the American settlement in 1863 to form the International Settlement which was about eight square miles. The French Concession extended from the International Settlement to Shanghai's old walled city and covered about four square

---

Records of the U.S. Customs Service, Records Group 36, National Archives Microfilm Publication M237, Roll 247.

[563]News Story, *The New York Times*, Tuesday, November 15, 1864, p. 8, "From the Pacific Coast," Library of Congress, Newspaper and Periodocal Reading Room, Washington, D.C.

[564]News Story, *The New York Times*, Tuesday, November 15, 1864, p. 10, "Passengers Arrived," Library of Congress, Newspaper and Periodical Reading Room, Washington, D.C.

miles. These two contiguous foreign settlements constituted the core of the city. The status of the foreign enclaves was extraterritorial, that is, Chinese law did not apply. The foreigners lived under their own laws and were guarded by their own warships docked on the Huangpu River.

Although Shanghai was run by foreigners, it was not a colony and most residents were Chinese who flocked to the foreign zones seeking safe haven from China's civil wars. Thus, there were, in fact, several Shanghais in existence at once, and there was little overlap between them. Westerners like Margaret (Gormley) Brashear would have encountered a western city. Living in Shanghai, she would have had little need of contact with the Chinese around her. She would not have needed to learn to speak even the most basic Chinese. Margaret (Gormley) Brashear's world was, no doubt, based on the classic British colonial model - the racecourse and the Club, and a church. Her outlook may also have been tinged with the arrogance of racial and cultural superiority arising in westerners on account of the difference in their point of view from that of the Chinese.

While she was living in Shanghai, Margaret (Gormley) Brashear wrote letters home to her family. Three of these letters and a note have survived. The letters and the note are in the possession of her great-grandnephew, Robert C. Gormley.[565]

LETTERS FROM SHANGHAI. Margaret (Gormley) Brashear appears to have directed all three of her letters to her brother, Robert Gormley and his wife, Hannah Jane (Johnson) Gormley. The letters mention both her parents as well as the names of all her brothers and sisters then living except Joseph and Letitia. She also makes comments about two of her nieces, Maggie Boyd, the daughter of Matilda (Gormley) Boyd, and Mary Wallace, the daughter of Letitia (Gormley) Wallace.

Her first letter from Shanghai read as follows:

> Shanghai China
> December 23th 1869
> Dear brother and sister
>
> once more I write to let you know that I am well I wrote to you by the last steamer which left here in November 20th with it a Draft enclosed for the old folks of thirty one Pounds 31 Pounds and fifteen shillings which will be equal to over two hundred $200,00 Dollars in Green backs your paper money which I think will be very acceptable and hope you have received it and have gotten the money I explained to you in my letter why I was obliged to get it on London you cannot get a Draft on an American Bank as there are none here but you can sell it there in any Bank Mr [Souder] will tell you I suppose if you

---

[565]Letter dated May 17, 1997 from Robert C. Gormley, 334 Brownsburg Road, Newtown, Pennsylvania 18940 to Kathryn C. Torpey, 5035 Domain Place, Alexandria, Virginia 22311-5066 provided copies of these letters for transcription.

do not know, I now enclose to you the second Draft[566] I keep the third in case of an
accident to the others it is very hard to get money sent from here to America all being
English else I should have sent before I wrote to the old folks and to Matilda months a go
and have been expecting an answer every steamer but none yet and it is over time now,
Matildas I sent to 1631 Locust St perhaps she has moved I am so anxious to hear from
you all and see you I would like so much to see little Mary Wallace what kind of a
looking girl, is she good looking and Maggie Boyd I think Maggie will be very course, I
want to know if all your young ones are good looking I do not like ugly children tell me
the names of James little ones and how he is doing, I hope well

Robert I want to know what you are working at also Janes husband and where Smith is
and what he is doing and if you are on familiar terms with his family for I do not wish any
of you to be on intimate terms with his wife or himself for I do not think them worthy I
am so pleased Billy did not start for California for he would have seen hard times in a
strange country without money tell him to be kind to our old father and mother and
remain as near as possible to them while they live for poor old father cannot have long to
remain on earth but I hope God will spare them both until we meet again once more it is
uncertain how long I shall remain in China but am certain to remain six months longer if I
live and if I die am bound <u>to remain</u> but I like China very much there is a great many
sights to be seen and some of the most handsome things in the world it is now Christmas
times and presents are flowing in I have received some very valuable ones to[o]
numerous to mention the most important are two very large [Solid] [silver] Goblets and a
satin quilt one side Red the other Blue satin very valuable I cannot send you home any
nice things as they would cost more than the value going through the Customs house but
will try when I return to take some with me silks are very cheap but very [often] only fit
for very warm weather I shall try and take you all a Dress when I return Maggie and
Mary Wallace included I hope they are nice girls tell me what colors Jane and you would
like stripped or plain there is no good black silk I know of nothing more that would
interest you hoping to hear from you soon and love to Jane and husband and Billy and
the same to yourself I remain your sister

    address as before   Margaret

Her second letter from Shanghai read as follows:

                                            Shanghai July 11th
                                                1870

My dear Brother and sister
I now sit down to answer your very [kind] and welcome letter and I am so pleased to hear

---

[566]The "second Draft," which is in the possession of Robert C. Gormley, 334 Brownsburg
Road, Newtown, Pennsylvania 18940, refers to the second copy of a Bank Note, dated November
19, 1869, payable to the order of Robert Gormley, Esq[er]. At the time Margaret (Gormley)
Brashear bought the Bank Note, the cashier made out three copies. On November 20, 1869,
Margaret (Gormley) Brashear sent the first copy of the Bank Note to her brother, Robert
Gormley. In the event the first copy of the Bank Note was lost in transit, she sent him the second
copy of the Bank Note on December 23, 1869. When he received the second copy of the Bank
Note, there was no need to cash it because he had already received and cashed the first copy.

you are all so well you do not know how much pleasure it gives me in this far off land to hear from you all and I am so pleased to see Hannah writes to me the greater part of the letter and gives me a little news of every thing when I receive your letter it takes me far back I can remember things I had forgotten I look back and cannot realize I ever worked in the fields in Mahoning, oh, how different my position now with any quantity of servants to wait on me here but with all this I would like to see you all again and particularly my dear old Father and Mother once again, before the[y] leave this world for I hope a better one Robert I notice particularly what you said, you did not treat yourself or any one else out of the money and I think so much more of you for it I would like to send you something for hannah and the children to buy clothes but I feel all I have to spare to give to the old folks while they are alive to make them comfortable I know none of the rest of the family can do anything for them after I shall not forget you my dear brother, you say your wages are small but I know your work is not hard you are now getting to have a little family and it will be [necessary] to have a little more if you have a horse and a dray could you do well do you think if so let me know what it will cost and I will try what I can do for you Robert if you think you can do better, but do not undertake it unless you think you can do well I received a very kind letter from James a few months ago and have not answered it yet but think I shall this steamer but do not know where to address it I see it was mailed in Tamaqua but he gives me no address to send to I have come to the conclusion I will not write this steamer to him I notice Jane never writes to me but no matter she can live without me and I am certain I can without her we expect fearful times here some fifty miles from here the Chinese have murdered all the Europeans they broke into the Convent and ravished and then murdered seventeen sisters of Charity they cut the breasts of[f] them all first also a number of Priests were murdered this place is in a frightful state any quantity of man of war vessels of all nations are here they expect they will march in here in the night and murder us all they have made every man a volunteer it is fearful times now so do not be [surprised] if you hear I [am reported] murdered for we all expect it now you will see I have not much space to write more but answer this as soon as you receive it hopefully you are all well and happy I am your sister

Margaret

you will hear from me by the next steamer God bless you and may we all meet again

The undated note is thought to have been enclosed with the second letter from Shanghai dated July 11, 1870 because the note makes reference to "the massacre" which may possibly refer to the murders described in the second letter from Shanghai.[567] The undated note read as follows:

---

[567]According to family tradition, the undated note is said to have been enclosed with the *third* letter from Shanghai dated March 12, 1871, however, three despatches from the Foreign Office in London state that the Secretary of the British Legation in Pekin (sic) reported all parts of China were quiet during the time period February 26 to March 16, 1871. These reports were published in the *Philadelphia Public Ledger* on March 15, March 27, and April 4, 1871, respectively. Furthermore, the first riot in Shanghai did not occur until May 3, 1874. The riot was centered in the French Concession after Westerners made known their plan to build a road through a Chinese cemetery located in that part of Shanghai. The Chinese authorities paid for the cost of damage to foreign property and the French paid the families of the Chinese who were

My dear sister I have not forgotten about Roberts pipe and I shall find a corner in my
trunk to take him a nice one if I am spared the massacre which I hope we will also your
[dress] but there is no telling when I shall return as I shall more than likely go by the way
of Europe and cross the Red Sea then I have been almost around the world I am
scribbling this off in a hurry the excitement is so great on account of the massacre we are
not fit for anything my mind now is not on anything else we are all in fear of being
murdered at any hour the Chinese are here in thousands I must close

Her third letter from Shanghai read as follows:

the 12 1871

Shanghai March

My dear brother and sister
I suppose you have been long looking and waiting for a letter from me and I have been
doing the same with you I did not receive your letter until a few weeks a go after an
absence of some seven or eight months I received it too late to answer by the last steamer
when I got your letter I was delighted but very sorry to think you had perhaps bought your
Horses and Dray and I suppose looking every month for a letter and some help from me I
now send you three hundred dollars $300 which will be a little help to you I only hope it
does not come too late for I suppose you have been much disappointed in not hearing
from me and I was as much in not hearing from you, besides my dear Sister you spelled
my name wrong my name is [Brashear] and you spelled it [Bradshear] Billy made a
mistake while I was in California[568] in the number of my Box in the Post Office through
carelessness on his part and through that he did not get the money to send him to school I
have always been particular in every letter to send send my name and address but I think I
have not done so with you but for the future you must be particular how you spell my
name I am sorry my letter did not reach in time for my dear old father to hear from me
how much I would give only to see him now but I hope I shall see him yet before he dies
at any rate if I do not have that pleasure on earth all I can do is to erect a handsome
monument to their memory for I think I shall be in China for the [next] two years but I
hope my dear old father and mother will survive a much longer time, oh how I do long to
see you all once more and particularly my dear little brother Billy I suppose he is not so
small but in looking back I only see him a little child in Mahoning my poor child he is
not strong but never mind should God spare me my dear little brother shall be taken care
of and should I die he will be still better off I am writing this in such a hurry I do hardly
know what to write I am only so anxious you shall have the money but am so afraid it is
too late should it be so and you have no horses and Dray then give one hundred dollars to
father and mother but if you require it all now give a trifle to them and by the time I
receive an answer to your letter I may be able to send them some but I hope my dear
brother and sister [it] is not too late if so it is not my fault the three hundred dollars I
send you in English money is sixty four pounds and I think five shillings it will bring
something over three hundred green backs I can write nothing more will send second
Draft on next steamer April I am happy and contented God bless you all may you ever

---

killed. No Westerners were killed during the first riot in Shanghai.

[568] According to the Native Daughters of the Golden West, 543 Baker Street, San
Francisco, California 94117-1405, their Roster of California Pioneers lists a Margaret A.
Gormley, (Volume 20, Page 203), but she is not the subject of this family history.

be happy the best [wishes] of your affectionate sister

Maggie

FINAL DISPOSITION UNKNOWN. Thus far, all attempts to locate Margaret (Gormley) Brashear in Shanghai have failed.[569] According to family legend, her letter dated March 12,

---

[569]There is no information concerning **Margaret (Gormley) Brashear** in any of the following letters, records, or publications:

1) Letter dated February 20, 2004 from John A. Vernon, Archivist, Access Programs (NWC), National Archives and Records Administration, 8601 Adelphi Road, College Park, Maryland 20740-6001 to Kathryn C. Torpey, 5035 Domain Place, Alexandria, Virginia 22311-5066 states that he searched the Death Notices of U.S. Citizens Abroad 1870-1917, (Inventory 15, entry 849) located in Stack 250, Row 48, Shelf 4 to Row 49, Compartment 1, Row 1 and did not find any entries for Brashear during that period.

2) Despatches From U.S. Consuls in Shanghai, China, 1847-1906, National Archives II, College Park, Maryland, National Archives Microfilm Publication M112, Rolls 10, 11, 12 covering the years 1869 to 1871.

3) Records of Shanghai, English-language newspapers in China c. 1861-1880, FHL Microfilm Roll 1208487 (item 12).

4) Card File of China Coast Residents, (A-D) mentioned in English-language newspapers of South China including the Daily Press, China Mail, South China Morning Post, Hong Kong Register, and Government Gazette, FHL Microfilm Roll 1208491.

5) Passport Index Cards, 1850-1852 and 1860-1880, FHL Microfilm Roll 1429878.

6) List of Residents on the China Coast, 1832-1878, FHL Microfilm Roll 1208488 (item 1) contains an inconclusive reference to the following company:

1868	Broadlear, Anthony, & Co., ship chandler, Praya, 62
	E.D. Broadlear
	T.J. Anthony
	C.H.E. Sermund
1872	Broadbear, Anthony, & Co., storekeeper & ship chandler, 62 Praya

7) Shanghai China Cemetery Records, Burials in Old & New Cemetery, 1859-1899 and Seamens Cemetery, 1864-1886, FHL Microfilm Roll 0418134.

8) Church of England, Holy Trinity Cathedral, Shanghai, China, 1849-1945, FHL Microfilm Roll 0397734 contains listings for men with the surname Braysher and Baessler, but none with the surname Brashear.

9) British Consulate Registers, 1851 - 1876, Shanghai, China, FHL Microfilm Roll 1484031 and FHL Microfilm Roll 1818454 (item 1).

10) RG33 - Foreign Registers and Returns for British Nationals in Shanghai and Wei Hai Wei, China, 1852 - 1930, FHL Microfilm Roll 181805 (item 1).

11) Lists of Arriving and Departing Passengers, *Supreme Court & Consular Gazette* (aka *The North China*

1871, turned out to be the last that her family ever heard from her and they believed she was murdered during an uprising against foreigners in China shortly after sending the letter.[570,571]

Herald), Shanghai, China, January 1868 to December 1869, Library of Congress, Newspaper and Periodical Reading Room, Washington, D.C., Microfilm Publication No. 2499.

12) Lists of Arriving and Departing Passengers and Notices of Births, Marriages and Deaths, *Supreme Court & Consular Gazette* (aka *The North China Herald*), Shanghai, China, March 1871 to December 1875, Library of Congress, Newspaper and Periodical Reading Room, Washington, D.C., Microfilm Publication No. 2499.

13) Mary Matheson Wilbur, *Vital Records of Americans in China*. (Shanghai, China: Shanghai Chapter DAR, 1940), DAR Library, Washington, D.C.

[570]Letter dated November 7, 2003 from Robert C. Gormley, 334 Brownsburg Road, Newtown, Pennsylvania 18940 to Kathryn C. Torpey, 5035 Domain Place, Alexandria, Virginia 22311-5066 contains a copy of an article by Ed Gildea entitled "Summit Hill Woman Murdered in China" that appeared in a June 1973 issue of *The Valley Gazette* in which John M. Gormley relates the family legend concerning the death of Margaret (Gormley) Beasler (sic).

[571]Find-A-Grave Memorial # 198446710, Margaret Gormley Brashear (no headstone photograph), added April 18, 2019, Lost at War, <<www.findagrave.com>>.

Joseph Gormley was born June 1836 in Mullinabrone, Aghadowey Parish, County Londonderry, Ireland.[572,573,574] He was buried on February 22, 1904, probably in Silver City Precinct, Lyon County, Nevada.[575,576,577]

U.S. CENSUS ENUMERATIONS. Joseph Gormley was enumerated with his parents in the 1840 census in Mauch Chunk Township then in Northampton County, Pennsylvania.[578] In the 1850 census he was enumerated with his parents in Mahoning Township, Carbon County, Pennsylvania. [579]

---

[572]Baptism of Joseph Gormley, July 18, 1836, First Garvagh Presbyterian Church, Garvagh, Errigal Parish, County Londonderry, Ireland, Public Records Office of Northern Ireland, Belfast, Northern Ireland, Microfilm MIC/1P/257.

[573]Entry for Margaret Gormley and Children, Ship Sheridan Passenger Manifest, December 12, 1839, page 3, line 19, Passenger List of Vessels Arriving at New York, NY, 1820-1897, Records of the U.S. Customs Service, Record Group 36, National Archives Microfilm Publication M237, Roll 40 says 3, i.e. born 1836 in Ireland.

[574]1900 U.S. Census (population), Nevada, Lyon County, Silver City Precinct, E.D. 29, page 8, line 98, National Archives Microfilm Publication T623, Roll 943, Household of Joseph Gormley, says born June 1836.

[575]California/Nevada Historical Research, Newspaper Death Notices, 1863-1930, Volume 2, D-G, FHL Microfilm Roll 1598457 (item 7), says:

> Death Notices from Various Newspapers, Nona Parkin. compiler
> Lyon County Coroner's Records
>
> 1904 FEB 22   Joseph Gormley Native of Pennsylvania   66

[576]Index to Births and Deaths in Book A, 1887-1911, Lyon County, Nevada, Microfilm Roll 1902307, item 1, says: "1904, March 4 (filing date), Gormley, Joseph, Book A, page 106."

[577]Births and Deaths, 1887-1911, Lyon County, Nevada, Book A, page 106, Certificate of Death for Joseph Gormley, FHL Microfilm Roll 1902307, item 2, says "...burial 22nd day of Feb. 1904..."

[578]1840 U.S. Census (population), Pennsylvania, Northampton County, Mauch Chunk Township, page 212, line 21, National Archives Publication M704, Roll 479, Household of Jos. Gramley (sic).

[579]1850 U.S. Census (population), Pennsylvania, Carbon County, Mahoning Township,

Thereafter, Joseph Gormley is said to have gone West in search of gold. Whether he traveled alone or in the company of his brother-in-law, John Boyd, the husband of Matilda (Gormley) Boyd, is unknown. In any event, by the time of the 1860 census, Joseph Gormley was living in Placer County, California, where he was enumerated with another miner.[580] The listing was as follows:

WISCONSIN HILL, TOWNSHIP 7, COUNTY OF PLACER, CALIFORNIA, JULY 5, 1860

Joseph Gormely	23 M	Miner	Penn (sic)
George Mason	35 M	Miner	Baden

In the 1870 census, Joseph Gormley was enumerated in Lyon County, Nevada, where he was living in a small hotel with a family of five and three other adult men, two of whom were Chinese cooks.[581,582] The listing concerning Joseph Gormley was as follows:

SILVER CITY PRECINCT, LYON COUNTY, NEVADA

Gormley, Jos.	33 M	works in Quartz mill	Pa (sic) U.S. Citizen

In the 1900 census, Joseph Gormley was enumerated in Lyon County, Nevada, where he

---

page 388, lines 11-18, National Archives Microfilm Publication M432, Roll 762, Household of Joseph Gormley.

[580]1860 U.S. Census (population), California, Placer County, Wisconsin Hill, page 873, lines 7-8, National Archives Microfilm Publication M653, Roll 62, Household of Joseph Gormely (sic).

[581]1870 U.S. Census (population), Nevada, Lyon County, page 228, lines 1-9, National Archives Microfilm Publication M593, Roll 834, Household of Thos. Woggon (sic), Hotel Keeper.

[582]1875 Nevada State Census, Lyon County, from *Report Booklet Published for the State in 1876*, (Carson City, Nevada: State Publishing Office, 1876), <<www.ancestry.com>>, downloaded August 30, 2019, states:

Name:	J. Jormly (sic)
Age:	38
Sex:	M
Race:	White
Occupation:	Laborer
Place of Birth:	Pennsylvania (sic)
Head of Household:	T. Wogan
Community:	Lyon

was living alone in a house he owned free and clear.[583] Apparently he was retired because he had not worked in the preceding 12 months. The listing concerning Joseph Gormley was as follows:

SILVER CITY PRECINCT, LYON COUNTY, NEVADA
Gormley, Joseph b June 1836   63 M   Millwright   Pa (sic)

SEARCHING FOR GOLD. Prior to the Civil War, Joseph Gormley may have accompanied his brother-in-law, John Boyd, the husband of Matilda (Gormley) Boyd, to California in search of gold where they may have worked as placer miners. Placer gold took the form of dust, flakes, or nuggets. In those days, the commonest way of recovering placer gold was with a gold pan. Gold prospectors such as Joseph Gormley would have usually panned upstream until they encountered the bedrock source (or the mother lode) of the gold. This type of gold was normally found in stream beds and in gravel laid down by ancient rivers. This supply of gold was quickly exhausted and the placer miners were forced to use more sophisticated and expensive techniques including deep mines that were dug to tap the original deposits of gold. This kind of mining required huge amounts of capital that were beyond the means of most individual placer miners so they were often forced to work as wage laborers, return home, or wander on to gold strikes in other places such as Colorado, Nevada, Idaho, Montana, and Arizona.

After relocating from California to Nevada, Joseph Gormley probably lived somewhere in the vicinity of Silver City where he worked in a quartz mill. In 1868, there were 31 quartz mills in operation in Lyon County which had an aggregate of 440 stamps and 227 pans. The men working in these quartz mills endured many difficulties in reducing the ores. Almost every mill superintendent had a plan of his own and it is impossible to know exactly where Joseph Gormley may have worked.[584]

During the time that Joseph Gormley lived in Nevada, the Silver City Precinct quartz mills were primarily engaged in processing the ore from the Comstock Lode. That effort yielded almost $300 million in silver and gold ore before production severely declined after 1882. The Comstock Lode mining operations also yielded innovations in ore processing and in timbering, ventilation, and drainage of extremely deep mines that encouraged other exploration and discovery particularly in California, Idaho, Montana, and the Southwest after 1880.

According to family tradition, Joseph Gormley eventually moved on to Bowie,

---

[583] 1900 U.S. Census (population), Nevada, Lyon County, Silver City Precinct, E.D. 29, page 8, line 98, National Archives Microfilm Publication T623, Roll 943, Household of Joseph Gormley.

[584] *History of Nevada, 1881, with Illustrations and Biographical Sketches of its Prominent Men and Pioneers*, (Berkeley, California: Howell-North, 1958), p. 502-504.

Montana.[585,586] Once there, he may have been employed in a deep mining operation. Nothing more is known about Joseph Gormley and his search for gold except that he had returned to Lyon County, Nevada, by the time of the 1900 census.[587]

DEATH AND BURIAL OF JOSEPH GORMLEY. Joseph Gormley died on or about February 22, 1904. His certificate of death read as follows:

CERTIFICATE OF DEATH

State of Nevada
County of Lyon

This is to certify that the undersigned, an Undertaker, did, on the 22nd day of Feb. 1904, officiate as Undertaker at the burial of Joseph Gormley Sex Male, Age 66, Nativity, Penn. Cause of Death, General Debility, In presence of E.T. Powers and witnesses.

Witness my hand this 22nd day of Feb. 1904.

G.C. Kuhn

Filed at the request of G.C. Huhn (sic) this 4 day of March 1904.

F.W. Downey
County Recorder of Lyon County[588]

On February 27, 1904, an obituary for Joseph Gormley appeared in the *Lyon County*

---

[585]Conversation on June 24, 1997 with Robert C. Gormley, 334 Brownsburg Road, Newtown, Pennsylvania 18940 in which he said that, according to family tradition, Joseph Gormley may have gone to Bowie, Montana, searching for gold.

[586]Letter dated November 7, 2003 from Robert C. Gormley, 334 Brownsburg Road, Newtown, Pennsylvania 18940 to Kathryn C. Torpey, 5035 Domain Place, Alexandria, Virginia 22311-5066 contains a copy of an article by Ed Gildea entitled "Summit Hill Woman Murdered in China" that appeared in a June 1973 issue of *The Valley Gazette* in which John M. Gormley, great-grandson of Joseph and Margaret (Montgomery) Gormley, relates the family legend concerning Joseph Gormley having gone to Bowie, Montana.

[587]1900 U.S. Census (population), Nevada, Lyon County, Silver City Precinct, E.D. 29, sheet 8, line 98, National Archives Microfilm Publication T623, Roll 943, Household of Joseph Gormley.

[588]Births and Deaths, 1887-1911, Lyon County, Nevada, Book A, page 106, Certificate of Death for Joseph Gormley, FHL Microfilm Roll 1902307.

Times.[589] It read as follows:

> SILVER CITY SIFTINGS:
>
> The funeral of Joseph Gormley took place last Monday afternoon. A number of his old time friends accompanied the remains to their last resting place. Mr. Gormley was a native of Pennsylvania, aged 66 years.

There was no indication in his Certificate of Death or in his obituary of his actual date of death or where he was buried. No record of his burial was found in a census of cemeteries in Silver City or Yerington.[590,591]

THE LEGACY OF JOSEPH GORMLEY. Despite having worked in gold mining operations in the West for at least forty years, no estate, probate, will, or other legal proceeding of any kind was found for Joseph Gormley in the records of the Clerk of Court for Lyon County, Nevada. A search of the deed indexes in the Lyon County Recorder's Office also yielded negative results for property owned by Joseph Gormley despite the fact that the 1900 census clearly indicated he owned his own home free and clear.[592] So, it appears that the worldly goods accumulated by Joseph Gormley during his lifetime were disposed of in ways other than through the probate process in Lyon County, Nevada.

---

[589]Obituary of Joseph Gormley, *Lyon County Times*, Saturday, February 27, 1907, p. 3, col. 5 as transcribed by Barbara L. Hodges, CGRS, GenResearcher, P.O. Box 303, Fallon, Nevada 89407-0303 in her research report dated December 9, 2003, to Kathryn C. Torpey, 5035 Domain Place, Alexandria, Virginia 22311-5066.

[590]Cemetery Census, Lyon County, Nevada, Volume 1, FHL Microfilm Roll 1598460 (item 5).

[591]Find-A-Grave Memorial # 93854134, Joseph Gormley (no headstone photograph), added July 19, 2012, Burial Details Unknown, <<www.findagrave.com>>.

[592]Report dated December 9, 2003 from Barbara L. Hodges, CGRS, GenResearcher, P.O. Box 303, Fallon, Nevada 89407-0303 to Kathryn C. Torpey, 5035 Domain Place, Alexandria, Virginia 22311-5066.

William Brown Gormley was born c. December 5, 1838 in Mullinabrone, Aghadowey Parish, County Londonderry, Ireland.[593,594] He probably died between 1843 and 1846 in Summit Hill, Carbon County, Pennsylvania.

THE BRIEF LIFE OF WILLIAM BROWN GORMLEY. William Brown Gormley was just over a year old when he arrived in New York with his mother and the rest of the family. After their arrival, the family proceeded to Summit Hill where they joined Joseph Gormley who was already established at that location.

THE DEATH OF WILLIAM BROWN GORMLEY. There is a family tradition that a member of the Gormley family died as a child as a result of a fire in the home in Summit Hill.[595,596] Since a second child named William Gormley was born to Joseph and Margaret (Montgomery) Gormley in 1846, it is likely that the member of the family who died, tragically, in the fire in Summit Hill was this child.

THE BURIAL OF WILLIAM BROWN GORMLEY. The Gormley family is known to have maintained a plot at the Old Presbyterian Cemetery in Summit Hill so it is possible that William Brown Gormley may have been one of those buried in the family plot even though his name does

---

[593]Baptism of William Brown Gormley, December 5, 1838, First Garvagh Presbyterian Church, Garvagh, Errigal Parish, County Londonderry, Ireland, Public Records Office of Northern Ireland, Belfast, Northern Ireland, Microfilm MIC/1P/257.

[594]Entry for Margaret Gormley and Children, Ship Sheridan Passenger Manifest, December 12, 1839, page 3, line 19, Passenger List of Vessels Arriving at New York, NY, 1820-1897, Records of the U.S. Customs Service, Record Group 36, National Archives Microfilm Publication M237, Roll 40 says 1 year old, i.e. born 1838 in Ireland.

[595]Letter dated October 3, 1996 from Robert C. Gormley, 334 Brownsburg Road, Newtown, Pennsylvania 18940 to Kathryn C. Torpey, 5035 Domain Place, Alexandria, Virginia 22311-5066.

[596]Letter dated November 7, 2003 from Robert C. Gormley, 334 Brownsburg Road, Newtown, Pennsylvania 18940 to Kathryn C. Torpey, 5035 Domain Place, Alexandria, Virginia 22311-5066 contains a copy of an article by Ed Gildea entitled "Summit Hill Woman Murdered in China" that appeared in a June 1973 issue of *The Valley Gazette* in which John M. Gormley, great-grandson of Joseph and Margaret (Montgomery) Gormley, relates the family legend concerning the death of "...a baby girl (sic) whose name is not known (she (sic) was burned to death in a fire in Summit Hill)...".

not appear in any of the cemetery records.[597,598,599,600,601]

---

[597]Letter dated October 8, 1996 from Robert C. Gormley, 334 Brownsburg Road, Newtown, Pennsylvania 18940 to Kathryn C. Torpey, 5035 Domain Place, Alexandria, Virginia 22311-5066 states that he was familiar with the Gormley plot having visited it when growing up in Summit Hill and that the cemetery was cleared in June 1972.

[598]Letter dated June 12, 1997 from Robert C. Gormley, 334 Brownsburg Road, Newtown, Pennsylvania 18940 to Kathryn C. Torpey, 5035 Domain Place, Alexandria, Virginia 22311-5066 containing extracts of Volumes I, II, and III of the Records of the First Presbyterian Church of Summit Hill and Tamaqua and the Presbyterian Cemetery in Summit Hill as prepared by an elderly member of the church states that the name Gormley does not appear in the cemetery records.

[599]Summit Hill Presbyterian Cemetery Web Page, <<freepages,genealogy.rootsweb.com/~mccem/sh-presbcem.htm>>, downloaded September 10, 2003 contains a list of 156 names of those buried in the Old Presbyterian Cemetery. It was prepared from the cemetery plot map. The name Gormley does not appear on the plot map, however, the 156 names on the plot map only represent a partial listing of those buried in the cemetery

[600]Letter dated May 12, 2004 from Robert C. Gormley, 334 Brownsburg Road, Newtown, Pennsylvania 18940 to Kathryn C. Torpey, 5035 Domain Place, Alexandria, Virginia 22311-5066 contains a copy of a page from a small notebook that may show the names of people buried in the Old Presbyterian Cemetery whose surname began with the letter G. The whereabouts of the original notebook are unknown, but may be in the possession of the GAR Cemetery in Summit Hill. The photocopy of the page from the notebook is in the possession of Robert C. Gormley and states the following with respect to the Gormley burials:

     Buried on Lot
     James Gormley, soldier
     Joe Gormley
     Margaret M. Gormley
     Samel (sic) Gormley
     Joe Gormley
     [Jane] Gormley

[601]Find-A-Grave Memorial # 198446515, William Brown Gormley (no headstone photograph), added April 18, 2019, First Presbyterian Church Cemetery, Carbon County, Pennsylvania, <<www.findagrave.com>>.

Jane Gormley was born c. March 1, 1841 in Summit Hill, Carbon County, Pennsylvania.[602,603] She died May 7, 1915 in West Bethlehem, Lehigh County, Pennsylvania.[604] She married Henry Erwin, the son of John and Nancy (Dougherty/Davis) Erwin, in 1866.[605,606] He was born May 5, 1842 in County Londonderry, Ireland.[607] He died February 12, 1912 in West Bethlehem, Lehigh County, Pennsylvania.[608,609] They were both buried in Nisky Hill Cemetery,

---

[602]Letter dated November 13, 2003 from Edith Ann Szczecina, Secretary, First Presbyterian Church of Panther Valley, 44 West White Street, P.O. Box 36, Summit Hill, Pennsylvania 18250 to Kathryn C. Torpey, 5035 Domain Place, Alexandria, Virginia 22311-5066 provided copies of three pages of the baptismal register containing entries # 34 to # 140, inclusive, which state the following with respect to the members of the Gormley family:

REGISTER OF BAPTISMS:

NO.	CHILD	PARENTS	BORN	BAPTIZED
40	Peggy (sic) Jane	Joseph & Jane (sic) Gormley	1841	May 16, 1841
89	John	Joseph & Jane (sic) Gormley	August 5, 1843	
133	William	Joseph & Jane (sic) Gormley		April 7, 1847

[603]Death Certificate for Jennie Erwin, May 7, 1915, # 45749 & # 77, Pennsylvania Department of Vital Statistics, New Castle, Pennsylvania, says she was born March 1, 1843 (sic) in Pennsylvania and that she was the daughter of Joseph Gormley and Margaret Montgomery.

[604]Death Certificate for Jennie Erwin, May 7, 1915, # 45749 & # 77, Pennsylvania Department of Vital Statistics, New Castle, Pennsylvania.

[605]1910 U.S. Census (population), Pennsylvania, Lehigh County, Bethlehem (Part of), E.D. 164, page 14B, lines 79-83, National Archives Microfilm Publication T624, Roll 1364, Household of Henry Erwin says they were married 44 years (i.e., 1866).

[606]*Portrait and Biographical Record of Lehigh, Northampton, and Carbon Counties*, (Chicago, Illinois: Chapman Publishing Company, 1894), 423 says:

In 1866 Mr. Erwin and Miss Jennie Gormly (sic) were united in marriage.

[607]Death Certificate for Henry Erwin, February 12, 1912, # 11928 & # 26, Pennsylvania Department of Vital Statistics, New Castle, Pennsylvania, says he was born March 5, 1842 in Ireland to John Erwin and Ann Davis (sic).

[608]Death Certificate for Henry Erwin, February 12, 1912, # 11928 & # 26, Pennsylvania Department of Vital Statistics, New Castle, Pennsylvania.

[609]Obituary of Henry Erwin, *The Allentown Public Call*, Tuesday, February 13, 1912, says:

Bethlehem. Northampton County, Pennsylvania.[610,611]

       U.S. CENSUS ENUMERATIONS. Although Jane Gormley appears to have been baptized under the name Peggy Jane Gormley, she was always known as Jennie.[612] In the 1850 census, she was enumerated in her parents' household on their property in Mahoning Township, Carbon County, Pennsylvania.[613] Her whereabouts at the time of the 1860 census are unknown.

       MARRIAGE OF JANE GORMLEY TO HENRY ERWIN. Jane Gormley is said to have married Henry Erwin in 1866, but where they were married and by whom is unknown.[614]

       HENRY ERWIN, PAINT MANUFACTURER. Jane (Gormley) Erwin's husband was a prominent paint manufacturer in South Bethlehem. He was the proprietor of the Blue Mountain Paint Works, which may later have been known as the firm of Henry Erwin and Sons, the largest manufacturer of paint in the Lehigh Valley.[615] The manufacturing plant was located on a five

---

       Henry Erwin, the well-known paint manufacturer and founder of Erwin's Paint Works along the Monocacy River near Bethlehem died yesterday. He was 71 years old. Death resulted from the effects of several strokes of paralysis, the first visitations being little more than six months ago.

[610]Death Certificate for Henry Erwin, February 12, 1912, # 11928 & # 26, Pennsylvania Department of Vital Statistics, New Castle, Pennsylvania, says he was buried at Nisky Hill Cemetery on February 15, 1912.

[611]Death Certificate for Jennie Erwin, May 7, 1915, # 45749 & # 77, Pennsylvania Department of Vital Statistics, New Castle, Pennsylvania, says she was buried at Nisky Hill Cemetery on May 10, 1915.

[612]Letter dated November 13, 2003 from Edith Ann Szczecina, Secretary, First Presbyterian Church of Panther Valley, 44 West White Street, P.O. Box 36, Summit Hill, Pennsylvania 18250 to Kathryn C. Torpey, 5035 Domain Place, Alexandria, Virginia 22311-5066 provided copies of three pages of the baptismal register containing entries # 34 to # 140, inclusive.

[613]1850 U.S. Census (population), Pennsylvania, Carbon County, Mahoning Township, page 388, lines 11-18, National Archives Microfilm Publication M432, Roll 762, Household of Joseph Gormley.

[614]*Portrait and Biographical Record of Lehigh, Northampton, and Carbon Counties*, (Chicago, Illinois: Chapman Publishing Company, 1894), 423.

[615]*National Register Listed Eligible Properties*, Pennsylvania Historical Museum Commission, Bureau of Historic Preservation, Northampton County, p. 198, states:

acre tract and employed about twenty people. The paints were shipped all around the country, but the principal markets were in New York and Chicago. The firm specialized in red and ochre (a reddish-yellow color) paints. They also dealt largely in imported umbers (a brown earthlike color) and siennias (a yellowish-brown color).

Henry Erwin immigrated to the United States in 1843 with his parents, John and Nancy (Dougherty/Davis) Erwin.[616] Initially, Henry Erwin's father was employed in the coal mines in Summit Hill. Later, he purchased a farm near Lehighton. The Erwin family farm appears to have been located partly in Mauch Chunk Township and partly in Mahoning Township along the same road where Margaret (Montgomery) Gormley bought 50 acres of land in 1859.[617]

At the age of eighteen, Henry Erwin was apprenticed to learn the blacksmith trade at Mauch Chunk, and later he went to Janesville where he became a machinist and boiler maker at the Janesville Locomotive Shops. In 1864, he accepted a position with a coal company and was put in charge of the mining machinery at Yorktown. In 1866, he relocated to Lehighton where he opened a blacksmith shop. It may have been then that Henry Erwin renewed his acquaintance with Jane Gormley whom he must have known since they were both children given that their

<hr>

Municipality:	Bethlehem City
Key No.	102486
Historic Name:	Henry Erwin & Sons Manufacturers of Mineral Paints
Address:	Schoenersville & Mauch Chunk Rds
Status:	Eligible
Status Date:	09/22/1994

[616]The following conflicting information exists concerning the name of Henry Erwin's mother:

1) *Portrait and Biographical Record of Lehigh, Northampton, and Carbon Counties*, (Chicago, Illinois: Chapman Publishing Company, 1894), p. 423, says Henry Erwin's mother was Nancy, the daughter of William, and Margaret (Davis) Dougherty.

2) Charles Rhoads Roberts, compiler, *History of Lehigh County, Pennsylvania, and a Genealogical and Biographical Record of Its Families*, (Allentown, Pennsylvania: Lehigh Valley Publishing Company, Ltd., 1914), p. 317, 318 says Henry Erwin's mother was Nancy, the daughter of William, and Margaret (Davis) Dougherty.

3) Death Certificate for Henry Erwin, February 12, 1912, # 11928 & # 26, Pennsylvania Department of Vital Statistics, New Castle, Pennsylvania says Henry Erwin's mother was Ann Davis.

4) Obituary of Henry Erwin, *Bethlehem Globe Times,* Tuesday, February 13, 1912, p. 1, Bethlehem Area Public Library, 11 West Church Street, Bethlehem, Pennsylvania, 18018-5888 says Henry Erwin's mother was Ann Davis.

[617]Deed from John Erwin & Wife to Thomas Erwin, March 26, 1861 (recorded July 26, 1866), Volume 13, p. 26, Deeds, Volumes 12-15, 1864-1867, Carbon County, Pennsylvania, FHL Microfilm Roll 2208977.

fathers worked together as coal miners in Summit Hill before they bought their farms.

In 1867, after Henry Erwin's marriage to Jane Gormley, he removed to Bethlehem where he engaged in mining iron ore. He leased ground for these purposes near Bath. He changed his place of business from time to time finally becoming the proprietor of a metallic paint and iron ore mine near the Lehigh Gap in Carbon County. He manufactured about 30 shades of paint. For this purpose he used about fifteen kinds of minerals some of which he imported. He also operated mines in other parts of Pennsylvania, New Jersey, and Virginia including the Bermuda Ochre Company which was incorporated with a capital of $32,000.00. The company owned 900 acres of land between Petersburg and City Point on the Appomattox River in Virginia.[618,619]

THE LATER YEARS. Henry and Jane (Gormley) Erwin appear to have spent their entire married life in Bethlehem.

In the 1870 census, Henry Erwin and his household were enumerated in South Bethlehem, Northampton County, Pennsylvania.[620] The enumeration was as follows:

SOUTH BETHLEHEM, NORTHAMPTON COUNTY, PENNSYLVANIA, AUGUST 5, 1870

Erwin, Henry	28 M	Teamster	$4,000 $2,000	Pa (sic)
, Jennie	27 F	Keeping House		Pa
, Willie	4 M			Pa
, Minnie	3 F			Pa
, Lillie	3/12 F			Pa
Boyd, Maggie	15 F	Dressmaker		Pa
Camsey, James	30 M	Laborer		Pa

In the 1880 census, Henry Erwin and his household were enumerated in Hanover Township, Lehigh County, Pennsylvania.[621] The enumeration was as follows:

---

[618]*Portrait and Biographical Record of Lehigh, Northampton, and Carbon Counties,* (Chicago, Illinois: Chapman Publishing Company, 1894), 423.

[619]Charles Rhoads Roberts, compiler, *History of Lehigh County, Pennsylvania, and a Genealogical and Biographical Record of Its Families,* (Allentown, Pennsylvania: Lehigh Valley Publishing Company, Ltd., 1914), 317, 318.

[620]1870 U.S. Census (population), Pennsylvania, Northampton County, South Bethlehem, page 335, lines 5-11, National Archives Microfilm Publication M593, Roll 1381, Household of Henry Erwin.

[621]1880 U.S. Census (population), Pennsylvania, Lehigh County, Hanover Township, E.D. 210, page 689A, lines 6-14, National Archives Microfilm Publication T9, Roll 1148, Household of Henry Erwin.

HANOVER TOWNSHIP, LEHIGH COUNTY, PENNSYLVANIA, JUNE 19, 1880

Erwin, Henry	M 37	Manufacturer of Paint	Ireland
, Jenny	F 35	Keeping House	Pa
, William	M 12	at school	Pa
, Minnie	F 11	at school	Pa
, Jenny	F 8	at school	Pa
, Harry	M 6		Pa
, John	M 4		Pa
, Joseph	M 2		Pa
, Maggie	F 8/12		Pa

In the absence of an 1890 census, Henry Erwin was found in the *Bethlehem City Directory* where he was listed as a paint manufacturer living at 120 Broad. w b, South Bethlehem.[622]

In the 1900 census, Henry Erwin and his household were enumerated in West Bethlehem, Lehigh County, Pennsylvania.[623] The enumeration was as follows:

WEST BETHLEHEM, LEHIGH COUNTY, PENNSYLVANIA, JUNE 7, 1900

Erwin, Henry	M May 1842	Ireland	Arrived 1840; Naturalized citizen Paint Manufacturer
, Jennie	F Mar 1843	Pa	8 children, 7 living
, Minnie	F Nov 1868	Pa	
, John	M Feb 1879	Pa	
, Margaret	F Sep 1880	Pa	

In the 1910 census, Henry Erwin and his household were again enumerated in Bethlehem, Lehigh County, Pennsylvania.[624] The enumeration was as follows:

BETHLEHEM (PART OF), LEHIGH COUNTY, PENNSYLVANIA, MAY 3, 1910

Erwin, Henry	M 70 Ireland		M 44 years	Arrived 1840 Naturalized citizen Own Income
, Jane	F 67 Pa		M 44 yrs	8 children, 7 living
Curtis, Minnie	F 41 Pa		M 8 yrs	3 children, 2 living
, Henry	M 7 Pa			
, Dorothy	F 3 Pa			

----

[622]Bethlehem, Pennsylvania Directory, 1890, <<www.ancestry.com>>, downloaded December 4, 2000.

[623]1900 U.S. Census (population), Pennsylvania, Lehigh County, West Bethlehem, E.D. 0033, page 12, lines 18-22, National Archives Microfilm Publication T623, Roll 1429, Household of Henry Erwin.

[624]1910 U.S. Census (population), Pennsylvania, Lehigh County, Bethlehem (Part of), E.D. 164, page 14B, lines 79-83, National Archives Microfilm Publication T624, Roll 1364, Household of Henry Erwin.

140

THE CHARACTER OF JANE (GORMLEY) ERWIN. In marrying Henry Erwin, Jane (Gormley) Erwin eventually became a well-to-do woman. Although she may have been somewhat vain in that she concealed the fact that she was born in 1841 in order to appear younger than her husband, Henry Erwin, who was born in 1842, she never forgot her roots or neglected the needs of her brothers and sisters.

Despite allegations to the contrary made by her sister, Margaret (Gormley) Brashear, Jane (Gormley) Erwin not only appears to have kept in touch with her family, but she helped them when they needed help.[625] At the time of the 1870 census, her niece, Maggie Boyd, the daughter of Matilda (Gormley) Boyd, was enumerated in the Erwin household in South Bethlehem.[626] And, in 1903, Jane (Gormley) Erwin was the executrix who handled the final disposition of her mother's estate after the death of her brother, William Gormley, who had been left a life estate in some property in Summit Hill owned by their mother.[627] In addition to assuring that William Gormley's children received clear title to the property in Summit Hill, Jane (Gormley) Erwin buried her brother in the Erwin family plot at Nisky Hill Cemetery.[628] She also appears to have helped her sister, Letitia (Gormley) Wallace, with the preparation of her will which was executed on July 13, 1903, just ten days after the death of their brother, William Gormley.[629]

THE DEATH AND BURIAL OF HENRY ERWIN. Henry Erwin died at the family home in

---

[625]Letter dated May 17, 1997 from Robert C. Gormley, 334 Brownsburg Road, Newtown, Pennsylvania 18940 to Kathryn C. Torpey, 5035 Domain Place, Alexandria, Virginia 22311-5066 provided copies of Margaret (Gormley) Brashear's letters from Shanghai, China, for transcription. In the letter dated July 11, 1870, from Margaret (Gormley) Brashear to her brother, Robert Gormley, she states, in part:

> I notice Jane never writes to me but no matter she can live without me and I am certain I can without her...

[626]1870 U.S. Census (population), Pennsylvania, Northampton County, South Bethlehem, page 335, lines 5-11, National Archives Microfilm Publication M593, Roll 1381, Household of Henry Erwin.

[627]Estate of Margaret Gormley, Summit Hill, # 1309, Carbon County Courthouse, Jim Thorpe, Pennsylvania, contains a document signed by Letitia (Gormley) Wallace on September 4, 1903, in Philadelphia renouncing her right to administer the final settlement of her mother's estate in favor of her sister, Jane (Gormley) Erwin.

[628]Henry Erwin Plot Profile, Lot # 185, Section F, Issued July 2, 1901, provided by the Superintendent, Nisky Hill Cemetery, 254 E. Church Street, Bethlehem, Pennsylvania 18018-6143 on August 22, 1997.

[629]Estate of Letitia Wallace, Philadelphia, # 19, 1915, Register of Wills, Philadelphia, Philadelphia County, Pennsylvania.

West Bethlehem on February 12, 1912, at 11:45 A.M.[630] His obituary appeared in the *Bethlehem Globe Times* on February 13, 1912.[631] It read as follows:

Henry Erwin

Henry Erwin died, yesterday at noon in his late home, 120 West Broad street, Bethlehem, of cerebral apoplexy. He was 69 years, 11 months, and 7 days old. He was born in County Derry, Ireland, March 5, 1842, a son of John and Ann Davis Erwin. He was successfully engaged as a paint manufacturer for about 40 years. He was a member of Wesley M.E. Church. He leaves his widow, four sons: William H., Harry, and Dr. Joseph of Bethlehem: and Dr. John of Richmond Hill, N.Y.; three daughters, Minnie, wife of the late B.O. Curtis, at home, Jenny, wife of Geo. Waltman of Bethlehem, and Margaret, wife of Judson Smull of Palmerton; four grandchildren, a sister in Ireland. The funeral will be held from his late home, on Tuesday, at 2:00 p.m. Service will be held in the house. Interment will be made in the family plot in Nisky Cemetery. The funeral will be private.

He was buried in the Erwin family plot at Nisky Hill Cemetery. The news story about his funeral read as follows:

Henry Erwin

The funeral of the late Henry Erwin took place, yesterday from his late home, 140 West Broad street, Bethlehem, at 2:00 p.m. Rev. W.C. Simpson of Wesley M.E. Church and Rev. James Robinson of the First Presbyterian Church officiated at the service. Interment was made in a family plot in Nisky Hill Cemetery. The pallbearers were four sons: William Erwin, Harry Erwin, John Erwin, and Joseph Erwin.[632]

THE DEATH AND BURIAL OF JANE (GORMLEY) ERWIN. Jane (Gormley) Erwin died at the family home in West Bethlehem on May 7, 1915, at 9 A.M.[633] Her obituary appeared in the *Bethlehem Globe Times* on May 7, 1915.[634] It read as follows:

Mrs. Henry Erwin

Jennie, widow of the late Henry Erwin, this 9:00 a.m. died of heart disease in the family home, 120 West Broad street, Bethlehem. Born in Mauch Chunk, March 1, 1843 (sic), a

---

[630]Lehigh County, Pennsylvania, Deaths, 1874 - 1918, FHL Microfilm Roll 2131072.

[631]Obituary of Henry Erwin, *Bethlehem Globe Times*, Tuesday, February 13, 1912, p. 1, Bethlehem Area Public Library, 11 West Church Street, Bethlehem, Pennsylvania, 18018-5888.

[632]Funeral of Henry Erwin, *Bethlehem Globe Times*, Tuesday, February 16, 1912, p. 1, Bethlehem Area Public Library, 11 West Church Street, Bethlehem, Pennsylvania, 18018-5888.

[633]Lehigh County, Pennsylvania, Deaths, 1874 - 1918, FHL Microfilm Roll 2131072.

[634]Obituary of Mrs. Henry Erwin, *Bethlehem Globe Times*, Friday, May 7, 1915, p. 12., Bethlehem Area Public Library, 11 West Church Street, Bethlehem, Pennsylvania, 18018-5888.

She, too, was buried in the Erwin family plot at Nisky Hill Cemetery in Bethlehem, Northampton County, Pennsylvania. The news story about her funeral read as follows:

Mrs. Henry Erwin

The funeral of the late Mrs. Henry Erwin yesterday afternoon took place from late home, 120 West Broad street, Bethlehem. Rev. James Robinson assisted by Rev. Dr. J.R.T. Gray, conducted the service in the house. Interment was made in Nisky Hill cemetery. Her four sons were the pallbearers.[635]

According to the plot diagram, there is a monument in the center of the Erwin family plot which is surrounded by seven burial stones including the stone of William M. (sic) Gormley, Jane (Gormley) Erwin's brother, who, ironically, was the first member of the family to be buried there.[636]

THE DESCENDANTS OF HENRY AND JANE (GORMLEY) ERWIN. Henry and Jane (Gormley) Erwin had eight children, one of whom died in infancy.[637]

Based on information contained in their parents' obituaries, their surviving children appear to have lived in and around Bethlehem and in New York City. They appear to have been well educated, financially secure, and to have married well.

One of their grandsons, the late Henry K. Erwin, an ophthalmologist, and the son of Henry H. and Anna (Kindt) Erwin, provided a brief written account of the Erwin family

---

[635]Funeral of Mrs. Henry Erwin, *Bethlehem Globe Times*, Tuesday, May 11, 1915, p. 1, Bethlehem Area Public Library, 11 West Church Street, Bethlehem, Pennsylvania, 18018-5888.

[636]Henry Erwin Plot Profile, Lot # 185, Section F, Issued July 2, 1901, provided by the Superintendent, Nisky Hill Cemetery, 254 E. Church Street, Bethlehem, Pennsylvania 18018-6143 on August 22, 1997.

[637]Letter dated July 28, 1997 from the late Henry K. Erwin, 803 N. Wahneta Street, Apt. 55, Allentown, Pennsylvania 18103-2414, to Kathryn C. Torpey, 5035 Domain Place, Alexandria, Virginia 22311-5066 provided a copy of the Erwin Family Tree dated 1936 containing the names and dates for the descendants of Henry and Jennie (Gormley) Erwin.

history.[638] It read as follows:

> Unfortunately we were never a closely knit family so while at one time I had a number of cousins we had very little contact with them even in the same city (Bethlehem).
>
> I don't remember hearing any family or Gormley stories as a youngster. I do know that my grandparents belonged to the Methodist Church which was recently sold and rebuilt on the outskirts of the city. It was an old church where services were held on the second floor making it difficult for the elderly and handicapped to attend. Incidentally my grandfather donated a stained glass window for the church - his name being included. We were raised in the Reformed Church which later became the Christ (sic) United Church of Christ.
>
> My grandparents were buried in the Nisky Hill Cemetery which at that time was probably the only cemetery in North Bethlehem other than the Moravian Cemetery (God's Acres). They had a plot there and it included a Wm. M. (sic) Gormley (1841-1903) - who he was or where the other Gormleys are buried I don't know. I just went to inspect the old plot today - I hadn't been there in years. Two of the names in the plot were Henry Erwin (1843-1915) and Jennie Erwin (1843-1915) - no middle name or initial.

---

[638]Letter dated August 20, 1997 from the late Henry K. Erwin, 803 N. Wahneta Street, Apt. 55, Allentown, Pennsylvania 18103-2414, to Kathryn C. Torpey, 5035 Domain Place, Alexandria, Virginia 22311-5066.

John Gormley was born August 5, 1843 in Summit Hill, Carbon County, Pennsylvania.[639] He died July 9, 1862, in Washington D.C.[640,641] He was buried at the U.S. Military Asylum Cemetery now known as the United States Soldiers' and Airmen's Home National Cemetery in Washington, D.C.[642,643]

U.S. CENSUS ENUMERATIONS. In the 1850 census and in the 1860 census, John Gormley was enumerated in his parents' household on their property located in Mahoning Township,

---

[639]Letter dated November 13, 2003 from Edith Ann Szczecina, Secretary, First Presbyterian Church of Panther Valley, 44 West White Street, P.O. Box 36, Summit Hill, Pennsylvania 18250 to Kathryn C. Torpey, 5035 Domain Place, Alexandria, Virginia 22311-5066 provided copies of three pages of the baptismal register containing entries # 34 to # 140, inclusive, which state the following with respect to the members of the Gormley family:

REGISTER OF BAPTISMS:

NO.	CHILD	PARENTS	BORN	BAPTIZED
40	Peggy (sic) Jane	Joseph & Jane (sic) Gormley	1841	May 16, 1841
89	John	Joseph & Jane (sic) Gormley	August 5, 1843	
133	William	Joseph & Jane (sic) Gormley		April 7, 1847

[640]Union Compiled Military Service Record of John Gormley, Cos. H & G, 81st Pennsylvania Infantry, Records of the Adjutant General's Office, Record Group 94, National Archives, Washington, D.C., states John Gormley died July 9, 1862.

[641]Margaret Gormley, Civil War Dependent Relative Pension Application File, MO 246,903, Records of the Veterans Administration, Record Group 15, National Archives, Washington, D.C., states John Gormley died July 9, 1862.

[642]Letter dated November 20, 1996, from Lincoln T. Berry, Superintendent, United States Soldiers' and Airmen's Home National Cemetery, 21 Harewood Road, N.W., Washington, D.C. 20011 to Kathryn C. Torpey, 5035 Domain Place, Alexandria, Virginia 22311 states, in part, "Our records reflect that John Gormenly (sic) is buried at this cemetery. He is buried in Section: C Grave: 2769."

[643]This cemetery is managed by the Department of the Army. It was originally known as the U.S. Military Asylum Cemetery, but later changed its name to the United States Soldiers' and Airmen's Home National Cemetery.

Carbon County, Pennsylvania.[644,645] According to the depositions that appeared in his mother's request for a dependent relative pension, he was single, lived at home, and worked as a hired hand on the farms in Mahoning Township principally to earn money to support his parents.[646]

SERVICE IN THE CIVIL WAR. During the Civil War, John Gormley served as a private in Company G of the 81st Regiment of the Pennsylvania Volunteers.[647,648,649]

John Gormley originally enlisted on August 22, 1861, in Summit Hill, as a Private in Company H of the 36th Regiment Pennsylvania Infantry for a period of three years. Company H of the 36th Regiment subsequently became Company H of the 37st Regiment Pennsylvania Infantry which subsequently became Company H of the 81st Regiment Pennsylvania Infantry. On November 1, 1861, John Gormley was officially transferred from Company H to Company G of the 81st Regiment Pennsylvania Infantry.

The 81st Regiment consisted of six companies from Philadelphia and four from Carbon and Luzerne Counties. Recruiting began in August 1861 and the men reported at the general camp of rendezvous near Easton, Northampton County, Pennsylvania. On October 10, 1861, the regiment proceeded to Washington, D.C., and went into camp at Kendall Green. Two weeks

---

[644]1850 U.S. Census (population), Pennsylvania, Carbon County, Mahoning Township, page 388, lines 11-18, National Archives Microfilm Publication M432, Roll 762, Household of Joseph Gormley.

[645]1860 U.S. Census (population), Pennsylvania, Carbon County, Mahoning Township, page 972, lines 11-20, National Archives Microfilm Publication M653, Roll 1089, Household of Joseph Gomly (sic).

[646]Margaret Gormley, Civil War Dependent Relative Pension Application File, MO 246,903, Records of the Veterans Administration, Record Group 15, National Archives, Washington, D.C.

[647]Union Compiled Military Service Record of John Gormley, Cos. H & G, 81st Pennsylvania Infantry, Records of the Adjutant General's Office, Record Group 94, National Archives, Washington, D.C.

[648]J.D. Laciar, *Patriotism of Carbon County, Pennsylvania*, (Mauch Chunk, Pennsylvania, n.s., 1867), 45, says:

> Gormerly (sic), John   Enlisted 1861   Died 1862

[649]Samuel P. Bates, *History of the Pennsylvania Volunteers - 1861 - 1865*, (Harrisburg, Pennsylvania: B. Singlerly, State Printer, 1869). Volume IV:1191, says:

> Gormerly (sic), John; Private; mustered in __ 61; term 3 years; died 1862

later it moved to a camp overlooking the East Branch of the Potomac River and the Navy Yard where it was engaged in the defense of Washington until March 1, 1862, when it began active operations in the area of Northern Virginia.[650,651,652]

Having completed its mission, the regiment retired to Alexandria and from there proceeded south where it engaged in the Peninsular Campaign.[653]

While John Gormley was stationed in Alexandria he wrote at least one letter home to his parents. This letter survived because it is contained in his mother's application for a dependent relative pension.[654] The letter read as follows:

---

[650]John Gormley enlisted at the same time and place as a man named John Boyd who served as a Sergeant in Company H of the 81st Regiment. Sergeant John Boyd died at Camp California, Alexandria, Virginia, on February 6, 1862, and was buried in the National Cemetery in Alexandria, Virginia. To date, it has not been possible to determine whether Sergeant John Boyd was related to the John Boyd who married Matilda (Gormley) Boyd.

[651]Additional information about Sergeant John Boyd is contained in the following application by his father for a dependent relative pension: James Boyd, Civil War Dependent Relative Pension Application File, FO 293,274, FC 280,814, Records of the Veterans Administration, Record Group 15, National Archives, Washington, D.C.

[652]Letter dated August 28, 2000 from Ted Dombroski, 81st PVI, Co. K, 768 McNair Street, Hazelton, Pennsylvania 18201-2639 to Kathryn C. Torpey, 5035 Domain Place, Alexandria, Virginia 22311-5066 states that his group is in possession of a letter from a Sergeant John Williamson, Co. K, to his wife in which he mentioned the death of Sergeant John Boyd of Co. H who enlisted with John Gormley, the subject of this family history. It is unknown whether Sergeant John Williamson who wrote the letter is related to the Henry Williamson who sold 50 acres of land in Mahoning Township to John Boyd, the husband of Matilda (Gormley) Boyd. Sergeant John Williamson was killed on June 29, 1862 at Charles City Cross Roads. His letter states, in part:

> Sergeant John Boyd of Company H died on Wednesday night and his company buried him at the forte on Friday. I believe he is only to be buried there till they find where his friends are and then he will be sent home.

[653]Samuel P. Bates, *History of the Pennsylvania Volunteers - 1861 - 1865*, (Harrisburg, Pennsylvania: B. Singlerly, State Printer, 1869). Volume IV:1167-1169.

[654]Margaret Gormley, Civil War Dependent Relative Pension Application File, MO 246,903, Records of the Veterans Administration, Record Group 15, National Archives, Washington, D.C., contains the original letter written by John Gormley.

Alexander Virginnia
March the 7, 1862

Dear father and mother and brother I now lift my pen to right to yous to let yous know
that I am well at present and hoping that these few lines will find yous in the same state of
health   I let you know that I receve you kind letter on the forth of March and I was glad
to here from yous and that yous all ar all well   I let yous know that I receve the mits and
tobacco wich yous sent to me   we had good liven as long as the boxes lasted   when you
right I wich yous wod send me some postage stamps   I send my best respect to Robbert
Sinard (sic) [Robert Sinyard] and all the rest and [-------]   So that['s] all at present but
remain your brothe John Gormley

John Gormley

yous can tell Ruben Selner (sic) [Reuben Zellner] that Henry sent a box home and for him
to go to Lehighton and get it

During the Peninsular Campaign, the 81st Regiment participated in building roads and
fatigue duty during the siege of Yorktown and the march upon Williamsburg. At Chickahominy,
the regiment participated in building the famous Sumner Bridge (aka the Grape Vine Bridge).
On May 30, 1862, the Confederates attacked the Union forces at Fair Oaks (aka Seven Pines).
From that time forward the duty in the trenches and upon the skirmish line was brutal. Many
men were wounded or killed in unfamiliar places with curious names such as the Nine Mile
Road, the Peach Orchard, Savage Station, and the White Oak Swamp. But, by far, the 81st
Regiment sustained its most severe losses during the Peninsular Campaign at the battle ground of
Charles City Cross Roads where the battle raged with unabated fury.[655]

THE DEATH OF JOHN GORMLEY. Exactly where John Gormley became a casualty of the
Peninsular Campaign is unknown.[656,657,658] The Casualty Sheet in his compiled military service

---

[655]Samuel P. Bates, *History of the Pennsylvania Volunteers - 1861 - 1865*, (Harrisburg,
Pennsylvania: B. Singlerly, State Printer, 1869). Volume IV:1167-1169.

[656]Letter dated December 3, 1996, from Robert C. Gormley, 334 Brownsburg Road,
Newtown, Pennsylvania 18940 to Kathryn C. Torpey, 5035 Domain Place, Alexandria, Virginia
22311-5066 recounts the family legend concerning the death and burial of John Gormley as
follows:

When I was born (in S. Hill) the town was sprinkled with Gormleys married and
unmarried. Among "the family" were at least seven nephews and nieces of (soldier) John,
my grandfather, of course, being one of them. At an early age (probably five or six) I was
informed by grandpop that his uncle John was killed at Antietam and was undoubtedly
buried in one of the unidentified graves in the national cemetery at Sharpsburg. Other
"old" members of the family recited the same story from time to time.

Curious about this, I finally went to Antietam in the late 50s and spoke with Park officials
there about Union dead ID'd in the cemetery. Unfortunately, they could only verify that

record states:

> This man was admitted to Douglas G.H., Washington, D.C., July 4; 62, with a gunshot
> wound (diagnosis also appears remittent fever) and died July 9th 1862, of typhoid fever
> and gunshot wound.[659]

The Surgeon General's Report that appears in John Gormley's mother's application for a dependent relative pension reiterates:

> John Gorman (sic) Priv. Co. G 81st Pa. Vol. was admitted to Douglas G.H. Washington,
> D.C. July 4, 1862 with vulnus sclopeticum[660] diagnosis also shown as remittent fever and
> died July 9, 1862, No further [-----] of soldier's treatment found. There are no records of

---

> the 81st PV participated in the battle and that according to Bates, John Gormerly (Co. G)
> died in 1862. This seemed to match the family legend; so I put in on the back burner,
> went to work, and didn't pick it up again until 1977, when, caught up in my relic hunting
> and collecting I wrote to the Archives for his records.

> By that time only Dad's generation of Gormleys survived in S. Hill, but the story of
> John's demise at Antietam persisted. Obviously, the War Dep't records changed that.
> Several of Dad's cousins, as I recall, were a mite skeptical of my declaration that John
> had been wounded at White Oak Swamp and died soon after in Washington, D.C. No
> one, they said, had ever mentioned that.

[657]Conversation in May 1995 with William S. Chambers, 9221 West Broward Boulevard, Plantation, Florida 33324-2415 in which he stated that he remembered his mother, Mary Ann (McCauley) Chambers, saying that her grandmother, Letitia (Gormley) Wallace, claimed her brother "Johnny" was killed in the war, but his mother mistakenly believed her great-uncle, John Gormley, was a Confederate soldier.

[658]Letter dated November 7, 2003 from Robert C. Gormley, 334 Brownsburg Road, Newtown, Pennsylvania 18940 to Kathryn C. Torpey, 5035 Domain Place, Alexandria, Virginia 22311-5066 contains a copy of an article by Ed Gildea entitled "Summit Hill Woman Murdered in China" that appeared in a June 1973 issue of *The Valley Gazette* in which John M. Gormley, great-grandson of Joseph and Margaret (Montgomery) Gormley, relates the family legend concerning the death of John Gormley. In the article John M. Gormley relates the erroneous belief that:

> Four of Mr. and Mrs. Joseph Gormley's sons served with Carbon County's famed Eighty-
> First Regiment. They were John, James, Robert, and Joseph. John never came home. He
> was killed in the battle of Antietam and was buried on the battlefield in a mass grave.

[659]Union Compiled Military Service Record of John Gormley, Cos. H & G, 81st Pennsylvania Infantry, Records of the Adjutant General's Office, Record Group 94, National Archives, Washington, D.C.

[660]i.e., a gunshot wound.

this regiment on file prior to Nov. 23 1862.[661,662]

THE BURIAL OF JOHN GORMLEY. John Gormley's funeral preparations were begun at 4 P.M. on July 9, 1862, and he was buried at the U.S. Military Asylum Cemetery the same day he died.[663] He was buried in Section C, Grave 2769. His headstone was mistakenly engraved with the name John Gormenly.[664,665]

---

[661]Margaret Gormley, Civil War Dependent Relative Pension Application File, MO 246,903, Records of the Veterans Administration, Record Group 15, National Archives, Washington, D.C., contains the Surgeon General's Report for the subject of this family history.

[662]Margaret Gormelly (sic), Civil War Dependent Relative Pension Application File, WO 2523, WC 610, Records of the Veterans Administration, Record Group 15, National Archives, Washington, D.C., reveals that there was a *second* man named John Gormley who served in Co. A, 88th New York Infantry. He died on June 15, 1862, while on picket duty during the Battle of Fair Oaks in the Peninsular Campaign. When Margaret (Montgomery) Gormley applied for a dependent relative pension, the records of both John Gormleys became somewhat co-mingled and documentation regarding the death of both men appears in the compiled military service record of the subject of this family history and in his mother's application for a dependent relative pension. The second John Gormley was from Philadelphia. He married Margaret Wilson at St. Augustine's Roman Catholic Church in Philadelphia on November 10, 1846, and had three children, Annie C., John, and Catharine. His widow, Margaret (Wilson) Gormley, was enumerated in the 1890 Census of Civil War Veterans and Their Widows. The 1890 census entry contains the following information concerning the second John Gormley:

> John Gormley, Pvt. Co. A, 88th New York Infantry
> 16 Dec 1861 to Jun 15 1862
> Killed at the Battle of Fair Oaks
> Widow, Margaret Gormley living at 1710 Latimer Street, Philadelphia

[663]*Alphabetical Index to Places of Interment of Deceased Union Soldiers in the Various States and Territories as Specified in Rolls of Honor Nos. I-XIII*, (Washington, D.C.: Government Printing Office, 1868), 35 concerning burials in the Military Asylum Cemetery, Washington, D.C., says: "Gorman (sic), John, Private, 81st Pennsylvania, Co. G, July 9, 1862.

[664]Letter dated November 20, 1996 from Lincoln T. Berry, Superintendent, United States Soldiers' and Airmen's Home National Cemetery, 21 Harewood Road, N.W., Washington, D.C. 20011 to Kathryn C. Torpey, 5035 Domain Place, Alexandria, Virginia 22311 states, in part: "According to the information you provided in your letter, the last name on the headstone and the last name recorded in the Cemetery files on your ancestor is incorrectly spelled. If you will mail an official document showing the correct spelling of the last name, I will order a new headstone."

[665]Letter dated December 17, 1996 from Lincoln T. Berry, Superintendent, United States Soldiers' and Airmen's Home National Cemetery, 21 Harewood Road, N.W., Washington, D.C.

The headstone was replaced.[666,667] It now reads:

JOHN
GORMLEY
PVT
CO. G
81 PA INF
JUL 9 1862

THE AFTERMATH. Margaret (Montgomery) Gormley's application for a Civil War dependent relative pension indicates that after the death of her son, she and her husband received his back pay and his bounty allowance.[668] There is no indication in the record that they ever knew exactly where he died or where he was buried, a mystery that was not unraveled for more than 135 years.

LEST WE FORGET. In 1908, J.F. Kessley wrote a booklet named *Patriotism* in order to preserve the names of the men who enlisted from the Mahoning Township School District and who served during the Civil War. The booklet contains the name of John Gormley among the names of the 66 men from the Mahoning Township School District and the names of 135 other men who served from Mahoning Township.

The Soldiers Memorial tablet containing these names was originally placed in the New Mahoning School building on September 12, 1908. As of 2001, the memorial tablet hung on the wall of the Mahoning Township Elementary School in Lehighton.[669]

20011 to Kathryn C. Torpey, 5035 Domain Place, Alexandria, Virginia 22311 states: "I received the documents [you sent] verifying the correct spelling of the last name of John Gormley. A new headstone has been ordered. It will take 4-6 months before the headstone is received. I will advise you when the new headstone is set."

[666]Site visit on May 23, 1998 to the United States Soldiers' and Airmen's Home National Cemetery revealed that the headstone for John Gormley had been replaced, as requested.

[667]Letter dated November 19, 1998 from Lincoln T. Berry, Superintendent, United States Soldiers' and Airmen's Home National Cemetery, 21 Harewood Road, N.W., Washington, D.C. 20011 to Kathryn C. Torpey, 5035 Domain Place, Alexandria, Virginia 22311 provided official confirmation that the headstone of John Gormley had been replaced, as requested.

[668]Margaret Gormley, Civil War Dependent Relative Pension Application File, MO 246,903, Records of the Veterans Administration, Record Group 15, National Archives, Washington, D.C.

[669]Carolyn Zimmerman Johns, *Beyond the Blue Mountain: Mahoning Township Records:*

On that tablet is said to appear the following information concerning the subject of this family history:

GORMLY (sic), John	Co. G 31st (sic) Regiment	Member Mahoning School District
GORMLY (sic), John	Co. G 81st Regiment	Member Mahoning School District

Tax, Census, Cemetery, and Military Veteran for Carbon County, Schuylkill County, and Northampton County, Pennsylvania, (Bowie, Maryland: Heritage Books, Inc., 2001), 305.

William B. Gormley was born February 12, 1846 in Summit Hill, Carbon County, Pennsylvania.[670,671,672] He died July 3, 1903, probably in the Borough of Fountain Hill, Lehigh County, Pennsylvania.[673,674,675] He married Mary Catherine Hartman the daughter of Alexander and Jane (Campbell) Hartman on March 21, 1874 in Mauch Chunk, Carbon County, Pennsylvania.[676,677,678,679] She was born September 12, 1856 in Weissport, Franklin Township,

---

[670]Deed of Release from Joseph Gormley & Wife to Smith Gormley, November 14, 1860 (recorded November 16, 1860), Volume 10, p. 554, Deeds, Volumes 10-12, 1859-1864, Carbon County, Pennsylvania, FHL Microfilm Roll 2208976 states that the youngest child, i.e., William Gormley, had attained the age of fourteen, thus his older brother, Smith Gormley, was being released from his obligation for maintenance and support of his younger brother. This suggests that William Gormley was born in 1846.

[671]1900 U.S. Census (population), Pennsylvania, Lehigh County, Fountain Hill, E.D. 0048, page 5, line 21, National Archives Microfilm Publication T623, Roll 1429, Saint Luke's Hospital, says born: February 1847.

[672]Henry Erwin Plot Profile, Lot # 185, Section F, Issued July 2, 1901, provided by the Superintendent, Nisky Hill Cemetery, 254 E. Church Street, Bethlehem, Pennsylvania 18018-6143 on August 22, 1997 erroneously states the date of birth of William B. Gormley was February 12, 1841 (sic).

[673]Edward J. Redding, *The History of Fountain Hill, Pennsylvania,* (n.s., Edward J. Redding, 1996), p. unk, states that in 1892 there was a concerted effort to unite the three Bethlehems - Bethlehem, South Bethlehem, and West Bethlehem, but the residents of the Lehigh County portion of South Bethlehem resisted this effort. Fountain Hill was then located in that portion of South Bethlehem that was in Lehigh County. The next year, on November 7, 1893, the residents of Fountain Hill voted to become the Borough of Fountain Hill in Lehigh County.

[674]Estate of William Gormley, # 3065, Carbon County Courthouse, Jim Thorpe, Pennsylvania, contains a petition dated March 12, 1904, stating that William Gormley died July 3, 1903 in Lehigh County, Pennsylvania.

[675]Letter dated July 10, 1997 from Thea M. Tarreto, Assistant Clerk Orphans' Court Division, Lehigh County Court of Common Pleas to Kathryn C. Torpey, 5035 Domain Place, Alexandria, Virginia 22311-5066 states that although the records of the court cover the period 1893 to 1905, there is no record of the death of William Gormley in their records. However, they believe that many deaths during that period were mistakenly not recorded.

[676]Conversation on June 24, 1997 with Robert C. Gormley, 334 Brownsburg Road, Newtown, Pennsylvania 18940 in which he provided Mary Kalphant as a possible maiden name

Carbon County, Pennsylvania.[680,681] She died April 11, 1922 in Allentown, Lehigh County, Pennsylvania.[682] They were buried in separate plots at Nisky Hill Cemetery, Northampton County, Pennsylvania.[683,684,685]

---

for William B. Gormley's wife is in error.

[677]1860 U.S. Census (population), Pennsylvania, Carbon County, Franklin Township, page 23, lines 23-27, National Archives Microfilm Publication M653, Roll 1089, Household of Alex Hartman.

[678]Death Certificate for Mary Gormley, April 11, 1922, # 38576 & # 453, Pennsylvania Division of Vital Statistics, New Castle, Pennsylvania 16103 incorrectly states her father's name was Jacob Hartman.

[679]Mauch Chunk Mission of the Evangelical Association, Carbon County, Pennsylvania, FHL Microfilm Roll 1305775 says:

| March 21, 1874 | William B. Gormley and Mary C. Hartman | Mahoning, Carbon Co. Weissport | B.F. Bohner Minister |

[680]Death Certificate for Mary Gormley, April 11, 1922, # 38576 & # 453, Pennsylvania Division of Vital Statistics, New Castle, Pennsylvania 16103 contains a date of birth that is consistent with her age as contained in the 1890 Census Directory of Northampton County and the 1920 Census for Lehigh County cited elsewhere in this section.

[681]Letter dated December 29, 2003 from Diane E. Owen, Bethlehem Area Moravians, Inc., 1021 Center Street, Bethlehem, Pennsylvania 18018 to Kathryn C. Torpey, 5035 Domain Place, Alexandria, Virginia 22311-5066 contains a copy of the Interment Record of Mrs. Mary Gormley that states she was born in Weissport, Pa.

[682]Death Certificate for Mary Gormley, April 11, 1922, # 38576 & # 453, Pennsylvania Division of Vital Statistics, New Castle, Pennsylvania 16103.

[683]Henry Erwin Plot Profile, Lot # 185, Section F, Issued July 2, 1901, provided by the Superintendent, Nisky Hill Cemetery, 254 E. Church Street, Bethlehem, Pennsylvania 18018-6143 on August 22, 1997 states that William Gormley's date of death was July 3, 1903.

[684]Death Certificate for Mary Gormley, April 11, 1922, # 38576 & # 453, Pennsylvania Division of Vital Statistics, New Castle, Pennsylvania 16103.

[685]Letter dated December 29, 2003 from Diane E. Owen, Bethlehem Area Moravians, Inc., 1021 Center Street, Bethlehem, Pennsylvania 18018 to Kathryn C. Torpey, 5035 Domain Place, Alexandria, Virginia 22311-5066 contains a plot profile for the plot owned by James and Harry Gormley, the sons of Mary (Hartman) Gormley, Section O, Southern One-Half of Plot No.

U.S. CENSUS ENUMERATIONS. William B. Gormley was the youngest of all the children of Joseph and Margaret (Montgomery) Gormley. In the 1850 census, the 1860 census and in the 1870 census, he was enumerated in his parents' household on their property located in Mahoning Township, Carbon County, Pennsylvania.[686] [687] [688]

THE EARLY YEARS. William B. Gormley was named after his brother who died, tragically, in a fire said to have been in the family home in Summit Hill. Much like his sister, Jane, and brother, John, who were also born in America, he, too, was baptized in the First Presbyterian Church of Summit Hill and Tamaqua.[689]

Shortly after he was born, the Gormley family moved to Mahoning Township where Joseph Gormley had bought a farm. William B. Gormley grew up on the farm and, after the death of his brother, John Gormley, in 1862, he appears to have been the son who took primary responsibility for the maintenance and support of his parents.

His sister, Margaret (Gormley) Brashear, made the following comments about her brother

---

15 showing that their mother was buried in their plot in Nisky Hill Cemetery.

[686]1850 U.S. Census (population), Pennsylvania, Carbon County, Mahoning Township, page 388, lines 11-18, National Archives Microfilm Publication M432, Roll 762, Household of Joseph Gormley.

[687]1860 U.S. Census (population), Pennsylvania, Carbon County, Mahoning Township, page 972, lines 11-20, National Archives Microfilm Publication M653, Roll 1089, Household of Joseph Gomly (sic).

[688]1870 U.S. Census (population), Pennsylvania, Carbon County, Mahoning Township, page 172, lines 38-30, National Archives Microfilm Publication M593, Roll 1320, Household of Joseph Gormley.

[689]Letter dated November 13, 2003 from Edith Ann Szczecina, Secretary, First Presbyterian Church of Panther Valley, 44 West White Street, P.O. Box 36, Summit Hill, Pennsylvania 18250 to Kathryn C. Torpey, 5035 Domain Place, Alexandria, Virginia 22311-5066 provided copies of three pages of the baptismal register containing entries # 34 to # 140, inclusive, which suggests that William Gormley was born in 1847:

REGISTER OF BAPTISMS:

NO.	CHILD	PARENTS	BORN	BAPTIZED
40	Peggy (sic) Jane	Joseph & Jane (sic) Gormley	1841	May 16, 1841
89	John	Joseph & Jane (sic) Gormley	August 5, 1843	
133	William	Joseph & Jane (sic) Gormley		April 7, 1847

in two of her letters from Shanghai.[690] The letter dated December 23, 1869, says:

> ... I am so pleased Billy did not start for California for he would have seen hard times in a strange country without money tell him to be kind to our old father and mother and remain as near as possible to them while they live...

The letter dated March 12, 1871, says:

> ...Billy made a mistake while I was in California in the number of my Box in the Post Office through carelessness on his part and through that he did not get the money to send him to school...

> ...oh how I do long to see you all once more and particularly my dear little brother Billy I suppose he is not so small but in looking back I only see him a little child in Mahoning my poor child he is not strong but never mind should God spare me my dear little brother shall be taken care of and should I die he will be still better off...

MARRIAGE TO MARY CATHERINE HARTMAN. On March 21, 1874, William B. Gormley married Mary Catherine Hartman at the Mauch Chunk Mission of the Evangelical Association.[691] She was the daughter of Alexander and Jane (Campbell) Hartman.[692] She had at least three siblings - William Harrison, James A., and Letitia Ann. There is some speculation, as yet unproven, that her family might have been related to the Hartman family that lived in Poughkeepsie, Dutchess County, New York, whose daughter, Louise E. Hartman, married George Stephen Wallace, the youngest son of Stephen and Letitia (Gormley) Wallace.

After they were married, William and Mary (Hartman) Gormley are believed to have lived initially in Summit Hill because, in 1874, William B. Gormley served as the executor of the estate of John Boyd, the husband of his sister, Matilda (Gormley) Boyd. In a legal document dated October 6, 1874, contained in John Boyd's estate file, William B. Gormley is said by his sister, Matilda (Gormley) Boyd, to be "of Summit Hill."[693]

---

[690]Letter dated May 17, 1997 from Robert C. Gormley, 334 Brownsburg Road, Newtown, Pennsylvania 18940 to Kathryn C. Torpey, 5035 Domain Place, Alexandria, Virginia 22311-5066 provided copies of these letters for transcription.

[691]Mauch Chunk Mission of the Evangelical Association, Carbon County, Pennsylvania, FHL Microfilm Roll 1305775.

[692]Death Certificate for Mary Gormley, April 11, 1922, # 38576 & # 453, Pennsylvania Division of Vital Statistics, New Castle, Pennsylvania 16103 incorrectly states that her father's name was Jacob Hartman.

[693]Estate of John Boyd, Placer County, California, # 0848, Carbon County Courthouse, Jim Thorpe, Pennsylvania.

THE LATER YEARS. By the time of the 1880 census, William B. Gormley and his family were enumerated in Lansford Borough living directly beside Margaret (Glenn) Gormley, the widow of his brother, James Gormley.[694] The enumeration was as follows:

LANSFORD BOROUGH, CARBON COUNTY, PENNSYLVANIA, JUNE 18, 1880

Gormly, (sic) Maggie	F 33			Pa.
, John	M 13	works in mine*		Pa.
, Samuel	M 11	works in mine*		Pa.
, James	M 8	at school		Pa.
, William	M 5	at school		Pa.
, Robert	M 4			Pa.
Gormly, (sic) William	M 32	laborer*	Pa.	
, Mary	F 32	keeping house		Pa.
, Emma	F 5			Pa.
, Matilda	F 2			Pa.
, Joseph	M 6/12 (Dec)			Pa.

*out of work 4 months during the census year

According to a deposition contained in his mother's estate file, by 1883 William B. Gormley and his family had moved back to Summit Hill where he helped his sister-in-law, Margaret (Glenn) Gormley Allen, nurse his mother through her final illness. In his deposition, William B. Gormley further stated that he and his family did not move to Bethlehem until four months previous to his making the deposition which was dated February 14, 1888.[695]

In the 1890 Bethlehem City Directory, William B. Gormley was listed as a laborer living at "Main n. borough line. b, South Bethlehem."[696] The Gormley family was also listed in the 1890 Census Directory of Northampton County.[697] The listing was as follows:

---

[694]1880 U.S. Census (population), Pennsylvania, Carbon County, Lansford Borough, page 332C, lines 41-50 and page 332D, line 1, National Archives Microfilm Publication T9, Roll 1107, Households of Maggie Gormley and William Gormley.

[695]Estate of Margaret Gormley, Summit Hill, # 1309, Carbon County Courthouse, Jim Thorpe, Pennsylvania, contains a deposition from Margaret Allen and a deposition from William Gormley both c. February 14, 1888.

[696]Bethlehem, Pennsylvania Directory, 1890, <<www.ancestry.com>>, downloaded September 5, 2019.

[697]Northampton County Residents in 1890, <<http://www.bethlehempaonline.com/ beth1890/communities.html>>, downloaded August 31, 2019, states that the information came from the Census Directory that was published in 1891. It lists the inhabitants of Northampton County furnished by the Census Bureau at Washington, D.C., in the Eleventh U.S. Census, 1890.

BETHLEHEM TOWNSHIP, MONOCACY & EASTERN DISTRICT,
NORTHAMPTON COUNTY, PENNSYLVANIA

Gormley, William	42
, Mary C.	33
, Matilda B.	12
, William E.	7
, James M.	5
, Harry B.	2

In the 1900 census, William B. Gormley and his wife and children were not living together. He was enumerated as a *widower* living and working at Saint Luke's Hospital in Fountain Hill.[698] The enumeration was as follows:

FOUNTAIN HILL, LEHIGH COUNTY, PENNSYLVANIA, JUNE [5], 1900
Gormley, William B.   servant M 53   Orderly   Pa.

His wife, Mary (Hartman) Gormley, was enumerated in the 1900 census as a *widow* living with their three sons on Vineyard Street in West Bethlehem Borough.[699] The enumeration was as follows:

WEST BETHLEHEM BOROUGH, HANOVER TOWNSHIP, LEHIGH COUNTY,
PENNSYLVANIA, JUNE 1, 1900

Gormeney (sic),	Mary C.	head	F 53	Upholstering	Pa..
	William B.	son	M 17	Barber	Pa.
	James M.	son	M 14	Silk Winder	Pa.
	Harry B.	son	M 13	Silk Lacer	Pa.

DEATH AND BURIAL OF WILLIAM GORMLEY. William B. Gormley died July 3, 1903.[700] As far as can be ascertained, he did not leave a will. He was buried at Nisky Hill Cemetery in the Erwin family plot belonging to the husband of his sister, Jane (Gormley) Erwin.[701] According to

---

[698] 1900 U.S. Census (population), Pennsylvania, Lehigh County, Fountain Hill, E.D. 0048, page 5, line 21, National Archives Microfilm Publication T623, Roll 1429, Saint Luke's Hospital.

[699] 1900 U.S. Census (population), Pennsylvania, Lehigh County, Hanover Township, West Bethlehem Borough, E.D. 0032, page 7A, lines 38-41, National Archives Microfilm Publication T623, Roll 1429, Household of Mary C. Gormeney (sic).

[700] Estate of William Gormley, # 3065, Carbon County Courthouse, Jim Thorpe, Pennsylvania, contains a petition dated March 12, 1904, stating that William Gormley died July 3, 1903 in Lehigh County, Pennsylvania.

[701] Henry Erwin Plot Profile, Lot # 185, Section F, Issued July 2, 1901, provided by the Superintendent, Nisky Hill Cemetery, 254 E. Church Street, Bethlehem, Pennsylvania 18018-

the records of the cemetery, William B. Gormley was the first person to be buried in the Erwin family plot.

INHERITANCE FROM MARGARET (MONTGOMERY) GORMLEY. Although William B. Gormley did not leave a will, he did leave an estate that needed to be settled. In his mother's will, she had bequeathed a house she owned in Summit Hill to him for his use as long as he lived.[702] At his death, the house was to become the property of his children.[703]

After William B. Gormley died on July 3, 1903, his surviving children, Matilda (Gormley) Buss, William E. Gormley, James M. Gormley, and Harry B. Gormley, inherited the property which was located at 75 East White Street. They sold it immediately to Robert Law for $400.00.[704] Because James M. Gormley and Harry B. Gormley were still minors at the time of their father's death, the Orphans Court of Lehigh County appointed the Lehigh Valley Trust and Safe Deposit Company to represent their interests in the sale of the property in Summit Hill.[705]

MARY CATHERINE (HARTMAN) GORMLEY, WIDOW OF WILLIAM. It is not known why William B. Gormley and his wife, Mary (Hartman) Gormley, were living apart at the time of the 1900 census. About two years after the death of William B. Gormley, his widow was remarried to a man named Carl Herzer.[706] Their relationship appears to have been short lived.

6143 on August 22, 1997.

[702]Will of Margaret Gormley, May 29, 1878, November 8, 1883, Will Book 1, page 431, Carbon County, Pennsylvania, FHL Microfilm Roll 1290573.

[703]General Index to Estates, Carbon County, Pennsylvania, FHL Microfilm Roll 1290570 contains a reference to the Estate of Margaret Gormley, Summit Hill, # 1309, in which Letters of Administration were issued September 4, 1903, to Mrs. Henry Erwin, an Order of Sale was issued April 11, 1904, and a Return of Sale was filed April 30, 1904, to dispose of the property inherited by William Gormley from his mother.

[704]Deed Index - Grantors, Carbon County, Pennsylvania, FHL Microfilm Roll 2209390 says:

> 1904 Gormley, Margaret Est to Robert Law Vol 55, p. 701, Apr 12, 1904, Summit Hill

[705]Estate of William Gormley of Lehigh County, # 3065, Carbon County Courthouse, Jim Thorpe, Pennsylvania.

[706]1910 U.S. Census (population), Pennsylvania, Lehigh County, Bethlehem Borough (Part of), E.D. 163, page 10B, lines 58-60, Family Number 219, National Archives Microfilm Publication T624, Roll 1364, Household of Mary Herzer states that Mary Herzer was married twice, the second marriage having taken place five years previous to the 1910 census.

On March 26, 1907, Carl and Mary E. (sic) Herzer sold two parcels of land on the north side of Vinyard Street in Lehigh County to Alice T. Boyd who then reconveyed the property to Mary E. (sic) Herzer on the same date.[707,708] Why the property was conveyed in this manner is unclear.

On January 27, 1908, Mary (Hartman) Gormley Herzer wrote a note on a postcard directed to her niece, Miss Margaret Reed, then living in Weissport.[709] It read as follows:

> Bethlehem
> Jan 27 1908
>
> I received your card and was glad to here (sic) from you but times is very dull down here Carl is out of work since Oct and does not know when he can get work so you can judge for yourself I was looking fore ma to come down I wish she would love to all
>
> Mary C. Herzer

In the 1910 census, Mary (Hartman) Gormley Herzer, widow of William B. Gormley and estranged wife of Carl Herzer, was found living on Vineyard Street.[710] Her son, Harry B. Gormley, was living with her. The enumeration was as follows:

> BETHLEHEM BOROUGH (PART OF), LEHIGH COUNTY, PENNSYLVANIA,
> APRIL 26, 1910
>
> | | | | |
> |---|---|---|---|
> | Herzer, Mary | Head | F 53 Pa M² | 5 years 7 children 4 living |
> | | | | Owns home, mortgaged |
> | Newman, John | Boarder M 27 Pa S | | brakeman, railroad |
> | Gormaly (sic), Harry | Son | M 22 Pa S | laborer, odd jobs |

The 1910 census enumeration clearly indicates that Mary (Hartman) Gormley Herzer had

----

[707]Deed from Carl Herzer and Mary E. Herzer, his wife, to Alice T. Boyd, December 26, 1907 (recorded December 27, 1907), Volume 220, p. 387, Recorder of Deeds, Lehigh County, Pennsylvania.

[708]Deed from Alice T. Boyd to Mary E. Herzer, wife of Carl Herzer, December 26, 1907 (recorded December 27, 1907), Volume 220, p. 389, Recorder of Deeds, Lehigh County, Pennsylvania.

[709]Letter dated February 5, 2004 from Jessica Fahey-Petrack, 1043 Main Road, Lehighton, Pennsylvania 18235 to Kathryn C. Torpey, 5035 Domain Place, Alexandria, Virginia 22311-5066 transmitting copies of four postcards from a postcard collection that she inherited from her great-aunt, Margaret Reed, the niece of Mary C. (Hartman) Gormley Herzer.

[710]1910 U.S. Census (population), Pennsylvania, Lehigh County, Bethlehem Borough (Part of), E.D. 163, page 10B, lines 58-60, Family Number 219, National Archives Microfilm Publication T624, Roll 1364, Household of Mary Herzer.

remarried since the death of William B. Gormley, the second marriage having occurred five years earlier. The whereabouts of her estranged husband, Carl Herzer, are unknown.

In the 1920 census, Mary (Hartman) Gormley Herzer was again enumerated at the Vineyard Street address.[711] The enumeration clearly indicates that Mary (Hartman) Gormley Herzer was divorced presumably from her second husband, Carl Herzer, and she had resumed using the surname Gormley. Her son, James Gormley, and his two young daughters were living with her. The enumeration was as follows:

<pre>
BETHLEHEM (PART OF), LEHIGH COUNTY, PENNSYLVANIA,
JANUARY 5 & 9, 1920
        Gormley, Mary K.   Head   F 63 Pa D   Owns home, free
        , James M.   Son   M 36 Pa M   Silk weaver, Silk Mill
        ,Virginia M.   GdD   F 12 Pa S
        , Katherine J.   GdD   F 9 Pa   S
</pre>

Mary (Hartman) Gormley Herzer died on April 11, 1922. According to her death certificate, which was issued under the name Mary Gormley, she was a widow. She died at Sacred Heart Hospital in Allentown.[712] The Nisky Hill Cemetery Interment Record of Mrs. Mary Gormley also indicates that she was a widow, presumably of William B. Gormley.[713]

Mary (Hartman) Gormley Herzer left a will executed on March 28, 1922, in the name Mary Catherine Gormley, in which she named all four of her children who were then living.[714] The will contained instructions that her executors pay her debts, procure a tombstone for her grave, divide her clothing agreeably among them, appraise and dispose of her household goods, and sell her real estate within one year of her death with the money derived from the sale to be divided between them. Proceeds from her life insurance were to revert back to her children.

Her property located at 328 Vineyard Street was sold by her children to their brother,

---

[711]1920 U.S. Census (population), Pennsylvania, Lehigh County, Bethlehem, 10th Ward, E.D. 194, page 6A, lines 45-48, National Archives Microfilm Publication T625, Roll 1589, Household of Mary K. Gormley states that Mary K. Gormley was divorced.

[712]Death Certificate for Mary Gormley, April 11, 1922, # 38576 & # 453, Pennsylvania Division of Vital Statistics, New Castle, Pennsylvania 16103.

[713]Letter dated December 29, 2003 from Diane E. Owen, Bethlehem Area Moravians, Inc., 1021 Center Street, Bethlehem, Pennsylvania 18018 to Kathryn C. Torpey, 5035 Domain Place, Alexandria, Virginia 22311-5066 contains a copy of the Interment Record of Mrs. Mary Gormley that states she was a widow.

[714]Estate of Mary Catherine Gormley, # 18104, Register of Wills, Lehigh County Courthouse, Allentown, Pennsylvania contains a copy of the will of Mary Catherine Gormley.

James M. Gormley. The deed of sale contains a statement that Mary E. Herzer was divorced from her husband, Carl Herzer, in 1919. The deed further states that Mary E. Herzer after her divorce from her husband, Carl Herzer, assumed her name prior to her marriage with Carl Herzer and executed her will under that name, namely Mary C. Gormley.[715]

THE CHILDREN OF WILLIAM AND MARY (HARTMAN) GORMLEY. Of the six children of William B. and Mary (Hartman) Gormley, the oldest three - Emma, Matilda, and Joseph - were probably born in Lansford, and the youngest three - William, James, and Harry - were probably born in Summit Hill. Emma and Joseph probably died before reaching their majority. The other four children are mentioned in 1904 in their father's estate file in Carbon County and in 1922 in their mother's estate file in Lehigh County.[716,717]

Matilda B. Gormley married Harvey A. Buss. They had four children - Harold, Isabelle, and twins, Addison and William. Harvey A. Buss worked in the furniture business.

Harvey and Matilda (Gormley) Buss were enumerated in the 1900 census in Bethlehem with the two oldest children. Harvey Buss was stated to be a day laborer.[718] In the 1910 census, they were enumerated in Nazareth with all four of their children. Harvey Buss was stated to be a salesman in furniture store.[719]

In the 1920 census, they were enumerated with their daughter, Isabelle Buss, in Nazareth, at 29 North Whitefield. Street. Harvey Buss was stated to be a laborer in a furniture store. There is no listing in the 1920 census for their twin sons which may have been an enumerator's error.[720]

---

[715]Deed from Tillie Buss, et. al. to James Gormley, May 7, 1924 (recorded May 7, 1924), Volume 403, p. 212, Recorder of Deeds, Lehigh County, Pennsylvania.

[716]Estate of William Gormley of Lehigh County, # 3065, Carbon County Courthouse, Jim Thorpe, Pennsylvania.

[717]Estate of Mary Catherine Gormley, # 18104, Register of Wills, Lehigh County Courthouse, Allentown, Pennsylvania.

[718]1900 U.S. Census (population), Pennsylvania, Northampton County, Bethlehem Township (Part of), E.D. 0097, page 7, lines 33-36, National Archives Microfilm Publication T623, Roll 1446, Household of Harvey A. Buss.

[719]1910 U.S. Census (population), Pennsylvania, Northampton County, Nazareth Borough, E.D. 102, page 4A, lines 3-9, Family Number 83, National Archives Microfilm Publication T624, Roll 1382, Household of Henry (sic) A. Buss.

[720]1920 U.S. Census (population), Pennsylvania, Northampton County, Nazareth Borough, E.D. 140, page 8A, lines 7-9, National Archives Microfilm Publication T625, Roll

In the 1930 census, they were enumerated in Nazareth at 8 East Center Street with their son, Addison Buss, and their niece, Kathryn Gormley, the daughter of James M. Gormley.[721] Harvey Buss was stated to be a merchant operating a furniture store. In the 1940 census, they were enumerated living together with no other family members in residence with them.[722] Harvey Buss was stated to be the proprietor of a furniture store.

Matilda (Gormley) Buss died on December 18, 1945.[723] Her husband, Harvey A. Buss died on August 7, 1954.[724] They are both buried in Fairview Cemetery along with their son, William Gormley Buss, who died on June 17, 1922 when he was only 14-years-old.[725]

William E. Gormley married Elizabeth "Lizzie" Schweibenz in the Church of the Transfiguration in New York City on July 22, 1906. William E. Gormley was reported to have been from South Bethlehem and a popular tonsorialist with a shop at Pacific House.[726] The bride was reported to have been a much respected young woman from Allentown.[727] In the 1910 census, William E. Gormley and his wife were enumerated in Nazareth Borough where he was

----

1609, Household of Harvey A. Buss.

[721]1930 U.S. Census (population), Pennsylvania, Northampton County, Nazareth Borough, 1st Ward, E.D. 48-73, page 8A, lines 20-23, National Archives Microfilm Publication T626, Roll 2088, Household of Harvey A. Buss.

[722]1940 U.S. Census (population), Pennsylvania, Northampton County, Nazareth, E.D. 48-97, page 3A, lines 3-4, National Archives Microfilm Publication T627, Roll 3593, Household of Harvey A. Buss.

[723]Find-A-Grave Memorial # 29129249, Tillie B. Buss (headstone photograph), added August 18, 2008, Fairview Cemetery, Bethlehem, Northampton County, Pennsylvania, <<www.findagrave.com>>.

[724]Find-A-Grave Memorial # 29129246, Harvey A. Buss (headstone photograph), added August 18, 2008, Fairview Cemetery, Bethlehem, Northampton County, Pennsylvania, <<www.findagrave.com>>.

[725]Find-A-Grave Memorial # 29129250, William Gormley Buss (headstone photograph), added August 18, 2008, Fairview Cemetery, Bethlehem, Northampton County, Pennsylvania, <<www.findagrave.com>>.

[726]i.e., a barber.

[727]Marriage Gormley - Schweibenz, *Bethlehem Globe Times,* Wednesday, July 25, 1906, p. 7, Bethlehem Area Public Library, 11 West Church Street, Bethlehem, Pennsylvania, 18018-5888.

working as a barber.[728] By the time of the 1920 census, they had moved to Philadelphia where they lived at 681 N. 52nd Street.[729] While living in Philadelphia, William E. Gormley operated Gormley's Barber Shop located at the S.E. corner of 52nd and Girard Avenue.[730] In 1922, he was named as one of the executors of his mother's estate, but he died unexpectedly, of pneumonia, on November 18, 1923, before her estate was settled.[731,732] His obituary appeared in both the *Philadelphia Public Ledger* and the *Philadelphia Inquirer*.[733,734] He was buried in Nisky Hill

---

[728]1910 U.S. Census (population), Pennsylvania, Northampton County, Nazareth Borough, E.D. 102, page 11A, lines 14-15, Family Number 260, National Archives Microfilm Publication T624, Roll 1382, Household of William E. Gormley.

[729]1920 U.S. Census (population), Pennsylvania, Philadelphia County, Philadelphia, 44th Ward, E.D. 1672, page 8A, lines 39-40, National Archives Microfilm Publication T625, Roll 1645, Household of William Gormley, erroneously states that his wife, Elizabeth, 31 years old, is his "daughter."

[730]Letter dated February 13, 2004 from Nancy (Riley) Gerechoff, 414 Parker Avenue, P.O. Box 409, Deal, New Jersey 07723 transmitted a picture postcard of Gormley's Barber Shop which stated it was located on the S.E. corner of 52nd and Girard Avenue, Philadelphia, Pennsylvania.

[731]Death Certificate of William Gormley, November 18, 1923, Philadelphia, Pennsylvania, Pennsylvania Death Certificates, 1906-1966, <<www.ancestry.com>>, downloaded September 1, 2019.

[732]Letter dated December 29, 2003 from Diane E. Owen, Bethlehem Area Moravians, Inc., 1021 Center Street, Bethlehem, Pennsylvania 18018 to Kathryn C. Torpey, 5035 Domain Place, Alexandria, Virginia 22311-5066 contains a copy of the Interment Record of William E. Gormley that states he died November 18, 1923, in Philadelphia.

[733]Obituary of William E. Gormley, *Philadelphia Public Ledger*, Tuesday, November 20, 1923, p. 22, and Wednesday, November 21, 1923, p. 21, Library of Congress, Newspaper and Periodical Reading Room, Washington, D.C. read as follows:

> GORMLEY - Nov 18, WILLIAM E., husband of Elizabeth Gormley. Relatives and friends, also Montgomery Lodge, No 18, F. and A.M.; Aerie of Camden, No. 65, F.O.E.; Phila. Lodge, No. 54, L.O.O.M., and all societies of which he was a member are invited to the funeral services, Wed., 8 P.M., late residence 681 N. 52nd st. Int. Bethlehem, Pa., Thurs., 3 P.M.

[734]Obituary of William E. Gormley, *Philadelphia Inquirer*, Tuesday, November 20, 1923, p. 23, Library of Congress, Newspaper and Periodical Reading Room, Washington, D.C.

Cemetery in the same plot as his mother.[735] He left an undated will that was written entirely by hand on a 3x5 card. It appears that his will was originally filed in Philadelphia in late 1923. In 1944, his will was authenticated by the Register of Wills in Philadelphia and re-filed in Lehigh County.[736] His will read in its entirety as follows:

> In case anything happens to me I make my wife boss of everything I want her to sell everything and give $1,000 each to my two brothers and sister Harry B. Gormley, J.M. Gormley and Mrs. Tilly Buss.   William E. Gormley

William E. and Elizabeth "Lizzie" (Schweibenz) Gormley had no children. Presumably, his widow settled his estate as directed by his will. On January 30, 1931, Elizabeth "Lizzie" (Schweibenz) Gormley married Charles Magrath in Allentown, Lehigh County, Pennsylvania.[737] She was widowed for a second time on June 6, 1961.[738] She died in Upper Darby, Delaware County, Pennsylvania on August 25, 1968.[739] She was buried in Union-West End Cemetery in Allentown, Lehigh County, Pennsylvania.[740]

---

[735]Letter dated December 29, 2003 from Diane E. Owen, Bethlehem Area Moravians, Inc., 1021 Center Street, Bethlehem, Pennsylvania 18018 to Kathryn C. Torpey, 5035 Domain Place, Alexandria, Virginia 22311-5066 contains a plot profile for the plot owned by James and Harry Gormley, Section O, Southern One-Half of Plot No. 15 showing that William E. Gormley was buried in that plot in Nisky Hill Cemetery.

[736]Estate of William E. Gormley, # 34370, Register of Wills, Lehigh County, Allentown, Pennsylvania. The authentication of the will by the Register of Wills in Philadelphia is dated February 25, 1944. The will appears to have been originally recorded in Philadelphia in Book 465, Page 205, Year 1923, Estate # 3495.

[737]Marriage of Charles Magrath to Elizabeth F. Gormley, January 30, 1931, Allentown, Lehigh County, Pennsylvania, Pennsylvania Marriages, 1852-1968, <<www.ancestry.com>>, downloaded September 1, 2019.

[738]Death Certificate of Charles Magrath, June 6, 1961, Philadelphia, Pennsylvania, Pennsylvania Death Certificates, 1906-1966, <<www.ancestry.com>>, downloaded September 1, 2019.

[739]1968 Death Index, Pennsylvania Department of Health, Pennsylvania State Archives, Harrisburg, Pennsylvania.

Magrath, Elizabeth F., 79yrs, Upper Darby Twp, Delaware Co, 08/26/68, file # 079891.

[740]Find-A-Grave Memorial # 76482071, Elizabeth Magrath (no headstone photograph), added September 13, 2011, Union-West End Cemetery, Allentown, Lehigh County, Pennsylvania, <<www.findagrave.com>>.

James M. Gormley was a weaver in a silk mill. In the 1910 census, he was enumerated with his wife, Ellen (Sterner) Gormley, and their daughter, Virginia Gormley.[741] In the 1920 census, he was enumerated with his mother, Mary Catherine (Hartman) Gormley, and his two daughters - Virginia and Kathryn.[742] His wife, Ellen (Sterner) Gormley, who was very sick, was enumerated as a patient at the State Homeopathic Hospital in Hanover Township.[743] Ellen (Sterner) Gormley died shortly thereafter on March 27, 1920, and was buried in the family plot at Nisky Hill Cemetery.[744,745] In 1922, James M. Gormley was an heir to his mother's estate and, in 1924, he bought her property on Vineyard Street from his sister, Matilda (Gormley) Buss, his brother, Harry B. Gormley, and Elizabeth (Schweibenz) Gormley, the widow of his brother, William E. Gormley. In the deed of sale, he is stated to be unmarried, but widower is the more accurate description of his marital status.[746] He never remarried and, because of the difficulty of working in a silk ribbon factory and raising his two young daughters all by himself, the two girls were sent to live with their aunt, Matilda (Gormley) Buss.[747] James M. Gormley died on May 18, 1960, and was buried in the family plot at Nisky Hill Cemetery alongside his mother, his wife,

---

[741]1910 U.S. Census (population), Pennsylvania, Lehigh County, Bethlehem Borough, E.D. 163, page 15B, line 54-56, Family Number 338, National Archives Microfilm Publication T624, Roll 1364, Household of James Gormley.

[742]1920 U.S. Census (population), Pennsylvania, Lehigh County, Bethlehem, 10th Ward, E.D. 194, page 6A, line 45-48, National Archives Microfilm Publication T625, Roll 1589, Household of Mary K. Gormley.

[743]1920 U.S. Census (population), Pennsylvania, Lehigh County, Hanover Township, E.D. 213, page 8B, line 72, National Archives Microfilm Publication T625, Roll 1589, State Homeopathic Hospital.

[744]Obituary of Mrs. Ellen Gormley, *Bethlehem Globe Times*, Monday, March 29, 1920, p. 6, Bethlehem Area Public Library, 11 West Church Street, Bethlehem, Pennsylvania, 18018-5888.

[745]Letter dated December 29, 2003 from Diane E. Owen, Bethlehem Area Moravians, Inc., 1021 Center Street, Bethlehem, Pennsylvania 18018 to Kathryn C. Torpey, 5035 Domain Place, Alexandria, Virginia 22311-5066 contains a plot profile for the plot owned by James and Harry Gormley, Section O, Southern One-Half of Plot No. 15 showing that Ellen Gormley was buried in that plot in Nisky Hill Cemetery.

[746]Deed from Tillie Buss, et. al. to James Gormley, May 7, 1924 (recorded May 7, 1924), Volume 403, p. 212, Recorder of Deeds, Lehigh County, Pennsylvania.

[747]Conversation on February 2, 2004, with Nancy (Riley) Gerechoff, 414 Parker Avenue, P.O. Box 409, Deal, New Jersey 07723, granddaughter of James M. Gormley.

and his brother, William E. Gormley.[748,749]

His obituary appeared in *The Morning Call* on May 19, 1960.[750] It read as follows:

James M. Gormley

> James M. Gormley of 1034 Elm St., Bethlehem, died yesterday in St. Luke's
> Hospital. Born in Summit Hill, he was a son of the late William E. and Mary
> Hartman Gormley. He was the husband of the late Ella Sterner Gormley.
> Surviving are two daughters, Mrs. Kathryn Riley, Asbury Park, N.J., and
> Virginia Gormley, address unknown; a brother Harry B., Bethlehem; one
> grandchild and two great-grandchildren. Services will be at 11 a.m. Saturday in
> the Steyers Funeral Home, 500 Linden St., Bethlehem. Viewing will be
> tomorrow evening.

Harry B. Gormley was known to his friends and family as "Mike."[751] According to his
obituary, he was a World War I veteran and a member of the Fairview Fire House and the
Reliance Fire Company. In the 1910 census, he was enumerated with his mother at the Vineyard
Street property.[752] His occupation was listed as a laborer. In the 1920 census, he was enumerated
with his first wife, Laura E. (Hausman) Gormley, at 201 Main Street in Bethlehem.[753] His

---

[748]Letter dated December 29, 2003 from Diane E. Owen, Bethlehem Area Moravians,
Inc., 1021 Center Street, Bethlehem, Pennsylvania 18018 to Kathryn C. Torpey, 5035 Domain
Place, Alexandria, Virginia 22311-5066 contains a plot profile for the plot owned by James and
Harry Gormley, Section O, Southern One-Half of Plot No. 15 showing that James M. Gormley
was buried in that plot in Nisky Hill Cemetery.

[749]Find-A-Grave Memorial # 67441914, James M. Gormley (headstone photograph),
added March 25, 2011, Nisky Hill Cemetery, Bethlehem, Northampton County, Pennsylvania,
<<www.findagrave.com>>.

[750]Obituary of James M. Gormley, *The Morning Call*, Thursday, May 19, 1960,
<<www.newspapers.com>>, downloaded September 5, 2019.

[751]Obituary of Harry (Mike) Gormley, *Bethlehem Globe Times*, Saturday, October 6,
1962, p.19, Bethlehem Area Public Library, 11 West Church Street, Bethlehem, Pennsylvania,
18018-5888.

[752]1910 U.S. Census (population), Pennsylvania, Lehigh County, Bethlehem Borough
(Part of), E.D. 163, page 10B, lines 58-60, Family Number 219, National Archives Microfilm
Publication T624, Roll 1364, Household of Mary Herzer.

[753]1920 U.S. Census (population), Pennsylvania, Lehigh County, Bethlehem, 10th Ward,
E.D. 194, page 2A, lines 1-3, National Archives Microfilm Publication T625, Roll 1589,
Household of Harry B. Gormley.

occupation was listed as the operator of a pool room. Later, he worked as a musical instrument salesman.[754] According to family legend, he also ran a juke box concession which is consistent with the 1940 census enumeration that states he was a salesman for an independent phonograph company.[755,756]

His first wife, Laura E. (Hausman) Gormley died on November 9, 1959, in Bethlehem, Lehigh County, Pennsylvania.[757] Her obituary appeared in *The Morning Call* on November 11, 1959.[758] It read as follows:

Gormley Services

Services for Mrs. Laura Gormley, 71, of 823 Spring St., Bethlehem, who died Monday in her home, will be at 2 p.m. Friday in the Steyers Funeral Home, 500 Linden St., Bethlehem. Viewing will be tomorrow evening. She was the wife of Harry B. Gormley. Born in East Texas, she was a daughter of the late Jacob and Marguerite Moyer Hausman. She was a member of Bethany United Church of Christ, Bethlehem. Surviving besides her husband are a brother, Raymond Hausman, Bethlehem, and several nieces and nephews.

About a year after the death of his first wife, Harry B. Gormley wrote his will in which he left his entire estate to his "housekeeper," Leila (sic) Reichenbach, provided she was in his employment at the time of his death.[759] He also left an annuity to her brother, Harry (sic) B. Reichenbach, in the form of a monthly annuity to be used for completion of his college education and he directed that some of the money in his estate be made available for the necessaries of

----

[754]1930 U.S. Census (population), Pennsylvania, Lehigh County, Bethlehem, E.D. 39-45, page 4A, lines 16-17, National Archives Microfilm Publication T626, Roll 2064, Household of Harry B. Gormley.

[755]Conversation on February 2, 2004 with Nancy (Riley) Gerechoff, 414 Parker Avenue, P.O. Box 409, Deal, New Jersey 07723, granddaughter of James M. Gormley.

[756]1940 U.S. Census (population), Pennsylvania, Lehigh County, Bethlehem, E.D. 39-45, page 3B, lines 53-54, National Archives Microfilm Publication T627, Roll 3545, Household of Harry B. Gormley.

[757]Death Certificate of Laura E. Gormley, November 9, 1959, Bethlehem, Lehigh County, Pennsylvania, Pennsylvania Death Certificates, 1906-1966, <<www.ancestry.com>>, downloaded September 2, 2019.

[758]Obituary of Mrs. Laura Gormley, *The Morning Call*, Allentown, Pennsylvania, Wednesday, November 11, 1959, <<www.newspapers.com>>, downloaded September 2, 2019.

[759]Estate of Harry B. Gormley, # 52358, Register of Wills, Lehigh County, Allentown, Pennsylvania contains the will of Harry B. Gormley which was dated August 9, 1960.

Leila (sic) Reichenbach's mother, Lilly Reichenbach. Finally, he directed that if Leila (sic) Reichenbach predeceased him, then he left his estate to his niece, Kathryn (Gormley) Riley, with the proviso that she mandatorily provide the necessary funds for the maintenance and support of Lilly Reichenbach.[760] Harry B. Gormley died on October 5, 1962.[761] His obituary appeared in *The Morning Call* on October 6, 1962.[762] It read as follows:

> Harry Gormley - Harry (Mike) Gormley, 74 of 823 Spring St., Bethlehem, died
> yesterday in St. Luke's Hospital. Born in Summit Hill, he was a son of the late
> William E. and Mary (Hartman) Gormley. Surviving is his widow, Lila (sic).
> Arrangements will be announced from the Stayers Funeral Home, Bethlehem.

Harry B. Gormley was buried in Cedar Hill Memorial Park in Allentown in the same plot as his first wife, Laura (Hausman) Gormley.[763]

When Harry B. Gormley's will was submitted for probate on October 20, 1962, the only heir was his second wife, Leila (sic) (Reichenbach) Gormley who lived for almost thirty years after the death of her husband. She died on April 3, 1992. Her obituary appeared in *The Morning Call* on April 6, 1992.[764] It read as follows:

> GORMLEY - Mrs. Lila (sic) B. (Reichenbach), 81 of Lynnwood Drive,
> Allentown, April 3, 1992, in Fountain Hill; wife of the late Harry Gormley.
> Services 11 a.m. Monday, Long Funeral Home, 500 Linden St., Bethlehem.
> Interment, Woodlawn Cemetery, Allentown. Call 10-11 a.m. Monday.
> Contributions to LARC, 336 W. Spruce St., Bethlehem 18018.

---

[760]The daughter of his brother, James M. Gormley.

[761]Index to Estates, Lehigh County, Pennsylvania, 1812-1965, (F-J), FHL Microfilm Roll 2108123.

[762]Obituary of Harry Gormley, *The Morning Call*, Allentown, Pennsylvania, Saturday, April 6, 1992, <<www.newspapers.com>, downloaded September 1, 2019.

[763]Letter dated March 22, 2004 from Charleen Williamson, Family Services Counselor, Cedar Hill Memorial Park to Kathryn C. Torpey, 5035 Domain Place, Alexandria, Virginia 22311-5066 stating that Harry Gormley and Laura Gormley are buried in Lot # 469, Section D

[764]Obituary of Lila (sic) B. Gormley, *The Morning Call*, Allentown, Pennsylvania, Monday, April 6, 1992, <<www.newspapers.com>, downloaded September 1, 2019.

AFTERWORD

The history of this Gormley family begins about 1790 with the birth of Joseph Gormley in County Londonderry, Ireland, and ends in 1915 with the death of his last surviving child, Jane (Gormley) Erwin, in West Bethlehem, Lehigh County, Pennsylvania.

Like many Protestant families that immigrated to America from Ulster during the first half of the 19th Century, Joseph Gormley's decision to leave home was probably motivated by the certain knowledge that there was nothing to be gained by staying in Ireland. Undoubtedly, he was possessed of an earnest desire to achieve economic independence, a comfortable self-sufficiency, and upward mobility in a new country that rewarded immigrants for hard work.

The odyssey of the Gormley family began when Joseph Gormley left home, alone, to establish himself in Summit Hill as a coal miner. A year-and-a-half later, he sent for his wife, Margaret (Montgomery) Gormley, and their nine children. Three more Gormley children were born in America, and, in 1847, Joseph Gormley fulfilled his lifetime dream of achieving economic independence by buying a small working farm in Mahoning Township where the family realized some measure of prosperity.

The children of Joseph and Margaret (Montgomery) Gormley all grew up to be dependable and trustworthy while at the same time being acquisitive and competitive. Some stayed home while others moved on to Bethlehem, Philadelphia, South Carolina, California, Nevada, and, in one case, clear across the Pacific Ocean to Shanghai. Yet, regardless of their differences in style and personality, the passage of time, and the distance that separated them, the evidence clearly indicates that the children of Joseph and Margaret (Montgomery) Gormley remained inextricably bound together by a deep sense of duty and moral obligation to help each other in times of need while never giving up the ever lasting hope that God would bless them and keep them until they were all together again.

Oh how I do long to see you all once more...
Your affectionate sister, Maggie
Shanghai, 12th March 1871

Births

Margarette Jane Gormley was
Born September 28th 1858
Mary A. Gormley was
Born November 24th 1860
Allice Gormley was Born
May 29th 1863
Matilda Gormley was
born August 13 1867
Martha Gormley was
born March 28 1869
James A. Gormley was born April
1874

Family Bible
of Smith Gormley

Family Bible
of James M. Gormley

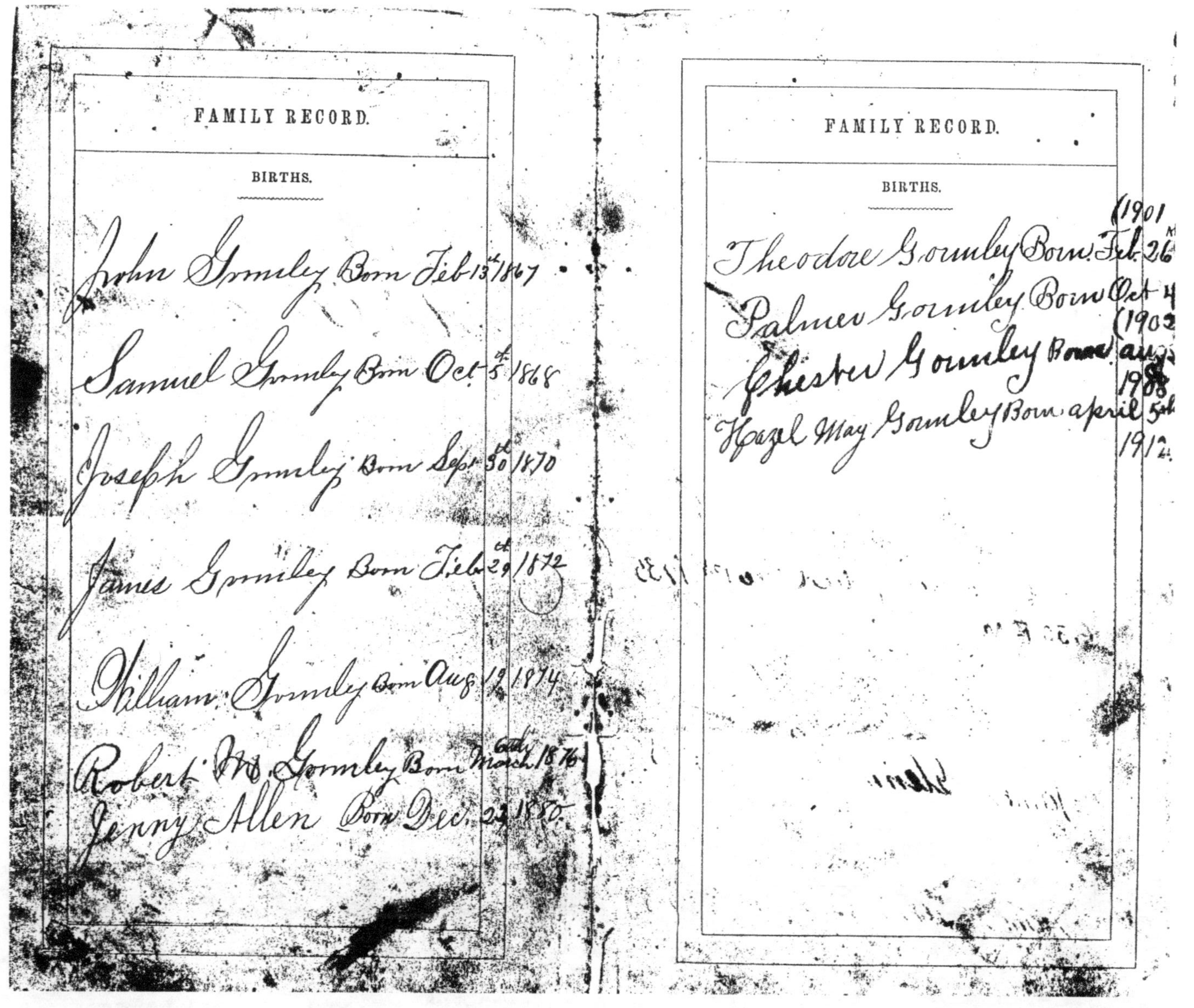

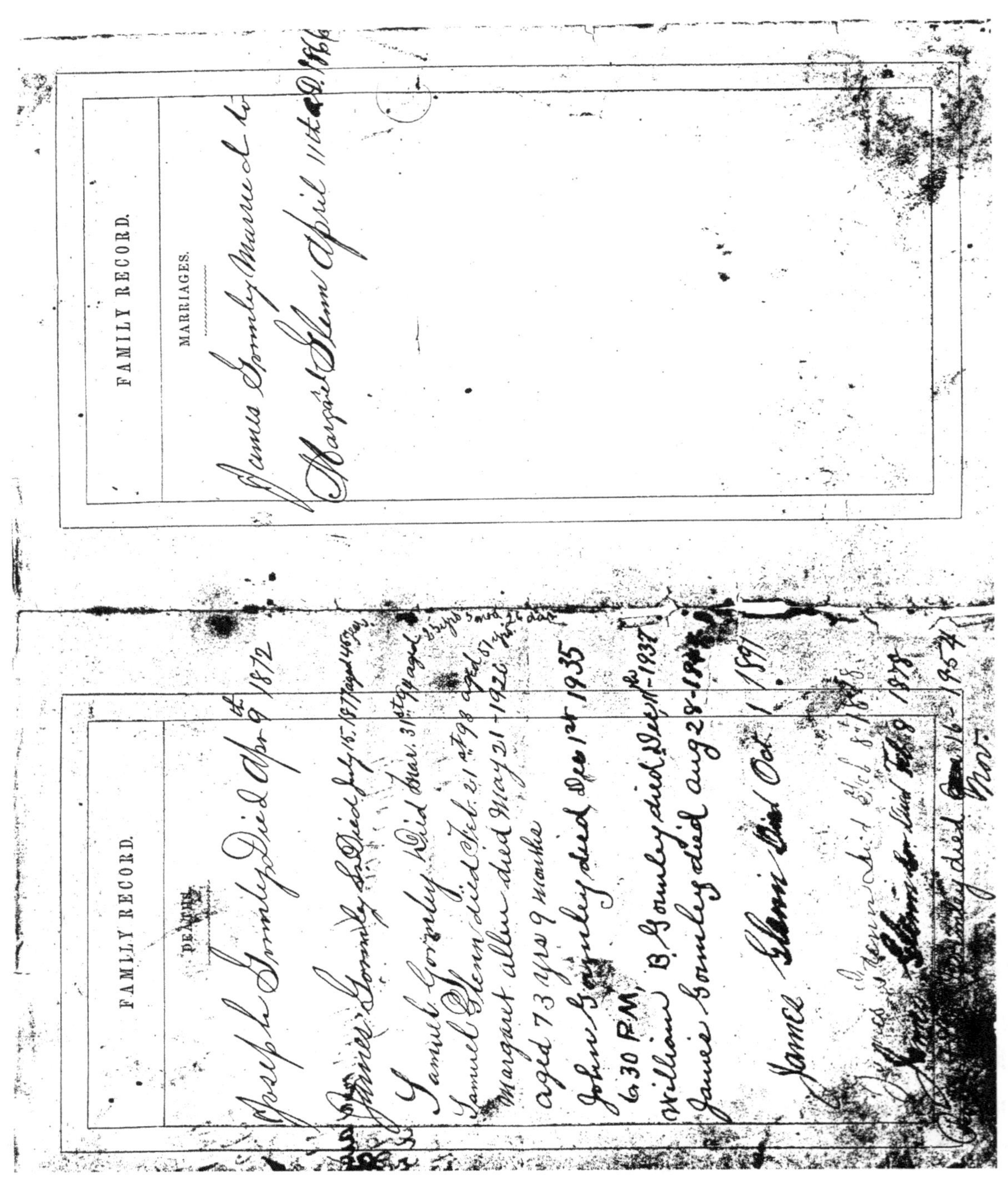

Buried on Lot.
James Gormley — soldier
Joe Gormley.
Margaret M. Gormey,
Samele Gormley C
Joe Gormley,
Cloid Gormley.

Robert Gormley gone
for generations 1934 $100.0

1885
John E. Griffiths 1905
Margaret Ann Patterson
Griffiths 1884 1907
in care of son
Mr John P. Griffiths
1916 west Moreland St
Phila
Pa

James Glenn Sr.
Samele Glenn Jun
Elisefeth Glenn
Mary "
Elisefeth Glenn Dr.

Eddward Griffith
old soldier Died 1873

177   Appendix C

Appendix C

Bann Valley
County Londonderry, Ulster, Ireland

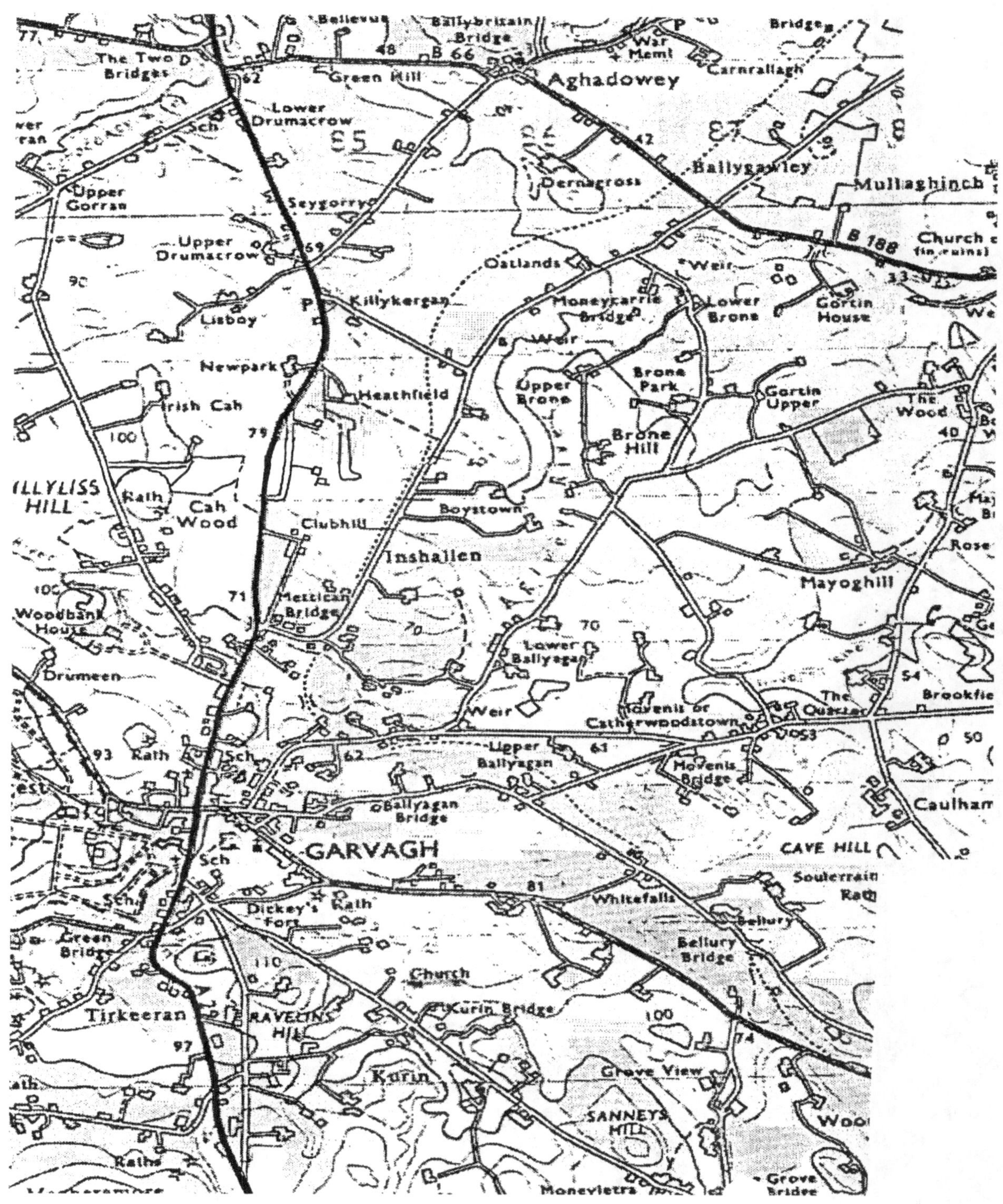

Carbon County, Pennsylvania

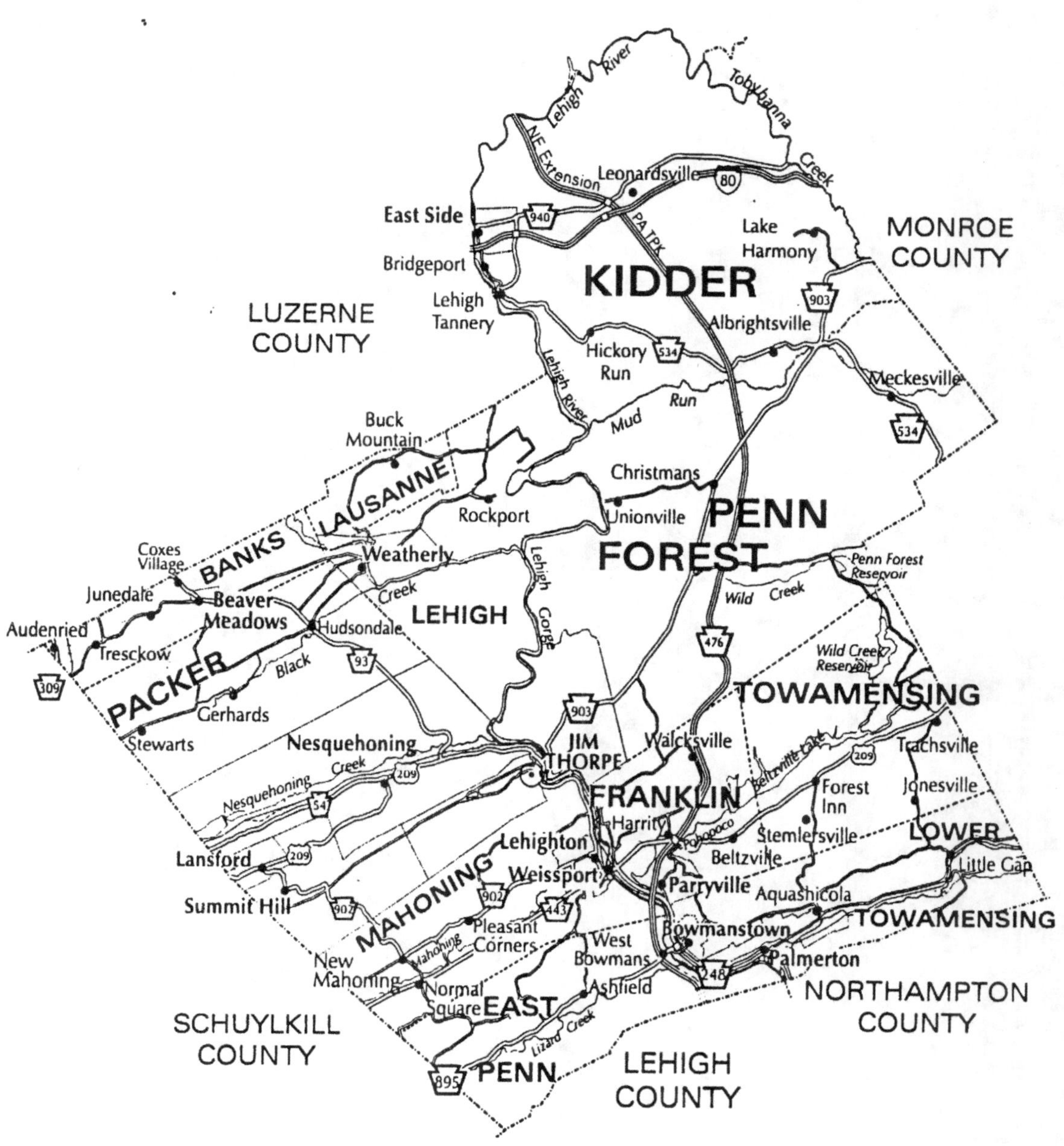

Appendix E

Declaration of Intent of Joseph Gormley
December 20, 1842

IN PURSUANCE of the Acts of Congress in such case made and provided, _Joseph Gormley_ a free white person, and an alien friend, desirous of being naturalized, makes a report and registry as follows:

Name.	Birth place.	Age.	Nation.	Allegiance.	Whence he emigrated	Time of arriv. U. S.	Intended place Settlement.
Joseph Gormley	County of Londonderry Ireland	45	Irish	Queen of Great Britain & Ireland	Londonderry	20 May 1835 at New York	Summit to the Northampton County

To the Prothonotary of the Court of Common Pleas of Northampton County, in Pennsylvania, in the United States of America.

Northampton County ss.

Joseph Gormley being duly sworn doth declare and say, that it is bona fide his intention to become a Citizen of the United States, and renounce forever, all allegiance and fidelity to any Foreign Prince, Potentate, State or Sovereignty whatever, and particularly to the Queen of Great Britain and Ireland of whom he is now a subject.

Sworn and subscribed, the _twentieth_ day of _December_ in the year of our Lord one thousand eight hundred and forty two and the sixty seventh year of the Independence of the United States.

Joseph Gormley
20 may

Joseph + Gormley
mark

Joseph + Gormley
mark

Wm. Hackett
Prot.

Naturalization Petition of Joseph Gormley
March 25, 1845

To the Honorable the Judges of the Court of Common Pleas of the County of *North*ampton, in the Commonwealth of Pennsylvania, now composing and holding the said Court.

THE PETITION OF *Joseph Gormley*
A Native of *Ireland*

RESPECTFULLY SHEWETH

THAT your petitioner arrived in the United States of America, more than five years since,

and that in pursuance of the acts of Congress of the United States, in that behalf made, he made a report and registry of his nativity, age, allegiance, emigration, arrival and intended place of settlement in the United States, conformably to the said Acts, a copy of which is herewith exhibited, and also in due form of law, made a declaration of his intention to become a citizen of the United States, on the *26* day of *December* A. D. 184*2* before the Court of *Common Pleas* in and for the County of *Northampton* a certificate whereof is hereunto annexed; and that he has resided within the limits, and under the jurisdiction of the United States for five years last past, and for one year last past, within the State of Pennsylvania; that he has never borne any hereditary title, or been of any of the orders of nobility in the kingdom whence he came, or elsewhere. He, therefore, prays he may be admitted to become a citizen of the United States.

Joseph X Gormley
mark

Thos. Broderick's *James Hanton*

Citizens of the United States, being duly *sworn* according to law, say, that they are well acquainted with the above named Petitioner, and that to their knowledge, he has resided within the limits, and under the jurisdiction of the United States for five years last past, and for one year last past, within the State of Pennsylvania; that during the same period, he has behaved himself as a man of good moral character, attached to the principles of the Constitution of the United States, and well disposed to the good order and happiness of the same.

Sworn, in open Court, this *25* day of *March* A. D. 184*5*

Thos. Broderick
James Denton
Wm. H. Brotzwell
Proth.

I *Joseph Gormley* the above named Petitioner, do on my solemn oath declare, that the contents of my Petition are true; that I will support the Constitution of the United States; and I do hereby renounce and relinquish any title or order of nobility to which I am or hereafter may be entitled; and that I do absolutely and entirely renounce and abjure all allegiance and fidelity to any foreign Prince, Potentate, State or Sovereignty whatever, and particularly to the *Queen Victoria* of whom I was heretofore a subject.

sworn in open Court, the *25* day of *March* A. D. 184*5*

Wm. H. Brotzwell
Proth.

Joseph X Gormley
mark

Appendix G

Will of Margaret (Montgomery) Gormley
May 29, 1878

Last Will and Testament of Margaret Gormely *(sic)*
Filed for Probate November 8 1883

I, Margaret Gormely *(sic)* of Summit Hill, Carbon County State of Penna do make this as my last will and testament (I being in good health and sound mind at this present writing). I bequeath to my son William the house I now occupy at the present time the same to be for his use as long as he lives but not to have any right to sell the same. At his death if any of his children are alive the *(sic)* are to have equal share of it. Should he die childless then the property to be equally divided amongst the children of Robert and James (my sons). The balance of my property real and personal to be divided as follows after paying all necessary expenses of my funeral and putting a headstone on my grave and that of my husband Joseph Gormley, my executor to have sole control of all my affairs without bonds. The following are the bequests I wish if there are enough money to do so, if not, my administrator to divide pro rata.

I bequeath to Mary Ann Wallis *(sic)* daughter of Letitia $100
I bequeath to Margaret Gormley daughter of Robert $200
I bequeath to Joseph Gormley son of Robert $100
I bequeath to John Gormley son of James $100
I bequeath to Matilda Gormley daughter of William $100

to each of the remaining four children of my son James each to receive fifty ($50) dollars.

All of the above bequests in money my administrator is to invest for them to *(sic)* the *(sic)* are of age. Should there be any money left after payment of all expenses of administrator the said administrator shall pay to my daughter Letitia if she is alive one hundred ($100) dollars, the balance of any to be divided pro rata amongst the persons named above. I hereby appoint and empower M.E. Sinyard of Summit Hill Carbon County Pa my legal administrator and executor of this my last will and testament.

her
Margaret X Gormley
mark

Signed and sealed in the presence of us this twenty-ninth day of May 1878.

Joseph Nevins
Palmer O'Donnell

Codicil

Having paid to Mary Ann Wallis *(sic)* through my daughter Letitia on or about the 25th day of March 1883 the sum of one hundred ($100) I do hereby annul and make void the bequest of one hundred dollars as mentioned in my will of 29th May 1878 to said Mary Ann Wallis (sic) as also the two ($200) hundred dollars willed to Margaret Gormley the daughter of my deceased son Robert. I want it changed as to read one hundred dollars ($100).

her
Margaret X Gormley
mark

Signed in presence of us this 31st day of October 1883

William Gormley
Margaret Allen

Joseph Gormely *(sic)* Born Nov 21st 1790 Died Oct 8th 1871
Margaret Gormley Born April 5th 1800 Died Nov 3rd 1883

187   Appendix H

Will of Margaret (Montgomery) Gormley
May 29, 1878

Carbon County S.S.

Registers Office Nov 21st 1883

There personally appeared William Gormley and Margaret Allen the subscribing witnesses to the foregoing Codicil of Margaret Gormley deceased and in their solemn oath did say that they were present and did see and hear Margaret Gormley of Summit Hill Carbon County Pa deceased, the testator herein named, seal publish and declare the same as and for her Codicil to her last will and testament and that at the doing thereof she was of sound disposing mind memory and understanding to the best of their knowledge and belief.

Wm Gormley
Margaret Allen

Sworn and subscribed before me the day and year aforesaid.

James H. Handwich
Reg. and Rec.

Carbon County S.S.

Registers Office Dec 18th 1883

There personally appeared James Nevins and Palmer O'Donnell the subscribing witnesses to the foregoing last will and testament of Margaret Gormley deceased and in their solemn oath did say that they were present and did see and hear Margaret Gormley of Summit Hill Carbon County Pa deceased the testator therein named seal publish and declare the same as and for her Last Will and Testament and that at the doing thereof she was of sound disposing mind memory and understanding to the best of their knowledge and belief.

Joseph Nevins
Palmer O'Donnell

Sworn and subscribed before me the day and year aforesaid.

James H. Handwich

Carbon County S.S.

Registers Office Dec 18th 1883

I, M.E. Sinyard do swear that as the executor of the foregoing last will and testament of Margaret Gormely *(sic)* of Summit Hill Carbon County deceased I will and truly administer the goods and chattels [right] and credit of the deceased equitable to law and that I will comply with the provisions of the law relating to collateral indentures.

M.E. Sinyard

Sworn and subscribed before me the day and year aforesaid and Letters Testamentary granted unto M.E. Sinyard.

James H. Handwich
Reg. and Rec.

June, 1973

Summit Hill woman murdered in China

By Ed Gildea

A member of one of Summit Hill's first families was murdered during an uprising in China in 1871. John Gormley, who works in Bright's, had this unusual story for the Gazette and to get the details I went to his home at 27 Walnut St. in Summit Hill one Sunday afternoon.

The woman, who was Gormley's great aunt, was Mrs. Margaret Beasler. She was the former Margaret Gormley, one of 11 children of Mr. and Mrs. Joseph Gormley, who settled in Summit Hill after coming from County Derry, Ireland. They were John Gormley's great grandparents.

Margaret married a tea merchant whom she met in Philadelphia and his business took him to Shanghai, China, where they lived for a few years.

They became victims of one of a series of periodic uprisings against foreigners.

John Gormley is shown with a painting of his great grandfather, Joseph Gormley, one of Summit Hill's first settlers. His daughter, Margaret, was a victim of an uprising in China in 1871.

Appendix I

John Gormley Letter
Alexandria, Virginia
March 7, 1862

Alexander verginnia
March the 7. 1862
Dear father and mother
and brother i now lift
my pu to rizht to yous
to lets yous know that
i aim well at presant
and hoping that these
few lins will find yous
in the same state
of hielth I let you know
that i receve you kind
letter on the forth of
march and i was glad
to here from yous and
that yous ar oll well
i let yous know that i
receve the nuts and tobacko
wich yous sent to me
we had good liven as long as
the boxes lasted

John Gormley Letter
Alexandria, Virginia
March 7, 1862

when you right i wich
yous wod send me some
postage stamps
i send my best respect
to robbert sinard and
oll the rest and camer's
so that oll is at prisant
but remains your
brother John Gormley
　　　John Gormley
yous can tel ruben
selner that henry sent
a box home and for him
to go to lehighton and
get it

Gormley Family Photographs

Joseph Gormley

Margaret Gormley

James Gormley

Letitia Gormley

Matilda Gormley

Margaret Gormley Jr

Joseph Gormley Jr

Descendants of Joseph Gormley

Generation 1

1. **JOSEPH[1] GORMLEY** was born between 21 Nov 1790-1792 in County Londonderry, Ireland. He died between 08-09 Oct 1871 in Mahoning Township, Carbon County, Pennsylvania. He married Margaret Montgomery, daughter of Robert Montgomery and Agnes (--?--) on 23 May 1822 in Garvagh, Errigal Parish, County Londonderry, Ireland. She was born on 05 Apr 1800 in Magheramore, Desertoghill Parish, County Londonderry, Ireland. She died between 03-04 Nov 1883 in Summit Hill, Carbon County, Pennsylvania.

Joseph Gormley and Margaret Montgomery had the following children:

2.   i.   SMITH M.[2] GORMLEY was born on 16 Mar 1823 in Magheramore, Desertoghill Parish, County Londonderry, Ireland. He died on 18 Mar 1883 in Buck Mountain, Lausanne Township, Carbon County, Pennsylvania. He married Margaret Ann McClellan, daughter of James McClellan and Margaret on 01 Nov 1857 in Buck Mountain, Lausanne Township, Carbon County, Pennsylvania. She was born on 12 Feb 1833 in Ireland. She died on 26 Jul 1910 in Mahanoy City, Schuylkill County, Pennsylvania.

       ii.   JANE GORMLEY was born in 1824 in Magheramore, Desertoghill Parish, County Londonderry, Ireland. She died between 1840-1841 in Ashton, then Northampton County now Carbon County, Pennsylvania.

3.   iii.   JAMES MONTGOMERY GORMLEY was born in 1825 in Magheramore, Desertoghill Parish, County Londonderry, Ireland. He died on 15 Jul 1877 in Lansford, Carbon County, Pennsylvania. He married Margaret Glenn, daughter of James Glenn and Elizabeth Bacon on 11 Apr 1866 in Summit Hill, Carbon County, Pennsylvania. She was born on 20 Aug 1846 in Ashton, Mauch Chunk Township, Carbon County, Pennsylvania. She died on 21 May 1920 in Summit Hill, Carbon County, Pennsylvania.

4.   iv.   LETITIA MONTGOMERY GORMLEY was born before 22 Jun 1827 in Magheramore, Desertoghill Parish, County Londonderry, Ireland. She died on 23 Oct 1914 in Philadelphia, Pennsylvania. She married Stephen Wallace, son of William Wallace and Mary Ann (--?--) on 04 Aug 1852 in Philadelphia, Pennsylvania. He was born about 1829 in Mullaghinch, Aghadowey Parish, County Londonderry, Ireland. He died about 1859 in Charleston, Charleston County, South Carolina.

5.   v.   MATILDA MONTGOMERY GORMLEY was born in Jun 1831 in County Londonderry, Ireland. She died on 15 Aug 1905 in Philadelphia, Pennsylvania. She married John Boyd on 05 Apr 1851 in Philadelphia,

Pennsylvania. He was born in 1827 in Ireland. He died about 1874 in Placer County, California.

6. vi. ROBERT MONTGOMERY GORMLEY was born before 03 Jan 1832 in Mullinabrone, Aghadowey Parish, County Londonderry, Ireland. He died on 02 Aug 1875 in Fountain Hill, Lehigh County, Pennsylvania. He married Hannah Jane Johnson, daughter of Andrew Johnson and Mary Gilmore in Bethlehem, Pennsylvania. She was born on 21 Mar 1842 in Nesquehoning, Mauch Chunk Township, Carbon County, Pennsylvania. She died on 22 Jan 1926 in Summit Hill, Carbon County, Pennsylvania.

  vii. MARGARET GORMLEY was born before 27 Mar 1834 in Mullinabrone, Aghadowey Parish, County Londonderry, Ireland. She died between 1871-1915. She married husband Brashear between 1850-1864.

  viii. JOSEPH GORMLEY was born in Jun 1836 in Mullinabrone, Aghadowey Parish, County Londonderry, Ireland. He died about 22 Feb 1904 in Silver City Precinct, Lyon County, Nevada.

  ix. WILLIAM BROWN GORMLEY was born before 05 Dec 1838 in Mullinabrone, Aghadowey Parish, County, Londonderry, Ireland. He died between 1843-1846 in Summit Hill, Carbon County, Pennsylvania.

7. x. JANE "JENNIE" GORMLEY was born about 01 Mar 1841 in Summit Hill, Carbon County, Pennsylvania. She died on 07 May 1915 in West Bethlehem, Lehigh County, Pennsylvania. She married Henry Erwin, son of John Erwin and Nancy Dougherty in 1866. He was born on 05 May 1842 in County Derry, Ireland. He died on 12 Feb 1912 in West Bethlehem, Lehigh County, Pennsylvania.

  xi. JOHN GORMLEY was born on 05 Aug 1843 in Summit Hill, Carbon County, Pennsylvania. He died on 09 Jul 1862 in Washington, D.C..

8. xii. WILLIAM B. GORMLEY was born on 12 Feb 1846 in Summit Hill, Carbon County, Pennsylvania. He died on 03 Jul 1903 in Borough of Fountain Hill, Lehigh County, Pennsylvania. He married Mary Catherine Hartman, daughter of Alexander Hartman and Jane Campbell on 21 Mar 1874 in Mauch Chunk, Carbon County, Pennsylvania. She was born on 12 Sep 1856 in Weissport, Carbon County, Pennsylvania. She died on 11 Apr 1922 in Allentown, Lehigh County, Pennsylvania.

2.   **SMITH M.**[2] **GORMLEY** (Joseph[1]) was born on 16 Mar 1823 in Magheramore, Desertoghill Parish, County Londonderry, Ireland. He died on 18 Mar 1883 in Buck Mountain, Lausanne Township, Carbon County, Pennsylvania. He married Margaret Ann McClellan, daughter of James McClellan and Margaret on 01 Nov 1857 in Buck Mountain, Lausanne Township, Carbon County, Pennsylvania. She was born on 12 Feb 1833 in Ireland. She died on 26 Jul 1910 in Mahanoy City, Schuylkill County, Pennsylvania.

Smith M. Gormley and Margaret Ann McClellan had the following children:

       i.   MARGARETTE "MAGGIE" JANE[3] GORMLEY was born on 28 Sep 1858 in Pennsylvania. She died on 26 Jul 1883 in Pennsylvania.

9.   ii.   MARY ANNA GORMLEY was born on 24 Nov 1860 in Pennsylvania. She died on 01 Sep 1922 in Mahanoy City, Schuylkill County, Pennsylvania. She married Harry Leopold Burkart, son of John B. Burkart and Marie Fehrnback on 26 Feb 1885 in Philadelphia, Pennsylvania. He was born on 24 May 1861 in Philadelphia, Pennsylvania. He died on 20 Feb 1920 in Philadelphia, Pennsylvania.

10.   iii. ALICE GORMLEY was born on 28 May 1863 in Buck Mountain, Lausanne Township, Carbon County, Pennsylvania. She died on 18 Mar 1931 in Mahanoy City, Schuylkill County, Pennsylvania. She married John W. Lowe, son of James Lowe and Catherine Dick on 10 Mar 1888 in Mahanoy City, Schuylkill County, Pennsylvania. He was born on 06 May 1861 in Nova Scotia, Canada. He died on 25 Mar 1939 in Mahanoy City, Schuylkill County, Pennsylvania.

11.   iv. MATILDA GORMLEY was born on 13 Aug 1867 in Buck Mountain, Lausanne Township, Carbon County, Pennsylvania. She died on 12 Jun 1946 in Kingston, Luzerne County, Pennsylvania,. She married Alfred McCollough, son of John McCollough and Anna Miller about 1884. He was born on 29 Jan 1862 in Pennsylvania. He died on 30 Apr 1913 in Winton, Lackawanna County, Pennsylvania.

      v.   MARTHA GORMLEY was born on 28 Mar 1869 in Pennsylvania. She died on 17 Mar 1887 in Pennsylvania.

     vi. JAMES A. GORMLEY was born on 18 Apr 1874 in Pennsylvania. He died on 06 Jan 1899 in Pennsylvania.

    vii. ROBERT LEONARD GORMLEY was born on 29 Jan 1878 in Buck Mountain,

Lausanne Township, Carbon County, Pennsylvania. He died on 16 Jan 1947 in St Louis, Missouri.

3. **JAMES MONTGOMERY[2] GORMLEY** (Joseph[1]) was born in 1825 in Magheramore, Desertoghill Parish, County Londonderry, Ireland. He died on 15 Jul 1877 in Lansford, Carbon County, Pennsylvania. He married Margaret Glenn, daughter of James Glenn and Elizabeth Bacon on 11 Apr 1866 in Summit Hill, Carbon County, Pennsylvania. She was born on 20 Aug 1846 in Ashton, Mauch Chunk Township, Carbon County, Pennsylvania. She died on 21 May 1920 in Summit Hill, Carbon County, Pennsylvania.

James Montgomery Gormley and Margaret Glenn had the following children:

 i. JOHN[3] GORMLEY was born on 13 Feb 1867 in Coaldale Schuylkill County, Pennsylvania. He died on 01 Dec 1935 in Summit Hill, Carbon County, Pennsylvania.

 ii. SAMUEL GORMLEY was born on 05 Oct 1868 in Lansford, Carbon County, Pennsylvania. He died on 31 Mar 1894 in Carbon County, Pennsylvania.

 iii. JOSEPH GORMLEY was born on 30 Sep 1870 in Lansford, Carbon County, Pennsylvania. He died on 09 Apr 1872 in Carbon County, Pennsylvania.

12. iv. JAMES GORMLEY was born on 29 Feb 1872 in Lansford, Carbon County, Pennsylvania. He died on 28 Aug 1944 in Summit Hill, Carbon County, Pennsylvania. He married Martha Haines Lewis on 16 Mar 1905 in Germantown, Philadelphia, Pennsylvania. She was born on 14 Aug 1877 in St. Clair, Schuylkill County, Pennsylvania. She died on 05 Dec 1965 in Coaldale, Schuylkill County, Pennsylvania.

13. v. WILLIAM B. GORMLEY was born on 19 Aug 1874 in Lansford, Carbon County, Pennsylvania. He died on 12 Dec 1937 in Coaldale, Schuylkill County, Pennsylvania. He married Hattie B. Lewis on 11 Feb 1904 in Summit Hill, Carbon County, Pennsylvania. She was born on 07 Dec 1878 in Lansford, Carbon County, Pennsylvania. She died on 20 Jan 1929 in Lansford, Carbon County, Pennsylvania.

14. vi. ROBERT MONTGOMERY GORMLEY was born on 06 Mar 1876 in Spring Tunnel (near Summit Hill), Carbon County, Pennsylvania. He died on 16 Nov 1954 in Lehighton, Carbon County, Pennsylvania. He married Ellen Mae Remaley, daughter of Daniel Remaley on 25 Aug 1900 in Summit Hill, Carbon County, Pennsylvania. She was born on 11 Jul 1882 in Summit Hill, Carbon County, Pennsylvania. She died on 14 Oct 1964.

4.   **LETITIA MONTGOMERY**[2] **GORMLEY** (Joseph[1]) was born before 22 Jun 1827 in Magheramore, Desertoghill Parish, County Londonderry, Ireland. She died on 23 Oct 1914 in Philadelphia, Pennsylvania. She married Stephen Wallace, son of William Wallace and Mary Ann (--?--) on 04 Aug 1852 in Philadelphia, Pennsylvania. He was born about 1829 in Mullaghinch, Aghadowey Parish, County Londonderry, Ireland. He died about 1859 in Charleston, Charleston County, South Carolina.

Stephen Wallace and Letitia Montgomery Gormley had the following children:

15.   i.   MARY ANN[3] WALLACE was born on 25 Nov 1853 in Charleston, Charleston County, South Carolina. She died on 31 Dec 1909 in Philadelphia, Pennsylvania. She married Thomas McCauley, son of Stephen McCauley and Margaret Wallace on 20 Nov 1879 in Philadelphia, Pennsylvania. He was born on 14 Feb 1854 in Philadelphia, Pennsylvania. He died on 08 Aug 1925 in Philadelphia, Pennsylvania.

16.   ii.   JOSEPH S. WALLACE SR. was born on 15 Dec 1855 in Charleston, Charleston County, South Carolina or Philadelphia, Pennsylvania. He died on 28 May 1915 in Philadelphia, Pennsylvania. He married Elizabeth Urwiler, daughter of Benjamin Urweiler and Elmira Brown about 1878. She was born on 10 Jul 1859 in Philadelphia, Pennsylvania. She died on 27 Aug 1939 in Philadelphia, Pennsylvania.

17.   iii.   GEORGE STEPHEN WALLACE SR. was born on 16 May 1858 in Charleston, Charleston County, South Carolina. He died on 26 Nov 1902 in Montgomery, Montgomery County, Alabama. He married Louise E. Hartman, daughter of Ambrose Ambrosius Hartman and Elizabeth Bontley in 1885. She was born on 13 Oct 1868 in Poughkeepsie, Dutchess County, New York. She died on 12 Oct 1946 in Poughkeepsie, Dutchess County, New York.

5.   **MATILDA MONTGOMERY**[2] **GORMLEY** (Joseph[1]) was born in Jun 1831 in County Londonderry, Ireland. She died on 15 Aug 1905 in Philadelphia, Pennsylvania. She married John Boyd on 05 Apr 1851 in Philadelphia, Pennsylvania. He was born in 1827 in Ireland. He died about 1874 in Placer County, California.

John Boyd and Matilda Montgomery Gormley had the following children:

18.   i.   JAMES M.[3] BOYD was born on 06 Apr 1852 in Pennsylvania. He died on 13 Aug 1930 in Summit Hill, Carbon County, Pennsylvania. He married Ellen Sinyard, daughter of William Sinyard and Mary Ann Margaret McMichael about 1874. She was born on 06 May 1850 in Pennsylvania. She died on 01 Dec 1916 in Summit Hill, Carbon County, Pennsylvania.

19.   ii.   MARGARET ANN BOYD was born in Oct 1853 in Philadelphia, Pennsylvania. She died on 28 Mar 1900 in Philadelphia, Pennsylvania. She married John Strawbridge on 17 Aug 1874 in Philadelphia, Pennsylvania. He was born on 03 Apr 1844 in Pennsylvania. He died on 21 Sep 1923 in Philadelphia, Pennsylvania.

6.   ROBERT MONTGOMERY[2] GORMLEY (Joseph[1]) was born before 03 Jan 1832 in Mullinabrone, Aghadowey Parish, County Londonderry, Ireland. He died on 02 Aug 1875 in Fountain Hill, Lehigh County, Pennsylvania. He married Hannah Jane Johnson, daughter of Andrew Johnson and Mary Gilmore in Bethlehem, Pennsylvania. She was born on 21 Mar 1842 in Nesquehoning, Mauch Chunk Township, Carbon County, Pennsylvania. She died on 22 Jan 1926 in Summit Hill, Carbon County, Pennsylvania.

Robert Montgomery Gormley and Hannah Jane Johnson had the following children:

    i.   JOSEPH[3] GORMLEY was born on 20 Dec 1866 in Bethlehem, Pennsylvania. He died on 02 Jul 1950 in Summit Hill, Carbon County, Pennsylvania.

    ii.   MARY E. GORMLEY was born on 12 Jan 1869 in South Bethlehem, Lehigh County, Pennsylvania. She died on 16 Jan 1926 in Summit Hill, Carbon County, Pennsylvania.

    iii.   ROBERT M. GORMLEY was born on 12 Jul 1870 in Bethlehem, Northampton County, Pennsylvania. He died on 24 Jan 1964 in Coaldale, Schuylkill County, Pennsylvania.

    iv.   MARGARET M. GORMLEY was born on 20 Dec 1873 in Bethlehem, Pennsylvania. She died on 18 Aug 1956 in Coaldale Schuylkill County, Pennsylvania.

    v.   WILLIAM A. GORMLEY was born on 30 Jul 1875 in Bethlehem, Pennsylvania. He died on 24 Nov 1955 in Summit Hill, Carbon County, Pennsylvania.

7.   JANE "JENNIE"[2] GORMLEY (Joseph[1]) was born about 01 Mar 1841 in Summit Hill, Carbon County, Pennsylvania. She died on 07 May 1915 in West Bethlehem, Lehigh County, Pennsylvania. She married Henry Erwin, son of John Erwin and Nancy Dougherty in 1866. He was born on 05 May 1842 in County Derry, Ireland. He died on 12 Feb 1912 in West Bethlehem, Lehigh County, Pennsylvania.

Henry Erwin and Jane "Jennie" Gormley had the following children:

20.   i.   WILLIAM HENRY[3] ERWIN was born on 03 Nov 1866 in Nesquehoning,

Mauch Chunk Township, Carbon County, Pennsylvania. He died on 03 May 1940 in Northampton, Northampton County, Pennsylvania. He married (1) OLIVIA S. STEM, daughter of William Stem and Eliza Kemmerer on 17 Nov 1897 in Lehigh County, Pennsylvania. She was born on 10 Mar 1871 in Pennsylvania. She died on 10 Jan 1919. He married (2) EDITH MORTON CRANSTON in 1920. She was born on 22 Dec 1887. She died on 12 Sep 1957.

21. ii. MINNIE ERWIN was born on 24 Nov 1868 in South Bethlehem, Northampton County, Pennsylvania. She died on 14 Aug 1946 in Flushing, Queens, New York, USA. She married Barton Olmsted Curtis on 26 Oct 1901 in Bethlehem, Lehigh County, Pennsylvania. He was born on 01 Aug 1868 in Iowa. He died on 03 Aug 1911 in Iowa.

 iii. JENNIE ERWIN was born on 10 Jun 1870 in South Bethlehem, Northampton County, Pennsylvania. She died on 06 Oct 1871 in West Bethlehem, Lehigh County, Pennsylvania.

22. iv. JENNIE ERWIN was born on 01 Apr 1872 in West Bethlehem, Lehigh County, Pennsylvania. She died on 05 May 1939 in Philadelpha, Pennsylvania. She married GEORGE HERBERT WALTMAN. He was born on 26 Feb 1871. He died on 03 May 1946.

23. v. HARRY H. ERWIN was born on 29 Nov 1874 in West Bethlehem, Lehigh County, Pennsylvania. He died on 28 Mar 1951 in Fountain Hill, Lehigh County, Pennsylvania. He married Anna M. Kindt, daughter of Stephen Kindt and Lucy in 1905. She was born on 23 Nov 1883 in New Jersey. She died on 11 Feb 1955.

24. vi. JOHN ERWIN was born in Feb 1875 in West Bethlehem, Lehigh County, Pennsylvania. He died on 08 Dec 1937 in Farmingdale, Nassau, New York. He married ETHEL RICKABY. She was born in 1884. She died in 1978.

25. vii. JOSEPH ERWIN was born in 1878 in West Bethlehem, Lehigh County, Pennsylvania. He died on 23 Jan 1936 in Brooklyn, Kings County, New York. He married (1) MATTIE JENNIE BROADHEAD, daughter of Joseph K. Broadhead in 1903. She was born in 1878 in Pennsylvania. She died in 1921. He married (2) EMELIE HIRZ after 1921. She died in 1935.

26. viii. MARGARET MONTGOMERY ERWIN was born in Sep 1879 in West Bethlehem, Lehigh County, Pennsylvania. She died on 16 Feb 1917 in Long Island,

New York. She married JUDSON GREY SMULL SR.. He was born on 02 May 1882 in Altoona, Blair County, Pennsylvania. He died on 21 Apr 1978 in Bethlehem, Lehigh County, Pennsylvania 18018.

8. **WILLIAM B.**[2] **GORMLEY** (Joseph[1]) was born on 12 Feb 1846 in Summit Hill, Carbon County, Pennsylvania. He died on 03 Jul 1903 in Borough of Fountain Hill, Lehigh County, Pennsylvania. He married Mary Catherine Hartman, daughter of Alexander Hartman and Jane Campbell on 21 Mar 1874 in Mauch Chunk, Carbon County, Pennsylvania. She was born on 12 Sep 1856 in Weissport, Carbon County, Pennsylvania. She died on 11 Apr 1922 in Allentown, Lehigh County, Pennsylvania.

William B. Gormley and Mary Catherine Hartman had the following children:

    i.   EMMA[3] GORMLEY was born about 1875 in Lansford, Carbon County, Pennsylvania. She died before 1890.

27.   ii.   MATILDA "TILLIE" B. GORMLEY was born on 12 Dec 1877 in Lansford, Carbon County, Pennsylvania. She died on 18 Dec 1945 in Northampton, Northampton, Pennsylvania, USA. She married Harvey Allen Buss on 03 Sep 1896 in Northampton, Pennsylvania. He was born on 21 Sep 1877 in Bethlehem, Northampton County, Pennsylvania. He died on 07 Aug 1954 in Nazareth, Northampton County, Pennsylvania.

    iii.   JOSEPH GORMLEY was born in Dec 1879 in Lansford, Carbon County, Pennsylvania. He died before 1890.

    iv.   WILLIAM E. GORMLEY was born on 06 Feb 1883 in Summit Hill, Carbon County, Pennsylvania. He died on 18 Nov 1923 in Philadelphia, Pennsylvania. He married Elizabeth Schweinbenz, daughter of John Schweibenz and Priscilla Frederick on 22 Jul 1906 in New York City, New York. She was born in 1889 in Pennsylvania. She died after 1923.

28.   v.   JAMES MONTGOMERY GORMLEY was born on 07 Oct 1884 in Summit Hill, Carbon County, Pennsylvania. He died on 18 May 1960 in Allentown, Lehigh County, Pennsylvania. He married ELLEN LOUISE STERNER. She was born on 09 Mar 1888 in Lower Saucon, Northampton County, Pennsylvania. She died on 27 Mar 1920 in Bethlehem, Lehigh County, Pennsylvania.

    vi.   HARRY B. "MIKE" GORMLEY was born on 28 Feb 1888 in Summit Hill, Carbon County, Pennsylvania. He died on 05 Oct 1962 in Bethlehem, Lehigh County, Pennsylvania. He married (1) LAURA E. HAUSMAN, daughter of Jacob Hausman and Marguerite Moyer about 1920. She was born on 15 Dec 1887 in East Texas, Lehigh, Pennsylvania, USA. She died on 09 Nov 1959 in Bethlehem, Lehigh County, Pennsylvania. He married (2) LILA REICHENBACH, daughter of Banks Reichenbach and Lillie Eisenhard between 1960-1962. She was born on 28 Dec 1910 in Allentown, Lehigh County, Pennsylvania. She died on 03 Apr 1992 in Fountain Hill, Lehigh County, Pennsylvania.

Generation 3

9.   **MARY ANNA**[3] **GORMLEY** (Smith M.[2], Joseph[1]) was born on 24 Nov 1860 in Pennsylvania. She died on 01 Sep 1922 in Mahanoy City, Schuylkill County, Pennsylvania. She married Harry Leopold Burkart, son of John B. Burkart and Marie Fehrnback on 26 Feb 1885 in Philadelphia, Pennsylvania. He was born on 24 May 1861 in Philadelphia, Pennsylvania. He died on 20 Feb 1920 in Philadelphia, Pennsylvania.

Harry Leopold Burkart and Mary Anna Gormley had the following child:
   i.   ROBERT THEODORE[4] BURKART was born on 30 May 1887 in Philadelpha, Pennsylvania. He died on 24 Feb 1970 in Pinellas County, Florida. He married (1) LYDIA MAY STIEF, daughter of Oscar R. Steif and Marie Mooney on 26 Mar 1920 in Manhattan, New York, New York. She was born on 28 Dec 1885 in Philadelphia, Pennsylvania. She died on 15 Mar 1957 in St. Petersburg, Pinellas County, Florida. He married (2) MARGARET MACCLELLAN SALISBURY about 07 Nov 1957 in Pinellas County, Florida. She was born on 23 May 1894. She died on 06 Aug 1978 in Pinellas County, Florida.

10.   **ALICE**[3] **GORMLEY** (Smith M.[2], Joseph[1]) was born on 28 May 1863 in Buck Mountain, Lausanne Township, Carbon County, Pennsylvania. She died on 18 Mar 1931 in Mahanoy City, Schuylkill County, Pennsylvania. She married John W. Lowe, son of James Lowe and Catherine Dick on 10 Mar 1888 in Mahanoy City, Schuylkill County, Pennsylvania. He was born on 06 May 1861 in Nova Scotia, Canada. He died on 25 Mar 1939 in Mahanoy City, Schuylkill County, Pennsylvania.

John W. Lowe and Alice Gormley had the following children:
   i.   JAMES A.[4] LOWE was born on 20 Jul 1888 in Buck Mountain, Lausanne Township, Carbon County, Pennsylvania. He died on 31 May 1964 in Sayre, Bradford County, Pennsylvania, USA. He married Ida E. Wagner, daughter of James Wagner and Laura Reese on 26 Aug 1915 in Mahanoy City, Schuylkill County, Pennsylvania. She was born in 1889 in Mahanoy City, Schuylkill County, Pennsylvania. She died in 1970.

    ii.   HILDA LOWE was born on 18 Feb 1890 in Buck Mountain, Lausanne Township, Carbon County, Pennsylvania. She died on 21 Sep 1948 in Mahanoy City, Schuylkill County, Pennsylvania.

    iii.   HARRY BURKART LOWE was born on 24 Jul 1892 in Mahanoy City, Schuylkill County, Pennsylvania. He died on 23 Sep 1924 in Coal City, Northumberland, Pennsylvania, USA. He married CATHERINE "KIT" M. ECKLER. She was born on 27 Nov 1895 in Mahanoy City, Schuylkill County, Pennsylvania. She died on 19 Dec 1983 in Atlanta, Fulton County, Georgia.

    iv.   MARGARET S. LOWE was born on 01 Apr 1897 in Pennsylvania. She died in Dec 1973 in probably New Jersey. She married WINFIELD "BARNEY" WENTZ. He was born on 21 Oct 1894 in Pennsylvania. He died in May 1968 in probably New Jersey.

    v.   JOHN GORMLEY LOWE was born on 01 Aug 1901 in Mahanoy City, Schuylkill County, Pennsylvania. He died in Feb 1969 in Linden, Union, New Jersey, USA.

    vi.   KATHRYN LOWE was born on 06 Dec 1905 in Pennsylvania. She died in Mar 1985 in Mahanoy City, Schuylkill County, Pennsylvania. She married WILLIAM RISMILLER. He was born on 07 Nov 1905. He died in Jun 1978 in Mahanoy City, Schuylkill County, Pennsylvania.

11.   **MATILDA³ GORMLEY** (Smith M.², Joseph¹) was born on 13 Aug 1867 in Buck Mountain, Lausanne Township, Carbon County, Pennsylvania. She died on 12 Jun 1946 in Kingston, Luzerne County, Pennsylvania,. She married Alfred McCollough, son of John McCollough and Anna Miller about 1884. He was born on 29 Jan 1862 in Pennsylvania. He died on 30 Apr 1913 in Winton, Lackawanna County, Pennsylvania.

Alfred McCollough and Matilda Gormley had the following children:

    i.   EDITH⁴ MCCOLLOUGH was born on 06 Mar 1885 in Eckley, Luzerne County, Pennsylvania. She died on 01 Aug 1957 in Kingston, Luzerne County, Pennsylvania, USA. She married Arthur D. Vincent on 12 Aug 1913 in Luzerne County, Pennsylvania. He was born on 12 Nov 1886 in Walkerton, St Joseph, Indiana, USA. He died on 10 May 1954 in Hanover Township, Luzerne County, Pennsylvania.

    ii.   HAZEL MCCOLLOUGH was born on 11 Dec 1890 in Silver Brook Schuylkill County Pennsylvania. She died on 09 Mar 1959 in Kingston, Luzerne

County, Pennsylvania, USA. She married (1) JOSEPH E. BRADLEY about 1919. He was born in 1889 in Pennsylvania. She married (2) CLARENCE MELVIN PETERS, son of Mahlon A. Peters and Catherine Eroh on 15 May 1933 in Kingston, Luzerne County, Pennsylvania, USA. He was born on 27 Oct 1891 in Dorrance, Luzerne, Pennsylvania, USA. He died on 05 May 1943 in Kingston, Luzerne County, Pennsylvania, USA. She married (3) JOSEPH WARNE RUBURY, son of Luke Rubury and Bessie Warner on 30 Nov 1944 in Luzerne County, Pennsylvania. He was born on 26 Dec 1885 in Nanticoke, Luzerne, Pennsylvania, USA. He died on 21 Jan 1958 in Kingston, Luzerne County, Pennsylvania,.

 iii. EMILY MCCOLLOUGH was born on 23 Sep 1895 in Tresckow, Carbon County, Pennsylvania, USA. She died on 15 Aug 1962 in Wilkes-Barre, Luzerne County, Pennsylvania, USA. She married Joseph Lampman, son of George Lampman and Louise Kuhl on 05 Dec 1917 in Luzerne County, Pennsylvania. He was born on 12 Nov 1893 in Wilkes-Barre, Luzerne, Pennsylvania, USA. He died on 21 Oct 1956 in Kingston, Luzerne County, Pennsylvania,.

12. **JAMES³ GORMLEY** (James Montgomery², Joseph¹) was born on 29 Feb 1872 in Lansford, Carbon County, Pennsylvania. He died on 28 Aug 1944 in Summit Hill, Carbon County, Pennsylvania. He married Martha Haines Lewis on 16 Mar 1905 in Germantown, Philadelphia, Pennsylvania. She was born on 14 Aug 1877 in St. Clair, Schuylkill County, Pennsylvania. She died on 05 Dec 1965 in Coaldale, Schuylkill County, Pennsylvania.

James Gormley and Martha Haines Lewis had the following children:

 i. ALLEN⁴ GORMLEY was born about 1907 in St. Clair, Schuylkill County, Pennsylvania. He died about 1910.

 ii. MARTHA HAINES GORMLEY was born on 21 Mar 1907 in Summit Hill, Carbon County, Pennsylvania. She died on 01 Nov 1986 in Hagerstown, Washington County, Maryland. She married Clyde L. Downs on 22 Apr 1929 in Tamaqua, Schuylkill County, Pennsylvania. He was born on 17 Oct 1908 in Williamsport, Washington County, Maryland. He died in Towson, Baltimore County, Maryland.

 iii. CHARLES LEWIS GORMLEY was born on 21 Jul 1910 in Summit Hill, Carbon County, Pennsylvania. He died on 13 Jan 1980 in Levittown, Pennsylvania. He married Marie Agnes McFadden in 1941. She was born on 11 May 1914 in Summit Hill, Carbon County, Pennsylvania. She died on 16 Jul 2002 in

Bristol, Bucks County, Pennsylvania.

    iv.   JOHN MONTGOMERY GORMLEY was born on 07 Jul 1913. He died on 16 Dec 1991 in Palmerton, Carbon County, Pennsylvania. He married Alice Mae Earley on 01 Jan 1946 in Lansford, Carbon County, Pennsylvania. She was born on 04 May 1915. She died on 05 Jun 1976.

    v.   JOSEPH LEWIS GORMLEY was born on 25 May 1916. He died in 1972. He married FRANCES BOYCE.

    vi.   COLEMAN HERBERT GORMLEY was born on 18 Sep 1918 in Summit Hill, Carbon County, Pennsylvania. He died on 17 Mar 2003 in St. Petersburg, Florida. He married Olga Porambo on 18 Sep 1941 in Summit Hill, Carbon County, Pennsylvania. She was born on 12 Jul 1918. She died on 01 Nov 2001 in St. Petersburg, Florida.

13.   **WILLIAM B.**[3] **GORMLEY** (James Montgomery[2], Joseph[1]) was born on 19 Aug 1874 in Lansford, Carbon County, Pennsylvania. He died on 12 Dec 1937 in Coaldale, Schuylkill County, Pennsylvania. He married Hattie B. Lewis on 11 Feb 1904 in Summit Hill, Carbon County, Pennsylvania. She was born on 07 Dec 1878 in Lansford, Carbon County, Pennsylvania. She died on 20 Jan 1929 in Lansford, Carbon County, Pennsylvania.

William B. Gormley and Hattie B. Lewis had the following child:
    i.   FRANK WILLIAM[4] GORMLEY was born on 26 Jun 1906. He died on 24 Feb 1973 in Lansford, Carbon County, Pennsylvania. He married OLIVIA MARGARET CREITZ. She was born on 18 Jan 1910.

14.   **ROBERT MONTGOMERY**[3] **GORMLEY** (James Montgomery[2], Joseph[1]) was born on 06 Mar 1876 in Spring Tunnel (near Summit Hill), Carbon County, Pennsylvania. He died on 16 Nov 1954 in Lehighton, Carbon County, Pennsylvania. He married Ellen Mae Remaley, daughter of Daniel Remaley on 25 Aug 1900 in Summit Hill, Carbon County, Pennsylvania. She was born on 11 Jul 1882 in Summit Hill, Carbon County, Pennsylvania. She died on 14 Oct 1964.

Robert Montgomery Gormley and Ellen Mae Remaley had the following children:
    i.   THEODORE[4] GORMLEY was born on 26 Feb 1901 in Summit Hill, Carbon County, Pennsylvania. He died in Jan 1954. He married May Major on 24 Dec 1921.

    ii.   PALMER GORMLEY was born on 04 Oct 1902 in Summit Hill, Carbon

County, Pennsylvania. He died on 11 May 1974 in Lehighton, Carbon County, Pennsylvania. He married Thelma Steigerwalt, daughter of Thomas Steigerwalt and Verna Druckenmiller on 03 Oct 1931. She was born on 29 Dec 1913 in Lehighton, Carbon County, Pennsylvania. She died on 20 Jun 2000 in Lehighton, Carbon County, Pennsylvania.

   iii. CHESTER GORMLEY was born on 03 Aug 1908 in Summit Hill, Carbon County, Pennsylvania. He died on 13 Mar 1974 in Harrisburg, Dauphin County, Pennsylvania. He married Ethel M. Arner, daughter of William Arner and Mary Margaret Siebott on 21 May 1934. She was born on 26 Apr 1914 in Summit Hill, Carbon County, Pennsylvania.

   iv. HAZEL MAY GORMLEY was born on 05 Apr 1912 in Summit Hill, Carbon County, Pennsylvania. She died on 26 Dec 1996. She married (1) HOMER MANTZ on 31 Dec 1932. He was born on 30 Nov 1911. He died on 14 Dec 1966. She married (2) ROBERT CARTER after 1954. He died on 18 Apr 1998 in Hazleton, Luzerne County, Pennsylvania.

15. **MARY ANN³ WALLACE** (Letitia Montgomery² Gormley, Joseph¹ Gormley) was born on 25 Nov 1853 in Charleston, Charleston County, South Carolina. She died on 31 Dec 1909 in Philadelphia, Pennsylvania. She married Thomas McCauley, son of Stephen McCauley and Margaret Wallace on 20 Nov 1879 in Philadelphia, Pennsylvania. He was born on 14 Feb 1854 in Philadelphia, Pennsylvania. He died on 08 Aug 1925 in Philadelphia, Pennsylvania.

Thomas McCauley and Mary Ann Wallace had the following children:

   i. LETITIA⁴ MCCAULEY was born on 06 Dec 1880 in Philadelphia, Pennsylvania. She died on 01 Jan 1883 in Philadelphia, Pennsylvania.

   ii. MARGARET MCCAULEY was born on 10 Oct 1883 in Philadelphia, Pennsylvania. She died on 01 May 1957 in Philadelphia, Pennsylvania. She married John Thomas Smith, son of John T. Smith and Sarah McNutt on 24 Oct 1925 in Philadelphia, Pennsylvania. He was born on 03 Mar 1872 in Harford County, Maryland. He died on 24 Feb 1949 in Philadelphia, Pennsylvania.

   iii. LETITIA WALLACE MCCAULEY was born on 26 Jul 1885 in Philadelphia, Pennsylvania. She died on 30 Jan 1908 in Philadelphia, Pennsylvania.

   iv. THOMAS WALLACE MCCAULEY was born in Oct 1888 in Philadelphia, Pennsylvania. He died on 05 Apr 1890 in Philadelphia, Pennsylvania.

v. MARY ANN MCCAULEY was born on 07 Jul 1892 in Philadelphia, Pennsylvania. She died on 08 Aug 1984 in Burlington Township, Burlington County, New Jersey. She married Henry Grafe Chambers, son of William Scott Chambers and Josephine Irene Reitze on 30 Jul 1918 in Philadelphia, Pennsylvania. He was born on 08 Jan 1897 in Philadelphia, Pennsylvania. He died on 11 Nov 1953 in Collingswood, Camden County, New Jersey.

vi. WILLIS SKILLMAN MCCAULEY SR. was born on 08 Sep 1896 in Philadelphia, Pennsylvania. He died on 10 Sep 1970 in Philadelphia, Pennsylvania. He married Mae Schwartz, daughter of John Schwartz and Mary on 30 Jan 1921 in Elkton, Maryland. She was born on 18 Feb 1894 in Philadelphia, Pennsylvania. She died on 28 Jun 1982 in Philadelphia, Pennsylvania.

16. **JOSEPH S.³ WALLACE SR.** (Letitia Montgomery² Gormley, Joseph¹ Gormley) was born on 15 Dec 1855 in Charleston, Charleston County, South Carolina or Philadelphia, Pennsylvania. He died on 28 May 1915 in Philadelphia, Pennsylvania. He married Elizabeth Urwiler, daughter of Benjamin Urweiler and Elmira Brown about 1878. She was born on 10 Jul 1859 in Philadelphia, Pennsylvania. She died on 27 Aug 1939 in Philadelphia, Pennsylvania.

Joseph S. Wallace Sr. and Elizabeth Urwiler had the following child:

i. JOSEPH S.⁴ WALLACE JR. was born on 04 Oct 1879 in Philadelphia, Pennsylvania. He died on 10 May 1934 in West Berlin, Camden County, New Jersey. He married Letitia "Lettie" Kennedy, daughter of John Kennedy and Letitia on 10 Apr 1904 in Philadelphia, Pennsylvania. She was born on 14 Dec 1873 in Philadelphia, Pennsylvania. She died on 12 Apr 1952 in Camden, Camden County, New Jersey.

17. **GEORGE STEPHEN³ WALLACE SR.** (Letitia Montgomery² Gormley, Joseph¹ Gormley) was born on 16 May 1858 in Charleston, Charleston County, South Carolina. He died on 26 Nov 1902 in Montgomery, Montgomery County, Alabama. He married Louise E. Hartman, daughter of Ambrose Ambrosius Hartman and Elizabeth Bontley in 1885. She was born on 13 Oct 1868 in Poughkeepsie, Dutchess County, New York. She died on 12 Oct 1946 in Poughkeepsie, Dutchess County, New York.

George Stephen Wallace Sr. and Louise E. Hartman had the following children:

i. GEORGE STEPHEN⁴ WALLACE JR. was born on 12 Sep 1888 in Edgewood, Elmore County, Alabama. He died on 12 Mar 1955 in Newark, Essex County, New Jersey. He married (1) MINNIE ALBERTINA SWITZER, daughter of Albert Joseph Switzer and Caroline "Carrie" Kessler on 08 Oct 1910 in

Poughkeepsie, Dutchess County, New York. She was born on 01 Oct 1885 in Poughkeepsie, Dutchess County, New York. She died on 31 Dec 1948 in Poughkeepsie, Dutchess County, New York. He married (2) JEAN TAIT on 26 Aug 1922 in Newark, Essex County, New Jersey. She was born on 12 Feb 1894 in Edinburgh, Midlothian, Scotland. She died on 11 May 1982 in Lyndhurst, Bergen County, New Jersey.

ii.   ROBERT EARL WALLACE was born on 04 Aug 1891 in Edgewood, Elmore County, Alabama. He died on 02 Jan 1948 in Poughkeepsie, Dutchess County, New York. He married Minnie Albertina Switzer, daughter of Albert Joseph Switzer and Caroline "Carrie" Kessler on 21 Sep 1922 in Poughkeepsie, Dutchess County, New York. She was born on 01 Oct 1885 in Poughkeepsie, Dutchess County, New York. She died on 31 Dec 1948 in Poughkeepsie, Dutchess County, New York.

iii.   VERA MATILDA WALLACE was born on 31 Jan 1895 in Edgewood, Elmore County, Alabama. She died on 28 Sep 1948 in Poughkeepsie, Dutchess County, New York. She married John Joseph Butler Sr., son of William Butler and Mary Brennan on 29 Oct 1916 in Poughkeepsie, Dutchess County, New York. He was born in 1892 in Milton, Ulster County, New York. He died on 30 Oct 1953 in Poughkeepsie, Dutchess County, New York.

iv.   MASTER WALLACE was born on 19 Feb 1895 in Weatherly, Carbon County, Pennsylvania. He died on 21 Feb 1895 in Weatherly, Carbon County, Pennsylvania.

v.   LETTIE MAY WALLACE was born on 25 Jan 1898 in Edgewood, Elmore County, Alabama. She died on 29 Oct 1962 in South Amboy, Middlesex County, New Jersey. She married Edward Buckalew, son of Jacob Buckalew and Caroline "Carrie" Render on 26 Mar 1916 in Poughkeepsie, Dutchess County, New York. He was born on 21 Oct 1893 in South Amboy, Middlesex County, New Jersey. He died on 11 Apr 1975 in Neptune Township, Monmouth County, New Jersey.

vi.   MARY LOUISE WALLACE was born on 14 Mar 1901 in Edgewood, Elmore County, Alabama. She died on 17 Mar 1970 in Poughkeepsie, Dutchess County, New York. She married William Henry Witzenbocker, son of William H. Witzenbocker and Margaret McCarroll on 18 Jun 1922 in Poughkeepsie, Dutchess County, New York. He was born on 14 Nov 1895 in Newburgh, Orange County, New York. He died on 08 Oct 1986 in

Poughkeepsie, Dutchess County, New York.

18. **JAMES M.**[3] **BOYD** (Matilda Montgomery[2] Gormley, Joseph[1] Gormley) was born on 06 Apr 1852 in Pennsylvania. He died on 13 Aug 1930 in Summit Hill, Carbon County, Pennsylvania. He married Ellen Sinyard, daughter of William Sinyard and Mary Ann Margaret McMichael about 1874. She was born on 06 May 1850 in Pennsylvania. She died on 01 Dec 1916 in Summit Hill, Carbon County, Pennsylvania.

James M. Boyd and Ellen Sinyard had the following children:

    i.   WILLIAM S.[4] BOYD was born on 04 Jan 1876 in Summit Hill, Carbon County, Pennsylvania. He died on 14 Feb 1940 in Philadelphia, Pennsylvania. He married MARY.

    ii.   ROBERT JOHN BOYD was born in Aug 1878 in Pennsylvania.

    iii.   MARY MATILDA BOYD was born in Sep 1881 in Pennsylvania. She married Raymond Lewis in 1909. He was born in 1879 in Pennsylvania.

    iv.   MATTHEW LESTER BOYD was born on 10 Jun 1884 in Summit Hill, Carbon County, Pennsylvania. He died on 03 Jan 1955 in Coaldale, Schuylkill County, Pennsylvania. He married SARAH ELIZABETH SHINGLER. She was born in 1884 in Pennsylvania.

    v.   LETITIA JANE BOYD was born on 28 Jul 1889 in Pennsylvania. She died on 01 Nov 1936 in Summit Hill, Carbon County, Pennsylvania.

    vi.   ELIZABETH "BETTY" (TWIN) BOYD was born on 04 Jul 1891 in Pennsylvania. She died in Mar 1966 in Summit Hill, Carbon County, Pennsylvania.

    vii.   JAMES "JAY" G. (TWIN) BOYD was born on 04 Jul 1891 in Pennsylvania. He died in May 1969 in Summit Hill, Carbon County, Pennsylvania. He married THEREINE. She was born in 1903.

19. **MARGARET ANN**[3] **BOYD** (Matilda Montgomery[2] Gormley, Joseph[1] Gormley) was born in Oct 1853 in Philadelphia, Pennsylvania. She died on 28 Mar 1900 in Philadelphia, Pennsylvania. She married John Strawbridge on 17 Aug 1874 in Philadelphia, Pennsylvania. He was born on 03 Apr 1844 in Pennsylvania. He died on 21 Sep 1923 in Philadelphia, Pennsylvania.

John Strawbridge and Margaret Ann Boyd had the following children:

    i.   MARGARET DULLES[4] STRAWBRIDGE was born in Jul 1876 in Pennsylvania.

She died about 03 Dec 1923 in Camden County, New Jersey. She married JESSE MILES BIRCKS. He was born in Sep 1876 in Delaware. He died on 16 Oct 1922 in Kirkwood, Voorhees Township, Camden County, New Jersey.

ii. MATILDA BOYD STRAWBRIDGE was born on 09 Jan 1877 in Philadelphia, Pennsylvania. She died on 01 Nov 1939 in Philadelphia, Pennsylvania. She married Sidney Morris Snyder Sr., son of Edward Snyder and Mary Johnson in 1903 in Philadelphia, Philadelphia County, Pennsylvania. He was born on 18 May 1877 in Philadelphia, Pennsylvania. He died on 18 Dec 1953 in Philadelphia, Pennsylvania.

iii. MARTHA J. STRAWBRIDGE was born on 16 Nov 1883 in Camden, Camden County, New Jersey. She died on 19 Apr 1964 in Philadelpha, Pennsylvania. She married Alfred Beradge Clemmency in 1926 in Pennsylvania. He was born on 02 Nov 1877 in Philadelphia, Pennsylvania. He died on 27 Sep 1958 in Philadelphia, Pennsylvania.

iv. ADELAIDE F. STRAWBRIDGE was born on 18 Aug 1887 in Camden, Camden County., New Jersey. She died on 06 Jan 1954 in Philadelphia, Pennsylvania. She married Wallace E. Braker, son of George E. Braker and Mary E. Voutier on 29 Jan 1913 in Delaware. He was born on 29 Jan 1888 in Philadelphia, Pennsylvania. He died on 01 May 1959 in Philadelphia, Pennsylvania.

v. FLORENCE T. STRAWBRIDGE was born on 14 Jun 1895 in Philadelphia, Pennsylvania. She died between 1954-1957. She married Franklin Carl Lawrence in 1914 in New Jersey. He was born on 22 Aug 1882 in Philadelphia, Pennsylvania. He died on 12 Aug 1945 in Atlantic City, Atlantic, New Jersey, USA.

20. WILLIAM HENRY[3] ERWIN (Jane "Jennie"[2] Gormley, Joseph[1] Gormley) was born on 03 Nov 1866 in Nesquehoning, Mauch Chunk Township, Carbon County, Pennsylvania. He died on 03 May 1940 in Northampton, Northampton County, Pennsylvania. He married (1) OLIVIA S. STEM, daughter of William Stem and Eliza Kemmerer on 17 Nov 1897 in Lehigh County, Pennsylvania. She was born on 10 Mar 1871 in Pennsylvania. She died on 10 Jan 1919. He married (2) EDITH MORTON CRANSTON in 1920. She was born on 22 Dec 1887. She died on 12 Sep 1957.

William Henry Erwin and Olivia S. Stem had the following children:

i. GEORGE HENRY[4] ERWIN was born on 12 Feb 1899 in Pennsylvania. He died in Dec 1951. He married MARION HOTTENSTEIN. She was born in 1904.

    ii.   ELIZA JANE ERWIN was born on 13 Apr 1900 in Pennsylvania. She died in Apr 1977 in 19041. She married WILLIAM MITMAN. He was born on 06 Jan 1897. He died in Jan 1968 in 19041.

    iii.   MARGARET MONTGOMERY ERWIN was born in 1902 in Pennsylvania. She married HENRY CHARLES SPRUKS. He was born in 1895.

    iv.   HENRY STEM ERWIN was born on 28 Feb 1906. He died on 30 Nov 1906.

    v.   WILLIAM STEM ERWIN was born on 26 Jun 1907 in Pennsylvania. He died in May 1980 in Bethlehem, Pennsylvania 18018.

William Henry Erwin and Edith Morton Cranston had the following child:

    vi.   NANCY ERWIN was born in 1922.

21.   **MINNIE**[3] **ERWIN** (Jane "Jennie"[2] Gormley, Joseph[1] Gormley) was born on 24 Nov 1868 in South Bethlehem, Northampton County, Pennsylvania. She died on 14 Aug 1946 in Flushing, Queens, New York, USA. She married Barton Olmsted Curtis on 26 Oct 1901 in Bethlehem, Lehigh County, Pennsylvania. He was born on 01 Aug 1868 in Iowa. He died on 03 Aug 1911 in Iowa.

Barton Olmsted Curtis and Minnie Erwin had the following children:

    i.   HENRY ERWIN "HANK"[4] CURTIS was born on 06 Feb 1903 in Pittsburgh, Allegheny County, Pennsylvania. He died on 31 Jul 1986 in Queens County, New York.

    ii.   RUTH CURTIS was born in Jul 1905 in Salt Lake City, Salt Lake County, Utah. She died on 15 Nov 1905 in Salt Lake City, Salt Lake County, Utah.

    iii.   DOROTHY S."DOCK" CURTIS was born on 01 Oct 1906 in Salt Lake City, Salt Lake, Utah. She died on 23 Aug 2005 in Dryden, Tompkins County, New York. She married (1) WILLIAM T. HOLSMAN on 03 Jan 1931 in Manhattan, Kings County, New York. He was born on 24 May 1905 in Cook County, Illinois. He died on 03 Mar 1988. She married CHARLES E. CURTIS.

22.   **JENNIE**[3] **ERWIN** (Jane "Jennie"[2] Gormley, Joseph[1] Gormley) was born on 01 Apr 1872 in West Bethlehem, Lehigh County, Pennsylvania. She died on 05 May 1939 in Philadelpha, Pennsylvania. She married **GEORGE HERBERT WALTMAN**. He was born on 26 Feb 1871. He died on 03 May 1946.

George Herbert Waltman and Jennie Erwin had the following children:

    i.   JEANETTE[4] WALTMAN was born on 08 May 1899. She died on 01 Sep 1995. She married FRANK MARTIN TURNER. He was born on 29 Aug 1899. He died on 07 Aug 1984.

    ii.   JOHN R. WALTMAN was born in 1902. He married LUCILLE L. THORNBURG. She was born in 1903.

    iii.   JOSEPHINE MONTGOMERY WALTMAN was born in 1907.

23.   **HARRY H.**[3] **ERWIN** (Jane "Jennie"[2] Gormley, Joseph[1] Gormley) was born on 29 Nov 1874 in West Bethlehem, Lehigh County, Pennsylvania. He died on 28 Mar 1951 in Fountain Hill, Lehigh County, Pennsylvania. He married Anna M. Kindt, daughter of Stephen Kindt and Lucy in 1905. She was born on 23 Nov 1883 in New Jersey. She died on 11 Feb 1955.

Harry H. Erwin and Anna M. Kindt had the following children:

    i.   HENRY KINDT[4] ERWIN was born on 07 Sep 1908 in Pennsylvania. He died on 11 Apr 2000 in Lehigh Valley, Northampton County, Pennsylvania.

    ii.   LUCY JEAN ERWIN was born in 1910 in Pennsylvania. She married FLOYD W. SHAFER. He was born in 1905.

24.   **JOHN**[3] **ERWIN** (Jane "Jennie"[2] Gormley, Joseph[1] Gormley) was born in Feb 1875 in West Bethlehem, Lehigh County, Pennsylvania. He died on 08 Dec 1937 in Farmingdale, Nassau, New York. He married **ETHEL RICKABY**. She was born in 1884. She died in 1978.

John Erwin and Ethel Rickaby had the following children:

    i.   JOHN HENRY[4] ERWIN was born in 1914.

    ii.   CHARLOTTE ALICE ERWIN was born in 1915.

25.   **JOSEPH**[3] **ERWIN** (Jane "Jennie"[2] Gormley, Joseph[1] Gormley) was born in 1878 in West Bethlehem, Lehigh County, Pennsylvania. He died on 23 Jan 1936 in Brooklyn, Kings County, New York. He married (1) **MATTIE JENNIE BROADHEAD**, daughter of Joseph K. Broadhead in 1903. She was born in 1878 in Pennsylvania. She died in 1921. He married (2) **EMELIE HIRZ** after 1921. She died in 1935.

Joseph Erwin and Mattie Jennie Broadhead had the following children:

    i.   JANE GORMLEY[4] ERWIN was born on 11 Aug 1904 in Bethlehem, Lehigh County, Pennsylvania. She died on 28 Aug 2000. She married WILLIAM B.

THREAPLETON. He was born on 20 Jul 1904. He died on 16 Feb 1988 in Duval County Florida, USA.

    ii.   ELLA BROADHEAD ERWIN was born in 1907 in Pennsylvania. She married WILLIAM ARRISON MACCALLA. He was born in 1908.

26.   MARGARET MONTGOMERY*3* ERWIN (Jane "Jennie"*2* Gormley, Joseph*1* Gormley) was born in Sep 1879 in West Bethlehem, Lehigh County, Pennsylvania. She died on 16 Feb 1917 in Long Island, New York. She married JUDSON GREY SMULL SR.. He was born on 02 May 1882 in Altoona, Blair County, Pennsylvania. He died on 21 Apr 1978 in Bethlehem, Lehigh County, Pennsylvania 18018.

Judson Grey Smull Sr. and Margaret Montgomery Erwin had the following children:

    i.   LOUISE MARGARET*4* SMULL was born on 26 Apr 1909. She died on 16 Aug 1992 in Sarasota County, Florida. She married AUGUST RUDOLPH WERFT. He was born on 26 Feb 1909 in Altoona, Blair County, Pennslyvania. He died on 15 Jan 1987 in Sarasota County, Florida.

    ii.   JUDSON GREY SMULL JR. was born on 08 Jul 1913 in Richmond Hill, Queens, New York, USA. He died on 18 Jun 1979 in Pennsylvania. He married GERTRUDE MILLER. She was born in 1914 in Bethlehem, Lehigh County, Pennsylvania. She died on 03 Feb 2015 in Bethlehem, Lehigh County, Pennsylvania.

27.   MATILDA "TILLIE" B.*3* GORMLEY (William B.*2*, Joseph*1*) was born on 12 Dec 1877 in Lansford, Carbon County, Pennsylvania. She died on 18 Dec 1945 in Northampton, Northampton, Pennsylvania, USA. She married Harvey Allen Buss on 03 Sep 1896 in Northampton, Pennsylvania. He was born on 21 Sep 1877 in Bethlehem, Northampton County, Pennsylvania. He died on 07 Aug 1954 in Nazareth, Northampton County, Pennsylvania.

Harvey Allen Buss and Matilda "Tillie" B. Gormley had the following children:

    i.   HAROLD J.*4* BUSS was born on 13 Feb 1897 in Bethlehem, Northampton County, Pennsylvania. He died on 21 May 1960 in Fountain Hill, Lehigh County, Pennsylvania. He married BESSIE E. KNECHT. She was born on 09 Jan 1902 in Pennsylvania. She died on 13 Mar 1981 in Nazareth, Northampton County, Pennsylvania.

    ii.   ISABELLE M. BUSS was born on 31 May 1899 in Bethlehem, Northampton County, Pennsylvania. She died on 29 May 1987 in Nazareth, Northampton County, Pennsylvania. She married LUTHER D. CLEWELL. He was born on 04

Apr 1898 in Pennsylvania. He died on 15 May 1966 in Nazareth, Northampton County, Pennsylvania.

iii.　ADDISON FRANKLIN (TWIN) BUSS was born on 24 Mar 1908 in Nazareth, Northampton County, Pennsylvania. He died on 22 Jan 1987 in Slatington, Lehigh County, Pennsylvania. He married MIRIAM C. BACHMAN.

iv.　WILLIAM GORMLEY (TWIN) BUSS was born on 24 Mar 1908 in Nazareth, Northampton County, Pennsylvania. He died on 17 Jun 1922 in Nazareth, Northampton County, Pennsylvania.

28.　**JAMES MONTGOMERY**[3] **GORMLEY** (William B.[2], Joseph[1]) was born on 07 Oct 1884 in Summit Hill, Carbon County, Pennsylvania. He died on 18 May 1960 in Allentown, Lehigh County, Pennsylvania. He married **ELLEN LOUISE STERNER**. She was born on 09 Mar 1888 in Lower Saucon, Northampton County, Pennsylvania. She died on 27 Mar 1920 in Bethlehem, Lehigh County, Pennsylvania.

James Montgomery Gormley and Ellen Louise Sterner had the following children:

i.　VIRGINIA MAE[4] GORMLEY was born on 05 Jan 1908 in Bethlehem, Northampton County, Pennsylvania. She married Augustus "Butch" Kresh, son of John Kresh and Annie Hoffens on 17 Oct 1924 in Bethlehem, Lehigh County, Pennsylvania. He was born on 27 Oct 1898 in Hazelton, Luzerne County, PA. He died on 23 Dec 1948 in Bethlehem, Northampton County, Pennsylvania.

ii.　KATHRYN TILLIE GORMLEY was born on 26 Jul 1910 in Bethlehem, Lehigh County, Pennsylvania. She died on 21 Nov 1985 in Deal, Monmouth County, New Jersey. She married Harold Smith Riley, son of Thomas H. Riley and Ruth Slade on 23 Sep 1931 in Nazareth, Northampton County, Pennsylvania. He was born on 21 Jan 1906 in Passaic City, Passaic County, New Jersey. He died on 13 Sep 1980 in Deal, Monmouth County, New Jersey.

INDEX